Lecture Notes of the Institute for Computer Sciences, Social Informatics and Telecommunications Engineering 371

More information about this series at http://www.springer.com/series/8197

Zeng Deze · Huan Huang ·
Rui Hou · Seungmin Rho ·
Naveen Chilamkurti (Eds.)

Big Data Technologies and Applications

10th EAI International Conference, BDTA 2020
and 13th EAI International Conference
on Wireless Internet, WiCON 2020
Virtual Event, December 11, 2020
Proceedings

 Springer

Editors
Zeng Deze
School of Computer Science
China University of Geosciences
Wuhan, China

Rui Hou
South Central University for Nationalities
Wuhan, China

Naveen Chilamkurti
Department of Computer Science
and Information Technology
La Trobe University
Melbourne, VIC, Australia

Huan Huang
South Central University for Nationalities
Wuhan, China

Seungmin Rho
Hongik University
Seoul, Korea (Republic of)

ISSN 1867-8211   ISSN 1867-822X   (electronic)
Lecture Notes of the Institute for Computer Sciences, Social Informatics
and Telecommunications Engineering
ISBN 978-3-030-72801-4   ISBN 978-3-030-72802-1   (eBook)
https://doi.org/10.1007/978-3-030-72802-1

This Springer imprint is published by the registered company Springer Nature Switzerland AG
The registered company address is: Gewerbestrasse 11, 6330 Cham, Switzerland

Preface

It is our great pleasure to introduce the proceedings of the 10th European Alliance for Innovation (EAI) International Conference on Big Data Technologies and Applications (BDTA 2020) and 13th EAI International Wireless Internet Conference (WiCON 2020). Although for the first time these conferences took place in an online-only form due to COVID-19, they also attracted many researchers, scholars and practitioners around the world who are involved in developing and researching big data technology theories and applications and wireless communication. The theme of BDTA 2020 was "Big Data Age: A Scientific Revolution to Construct New Knowledge-based Systems".

The technical program of BDTA 2020 received 22 full paper submissions and finally accepted 9 of them after rigorous reviewing. The main scope of the conference included all the big data technologies, such as big data storage, search and management, big data visualization, natural language processing, image processing, deep learning algorithms, and new domains and novel applications related to these technologies. Beside high-quality technical paper presentations, the conference technical program also featured one keynote speech by Prof. Changqin Huang, who is from Zhejiang Normal University, Jinhua, China. The keynote speech mainly focused on intelligent educational applications driven by big data, and the mechanisms, characteristics and application scope of educational intelligence driven by big data were extensively introduced and discussed.

WiCON 2020 received 18 full paper submissions and after rigorous reviewing accepted 5 of them. The main topics of the conference include wireless and communication networks, wireless communication security, green wireless network architectures and communication protocols, Internet of Things (IoT)-based applications and industrial IoT. The keynote speaker was Prof. Abbas Jamalipour from The University of Sydney whose speech centered around edge computing and aerial support in 6G wireless networks.

We deeply appreciate the guidance from and coordination with the steering committee, Imrich Chlamtac, Honghao Gao and Jason J. Jung, and Xudong Wang and Der-Jiunn Deng who were essential for the success of the conferences. The same appreciation is also given to the excellent organizing committee team for their efforts in organizing and supporting the conferences, and especially for the construction of a fully-fledged online platform. In particular, we thank the Technical Program Committee, Prof. Rui Hou, Prof. Huan Zhou, Prof. Xiaobin Tan, Prof. Guisong Xia and Dr. Huan Huang, and Neeraj Kumar, B.G. Kim and Mohammed Hammoudeh who helped to arrange the peer-review process and scheduled a high-quality technical program. We also greatly appreciate the Conference Managers, Aleksandra Sledziejowska, Lukas Skolek and Karolina Marcinova, who devoted themselves to the preparation and organization of the conferences. Finally, we are grateful to all the authors who gave strong support to BDTA 2020 and WiCON 2020.

We strongly believe that the BDTA and WiCON conferences provide a wonderful platform for all researchers, scholars and practitioners to extensively discuss all scientific and technological aspects relevant to big data. We confidently hope that future BDTA and WiCON conferences will be even more strongly attended, more attractive and more successful.

Deze Zeng
Huan Huang
Rui Hou
Seungmin Rho
Naveen Chilamkurti

Organization

Conference Organization (BDTA 2020)

Steering Committee

Imrich Chlamtac	University of Trento, Italy
Honghao Gao	Shanghai University, China
Jason J. Jung	Chung-Ang University, Korea

Organizing Committee

General Chair

Cuiping Kang	South-Central University for Nationalities, China

General Co-Chair

Deze Zeng	China University of Geosciences, China

TPC Chair and Co-chairs

Huan Zhou	China Three Gorges University, China
Rui Hou	South-Central University for Nationalities, China
Xiaobin Tan	University of Science and Technology of China, China
Gui-Song Xia	Wuhan University, China

Sponsorship and Exhibit Chair

Chuanhui Huang	South-Central University for Nationalities, China

Local Chairs

Jing Zhao	South-Central University for Nationalities, China
Yang Wu	South-Central University for Nationalities, China

Workshops Chair

Liyong Wan	South-Central University for Nationalities, China

Publicity and Social Media Chairs

Huan Huang	South-Central University for Nationalities, China
Jason J. Jung	Chung-Ang University, Republic of Korea
Manik Sharma	DAV University, India

Publications Chairs

Fulan Fan	South-Central University for Nationalities, China
Marco Zapattore	University of Salento, Italy

Web Chairs

Shuai Yuan	South-Central University for Nationalities, China
Douglas Macedo	Federal University of Santa Catarina, Brazil

Technical Program Committee

Dawei Li	Montclair State University, USA
Xuxun Liu	South China University of Technology, China
Shouzhi Xu	China Three Gorges University, China
Chunsheng Zhu	Southern University of Science and Technology, China
Xiuhua Li	Chongqing University, China
En Wang	Jilin University, China
Ying He	Shenzhen University, China
Xin Li	Nanjing University of Aeronautics and Astronautics, China
Bohao Feng	Beijing Jiaotong University, China
Tian Wang	Huaqiao University, China
Xiaoyan Wang	Ibaraki University, Japan
Shengli Pan	China University of Geosciences, China
Xiaobo Zhou	Tianjin University, China
Shigeng Zhang	Central South University, China
Xiaojun Hei	Huazhong University of Science and Technology, China
Peng Liu	Hangzhou Dianzi University, China
Shibo He	Zhejiang University, China
Zhibo Wang	Wuhan University, China
Anfeng Liu	Central South University, China
Zheng Liu	China University of Geosciences, China
Linjing Wu	Central China Normal University, China
Min Hu	Hubei University of Chinese Medicine, China
Jingxiu Huang	South China Normal University, China

Conference Organization (WiCON 2020)

Steering Committee

Imrich Chlamtac	Bruno Kessler Professor, University of Trento, Italy
Xudong Wang	Shanghai Jiao Tong University, China
Der-Jiunn Deng	National Changhua University of Education, Taiwan

Organizing Committee

General Chair

Naveen Chilamkurti	La Trobe University, Australia

General Co-chair

Abbas Jamalipour	University of Sydney, Australia

TPC Chair and Co-chairs

Neeraj Kumar	Thapar Institute of Engineering and Technology, India
B. G. Kim	Sookmyung Women's University, South Korea
Mohammad Hammoudeh	Manchester Metropolitan University, UK

Sponsorship and Exhibit Chair

Khoa Phan	La Trobe University, Australia

Local Chair

Rabei Alhadad	La Trobe University, Australia

Workshops Chairs

Sharif Abuadbba	Data61, Australia
Nalin Asanka	La Trobe University, Australia
Jong-Hyouk Lee	Sangmyung University, South Korea

Publicity and Social Media Chair

Arun Kumar Sangaiah	Vellore Institute of Technology, India

Publications Chair

Seungmin Rho   Sejong University, South Korea

Web Chair

Abebe Diro   La Trobe University, Australia

Technical Program Committeess

Achyut Shankar   Amity University, India
Ashutosh Sharma   Lovely Professional University, India
A. S. M. Kayes   La Trobe University, Australia
Nalin Arachchilage   La Trobe University, Australia
Abebe Diro   La Trobe University, Australia
Sharif Abuadbba   Data61, Australia
Byung-Gyu Kim   Sookmyung Women's University, South Korea
Mohammad Hammoudeh   Manchester Metropolitan University, UK

Contents

BDTA 2020

Constructing Knowledge Graph for Prognostics and Health Management
of On-board Train Control System Based on Big Data and XGBoost 3
   Jiang Liu, Bai-gen Cai, Zhong-bin Guo, and Xiao-lin Zhao

Early Detecting the At-risk Students in Online Courses Based on Their
Behavior Sequences 17
   Shuai Yuan, Huan Huang, Tingting He, and Rui Hou

Do College Students Adapt to Personal Learning Environment (PLE)?
A Single-Group Study 34
   Changsheng Chen, Xiangzeng Meng, Junxiao Liu, and Zhi Liu

A Big Data Intelligence Marketplace and Secure Analytics Experimentation
Platform for the Aviation Industry 48
   Dimitrios Miltiadou, Stamatis Pitsios, Dimitrios Spyropoulos,
   Dimitrios Alexandrou, Fenareti Lampathaki, Domenico Messina,
   and Konstantinos Perakis

A Multi-valued Logic Assessment of Organizational Performance
via Workforce Social Networking 63
   José Neves, Florentino Fdez-Riverola, Vitor Alves, Filipa Ferraz,
   Lia Sousa, António Costa, Jorge Ribeiro, and Henrique Vicente

Research on the Sharing and Application of TCM Digital Resources 78
   Min Hu and Hao Li

Statistical Research on Macroeconomic Big Data: Using a Bayesian
Stochastic Volatility Model 90
   Minglei Shan

Introducing and Benchmarking a One-Shot Learning Gesture
Recognition Dataset 104
   Panagiotis Kasnesis, Christos Chatzigeorgiou,
   Charalampos Z. Patrikakis, and Maria Rangoussi

NetFlow Datasets for Machine Learning-Based Network Intrusion
Detection Systems 117
   Mohanad Sarhan, Siamak Layeghy, Nour Moustafa,
   and Marius Portmann

WiCON 2020

Performance Evaluation of Energy Detection, Matched Filtering and KNN
Under Different Noise Models   139
  Xiaoyan Wang, Jingjing Yang, Tengye Yu, Rui Li, and Ming Huang

Hybrid Deep-Readout Echo State Network and Support Vector Machine
with Feature Selection for Human Activity Recognition   150
  Shadi Abudalfa and Kevin Bouchard

Research on User Privacy Security of China's Top Ten Online
Game Platforms   168
  Lan-Yu Cui, Mi-Qian Su, Yu-Chen Wang, Zu -Mei Mo, Xiao-Yue Liang,
  Jian He, and Xiu-Wen Ye

Spectrum Sensing and Prediction for 5G Radio.   176
  Małgorzata Wasilewska, Hanna Bogucka, and Adrian Kliks

Towards Preventing Neighborhood Attacks: Proposal
of a New Anonymization's Approach for Social Networks Data   195
  Requi Djomo and Thomas Djotio Ndie

Author Index   209

BDTA 2020

Constructing Knowledge Graph for Prognostics and Health Management of On-board Train Control System Based on Big Data and XGBoost

Jiang Liu[1,3]([envelope]), Bai-gen Cai[2,3], Zhong-bin Guo[1], and Xiao-lin Zhao[1]

[1] School of Electronic and Information Engineering,
Beijing Jiaotong University, Beijing 100044, China
jiangliu@bjtu.edu.cn
[2] School of Computer and Information Technology,
Beijing Jiaotong University, Beijing 100044, China
[3] Beijing Engineering Research Center of EMC and GNSS Technology
for Rail Transportation, Beijing 100044, China

Abstract. Train control system plays a significant role in safe and efficient operation of the railway transport system. In order to enhance the system capability and cost efficiency from a full life cycle perspective, the establishment of a Condition-based Maintenance (CBM) scheme will be beneficial to both the currently in use and next generation train control systems. Due to the complexity of the fault mechanism of on-board train control system, a data-driven method is of great necessity to enable the Prognostics and Health Management (PHM) for the equipments in field operation. In this paper, we propose a big data platform to realize the storage, management and processing of historical field data from on-board train control equipments. Specifically, we focus on constructing the Knowledge Graph (KG) of typical faults. The Extreme Gradient Boosting (XGBoost) method is adopted to build big-data-enabled training models, which reveal the distribution of the feature importance and quantitatively evaluate the fault correlation of all related features. The presented scheme is demonstrated by a big data platform with incremental field data sets from railway operation process. Case study results show that this scheme can derive knowledge graph of specific system fault and reveal the relevance of features effectively.

Keywords: Knowledge graph · Prognostics and health management · Train control system · Big data · Machine learning · Extreme gradient boosting

1 Introduction

As the economic and social development all over the world, the demand for railway passenger and freight transport is expected to grow in the future. It is a common sense that safety is the heart of all the operation-related activities in railway transportation. As the core safety system controlling the movements of all moving trains, the Train

Z. Deze et al. (Eds.): BDTA 2020/WiCON 2020, LNICST 371, pp. 3–16, 2021.
https://doi.org/10.1007/978-3-030-72802-1_1

Control System (TCS) is responsible of setting up non-conflicting and safe routes for trains, defining safe limits of movement, and transmitting instructions or commands to train drivers. The high-speed railway is experiencing a rapid development in many countries. Presently, the railway industry has taken a great effort and is focused on the exploitation of advanced ABCDE (Artificial intelligence, Block chain, Cloud computing, big Data, Everything is connected) technologies in the new generation train control systems. Specifically, the big data technology has been applied in many aspects of railway operation and maintenance, including railway condition monitoring [1], train delay analysis and prediction [2], passenger route choice and demand forecasting [3], railway event and accident analysis [4], and optimization of time scheduling [5]. The integration of improved information conditions and advanced information processing technologies makes it possible of achieving a flexible, real-time, intelligent, integrated and fully automated railway operation and management system.

In the operation of the high-speed railway, fault diagnosis and equipment maintenance for train control systems play a significant role in ensuring safety and efficiency of the trains. In order to effectively extend the system life cycle, several new maintenance concepts have been proposed and utilized in many industrial branches. Particularly, the Prognostics and Health Management (PHM) technique, which aims to carry out fault detection, condition assessment and failure prediction, has been successfully implemented in the railway domain [6, 7]. However, conventional corrective maintenance and time-based maintenance strategies are still adopted in the maintenance and management of high-speed train control systems in China. Due to the limitations and conservative characteristics of the in-use maintenance rulebook, there is still space for improving the utilization of Remaining Useful Life (RUL) of train control systems, which is of great importance to optimize the cost efficiency of maintenance activities from a full-life-cycle perspective. The development of the novel train control systems requires the concentration on advanced methodologies and intelligent technologies to enable the Condition-based Maintenance (CBM), which is regarded as the key issue to cope with the increasing complexity of influencing factors on the competitiveness.

For the on-board train control system, CBM can be realized based on the enhancement of state monitoring conditions to the whole system and its components. However, it is difficult to add extra monitoring sensors or units, which are not dedicated to train control functions, to precisely collect the expected state variables. Consideration to the safety-critical characteristic and risk controlling against the system complexity makes it difficult to collect required system performance metrics directly for generating optimized maintenance decisions. Fortunately, the on-board train control system is designed with a capability of recording data logs in real-time during the field operation. In these log files, a number of status and state data fields at both the component level and system level are recorded along with fault/failure flags with respect to corresponding predefined fault modes. The accumulative data logs enable the opportunity to investigate the fault causes and the development characteristics under a rich information condition, which encourages us to establish a specific decision support system for the condition-based maintenance of the on-board train control equipments under the PHM framework through a big data-based approach.

In this paper, we mainly focus on the construction of the Knowledge Graph (KG) of specific on-board train control systems, which is an important foundation to realize the quantitative prediction of fault probability and risks to perform decision making in active maintenance. The characteristics of fault modes adopted in field operations are analyzed. Architecture of the big data platform and the XGBoost-enabled knowledge graph generation method by model training are introduced. Case study results with historical data sets from practical on-board train control equipments are given to show the capability of the presented solution.

The rest of this paper is organized as follows. Section 2 gives a global description to the architecture of the big data-based platform. In Sect. 3, the knowledge graph construction method using the XGBoost algorithm is introduced in detail. Section 4 depicts the realization of the platform and reports the results in the case study. Finally, conclusions and future plans are presented in Sect. 5.

2 Architecture of Big Data-Based Platform

The on-board train control equipment is a core part of Chinese Train Control System (CTCS), which is designed for safety assurance of the railway system by preventing the trains from over-speeding during the tracing between a train and its leading target train. Enormous effort has been devoted to enhance the safety protection capability of the whole system by advanced redundant architectures, fail-safe logics and interfaces, complete system testing and the verification specifications. The status monitoring and event recording of the on-board equipment provides direct information sources for the operators to analyze the operation state and find out the causes of the recent malfunction(s). Taking the 200H on-board equipment for high-speed railway as an example, the system developers have concerned the data logging function for a fault diagnostic purpose by using a PCMCIA card in the Data Record Unit (DRU). The maintenance staff will download the log files within the PCMCIA card when the train finished the planned operations. By using specific software tools, it is usually easy and intuitive to review and inspect the practical running status of equipment, actions of the Automatic Train Protection (ATP) unit, manual operation activities of the driver and the reported fault events. Through association analysis with data fields, curves and descriptions of the tools, the users can achieve fault diagnosis and maintenance determination according to the specifications and technical experience. However, the current event-driven maintenance mode only considers the local effect and possible responses to a specific fault report, and that is not sufficient to achieve a global system-level coverage to the equipment's whole life cycle. Under this circumstance, we proposed and developed a big data platform aiming at enabling a data-driven framework for the condition-based maintenance. By utilizing all the historical operation data, the association knowledge and occurrence regularity of different faults for the on-board train control equipment can be effectively obtained, which is of great value for the realization of the prognostics and health management over the current operation management rules.

Figure 1 shows the architecture of the big data-based platform for data management and CBM decision assistance of the on-board train control equipment. It can be found that the platform consists of four layers, which will be introduced as follows.

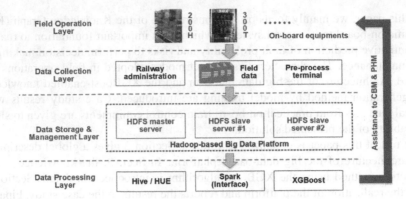

Fig. 1. Architecture of the big data-based platform.

2.1 Field Operation Layer

In this layer, on-board train control equipments record data logs to PCMCIA cards during the filed operation. Both the 200H and 300T on-board equipments are involved in the current version. System specifications and data extraction tools are involved in this front stage to collect useful data from the log files. With similar procedures, this platform is able to be compatible with other types of on-board equipments. Data acquisition based on this layer provides the foundation to reflect the equipment status in the time domain. At the same time, the derived knowledge graph and fault probability prediction results will provide feedback to this layer to affect the application of these on-board train control equipments in practical operation.

2.2 Data Collection Layer

The data collection layer is in charge of extracting and transforming raw data sets, which are obtained from the railway administration periodically. Specific tools and program scripts have been developed for automatic pre-processing, including the data classification, format transformation, code conversion and data cleaning. After these procedures, the characteristics corresponding to the fault labels, which are defined in the data logging tools according to the design of specific on-board equipments, would be prepared for incremental updating of the data storage and the following data processing operations.

2.3 Data Storage and Management Layer

This layer realizes the storage and management of the accumulative data collected from the equipments. The Hadoop Distributed File System (HDFS) [8, 9], which is an effective solution designed to run on the commodity hardware and has been proved suitable for the applications based on very large data sets, is adopted as the data storage framework. Three high level servers have been involved in this platform under a master/slave architecture. One server is configured as the NameNode to provide the service of managing the directory tree of all files and metadata about files and directories. The other two servers act as DataNodes in this Hadoop cluster to store the actual data files. This architecture ensures a flexible system extension capability corresponding to the increasing requirement and data quantity.

2.4 Data Processing Layer

The data processing layer achieves the exploration of the value from the field data files. Firstly, Hive is utilized as a data querying engine for the large-scale data stored in Hadoop. Through specific Python scripts, querying, sieving and statistical analysis can be realized according to the demand of the operators for equipment maintenance. The HUE (Hadoop User Experience) interface enables the users to access all the data files stored in HDFS and Hive-based data processing results. Secondly, Spark is integrated into the platform due to its advantages in iterative computing and accessibility to a set of machine learning APIs. Furthermore, the interface to the Extreme Gradient Boosting (XGBoost) models makes it possible to integrate the advanced algorithms with an enhanced computational efficiency level. Thirdly, XGBoost-based machine learning system is introduced for tree boosting to derive the feature importance scores for generating the knowledge graph under the Spark framework. Results of this layer finally achieve the goal of data-driven knowledge regularization for the different fault modes against the complicated and difficult mechanism modeling schemes.

3 Knowledge Graph Generation Method

Using a large amount of field data, it is difficult to clearly describe the mechanism of different faults or failures using analytical models that fit the data significantly better. From a data-driven perspective, the big data condition enables a different way to build knowledge models based on the long term state monitoring to the on-board train control equipment. The knowledge graph explores the potentials of heterogeneous data to reveal the relationship between a specific fault and all the related features. It provides a knowledge base of graph, where nodes indicate the entities and edges represent the relationship [10]. Through data training-based modeling, the derived KG is capable of identifying the contribution rate of each feature to a certain fault mode, and predicting the risks of the faults in future when the new-coming features are obtained. The most critical issue is the effectiveness of the knowledge graph. From the big data platform, we can extract sufficient training samples covering a long time period to ensure a rich information condition for model training. Thus, the adopted modeling solution will be the core issue that affects the performance of the derived KG and the trustworthiness of the KG-based prediction. In this paper, the XGBoost algorithm is adopted to build the knowledge graph based on big data. The identification of features and labels and the adopted algorithm are introduced as follows.

3.1 System Fault-Related Features

For the data logging tool of the 200H on-board equipments, the reported faults mainly attribute to six broad categories, including the controlling fault information, FSC error,

SBUS error, DRU fault information, A/B system inconsistency and the STM fault information. Furthermore, each of the category corresponds to several sub-categories that describe the failures or abnormal states of certain components or units of an on-board equipment. Taking SBUS error as an example, there are seven sub-categories covering the information from the OPE, BUF and FSC. The fault status information is extracted as the labels to enable the model training.

Except the fault label information, there are still 121 data fields for a piece of log record. The data items indicate the time information, identity information, train operation condition, running state information, action status of key components, Driver Machine Interface (DMI) data and system parameters. A brief summary to these data entities for each class in one piece of record is given as follows.

(1) Time information

This class contains the data entities corresponding to the time instant when the data was recorded. The typical entities belong to this class include year, month, date, hour, minute, second, millisecond, etc.

(2) Identity information

The identity information indicates train unit number, active driver ID, train ID, etc. This information illustrates the identity of the train, on-board equipment and the driver to identify the target labels corresponding to each fault event.

(3) Train operation condition

The operation conditions resulted by the train control system describe the authority and moving space that the train has to follow. There are a series of condition-related data fields, e.g. the current track circuit length, next track circuit length, EBP (Emergency Brake Profile) speed, NBP (Normal Brake Profile) speed and the LMA (Limit of Movement Authority).

(4) Running state information

This class describes the in-trip running states of the target train, including the track location, actual speed, control speed, acceleration, accumulative running distance, etc.

(5) Action status of key components

The actions and operation status of specific components of the on-board train control equipment are recorded in real-time. This class includes action mode, brake order (VC1/VC2), EB brake indication, B7N brake indication, LSI information ('A' system /'B' system), online/inactive track circuit information, DRU information, OPE state, FSC state, STM state information, LKJ information, etc.

(6) DMI data

The DMI-related information reflects the operation-related information provided to the drivers for specific train control activities, e.g. DMI text information, DMI brake alert time, DMI target speed, DMI target distance, DMI switch category.

(7) System parameters

This class corresponds to parameters and configurations for the train and on-board equipment, e.g. the wheel diameter, train type, equipment/manual priority, DRU FSC ROM version, message class code.

Before the data sets are utilized in model training, all the features and labels represented by specific data entities have to be formatted in the data pre-processing stage, which enhances the storage efficiency and accessibility to the modeling algorithms.

3.2 XGBoost-Based Model Training

The XGBoost method, which was proposed in 2016 [11], is one effective supervised machine learning algorithm to realize a scalable tree boosting system. It has successfully attracted much attention due to its outstanding efficiency and high prediction accuracy in solving a number of practical problems [12–14]. Given a training dataset $D = \{(x_i, y_i)\}$ with n samples, $i = 1, 2, \cdots, n$, where $x_i \in R^m$ represents the variable with m features and y_i denotes the corresponding label, a tree ensemble model predicts the dependent variable $\hat{y}_i$ using the following model

$$\hat{y}_i = \Phi(x_i) = \sum_{k=1}^{K} f_k(x_i) \tag{1}$$

where $f_k \in F$ denotes an regression tree with leaf scores, and F represents the space of trees as $F = \{f(y) = \omega_{h(y)}\}$ with the leaf node $h(y)$ of the yth sample and the leaf score $\omega_{h(y)}$.

For the tth iteration, the prediction results can be

$$\hat{y}_i^t = \hat{y}_i^{t-1} + f_t(x_i) \tag{2}$$

Thus, the objective function of the model can be written as the following form

$$J(f_t) = \sum_{i=1}^{n} L(y_i, \hat{y}_i^t) + \Gamma(f_t) = \sum_{i=1}^{n} L(y_i, \hat{y}_i^{t-1} + f_t(x_i)) + \Gamma(f_t) \tag{3}$$

where $L(*)$ represents the loss function, $\Gamma(*)$ indicates the complexity of the model, and it can be defined using the number of leaf nodes T and score ω as follows

$$\Gamma(f_t) = \gamma T + \frac{\lambda}{2} \sum_{j=1}^{T} \omega_j^2 \tag{4}$$

By simplification of $\Gamma(f_t)$ using the second-order Taylor expansion, the objective function can be re-written as

$$J(f_t) = \sum_{i=1}^{n} \left[g_i \omega_{h(x_i)} + \frac{1}{2} q_i \omega_{h(x_i)}^2 \right] + \gamma T + \frac{\lambda}{2} \sum_{j=1}^{T} \omega_j^2 \tag{5}$$

$$g_i = \frac{\partial L(y_i, \hat{y}_i^{t-1})}{\partial \hat{y}_i^{t-1}} \tag{6}$$

$$q_i = \frac{\partial^2 L(y_i, \hat{y}_i^{t-1})}{\partial \hat{y}_i^{t-1}} \tag{7}$$

It can be optimized and the optimal solution can be represented by the optimal value of ω_j and the corresponding value of $\Gamma(f_t)$ as

$$\omega_j^* = -\frac{\sum_{i\in I_j} g_i}{\sum_{i\in I_j} q_i + \lambda} \tag{8}$$

$$J(f_t) = -\frac{1}{2}\sum_{j=1}^{T}\frac{\left(\sum_{i\in I_j} g_i\right)^2}{\sum_{i\in I_j} q_i + \lambda} + \gamma T \tag{9}$$

By training the XGBoost model, a series of decision trees can be obtained and used in classification with specific labels as described in the former section. Utilization of the second order Taylor expansion to a loss function as (4) and normalization against the over-fitting make it different from conventional methods like Gradient Boosting Decision Tree (GBDT) solution [15]. Details of this algorithm can be found in [11].

3.3 Generation of Knowledge Graph

Through the model training based on data samples with all related features and labels extracted from the big data platform, a set of trees can be obtained to reflect the importance of each feature. The derived model describes the relationship between features and the labels representing specific fault modes. It is obvious that the involved features contribute differently to a certain fault mode. The value of feature importance provides us a reference to quantitatively evaluate the content of contribution by each feature to a fault label.

By utilizing the feature importance values, the knowledge graph corresponding to a specific fault is represented by a set of triples {$Node(fault)$, $Link$, $Node(feature)$}. As shown in Fig. 2, the structure of a local KG corresponding to a specific fault mode is based on a central node, m surrounding nodes and their links. $Node(fault)$ denotes the local center entity node indicating a specific fault mode from the fault label base. $Node(feature)$ represents the distributed graph node with respect to each of the features mentioned in Sect. 3.1. $Link$ in a triple formally illustrates a line connects $Node(fault)$ and $Node(feature)$, and it reveals the relationship between a feature and the fault mode quantitatively by the derived feature importance. It should be noticed that this example in Fig. 2 only shows a local area of the whole graph, which means there are more triples covering other central nodes {$Node(fault)$} for different faults connecting all the involved m neighborhood feature nodes {$Node(feature)$}.

It has to be noticed that the knowledge graph established with the big data platform and the presented procedures is a typical data-driven solution. That means knowledge of the target fault modes reflected by the KG does not concerns the physical mechanism of the on-board train control system and the evolution rules of faults. It just explores the capabilities of huge historical data sets to build models that could reach a determination to the future health status and maintenance decisions to a target on-board train control equipment. This solution would not completely replace conventional mechanism-based models or analytical models, but enables a new path to reveal the feature correlation rules and patterns in the data domain. The derived knowledge graph and data/models behind

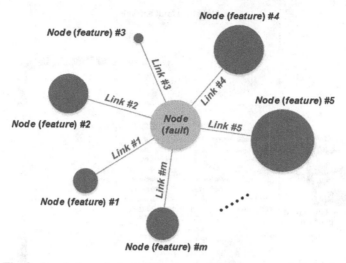

Fig. 2. Local view of a knowledge graph with respect to a fault mode.

it consolidate the knowledge base of the operators and maintenance staff to improve the field operation and management.

4   Results and Analysis

4.1   Datasets and Experimental Platform

The proposed system framework as Fig. 1 has been implemented using real case data sets from the high-speed railway administration. Since 2015, field data log files of on-board train control equipments used in practical railway operations were collected to build the big data-based system, where both the 200H and 300T on-board equipments were involved. In the laboratory, the big data platform was established using a master server and two slave servers. The four layers mentioned in Fig. 1 have been realized with specific software tools. Through the data pre-processing, the structured data sets, including all the features and fault mode labels, can be utilized in model training and derivation of the knowledge graphs. The procedures of knowledge graph construction based on the big data platform are described in Fig. 3.

The continuous accumulation of the filed data sets gradually consolidates the foundation of KG construction by this platform. By the end of 2019, there had been over 80 thousand log files of 200H on-board train control equipments, and the data amount almost reached 1TB. By integrating the Spark framework into the big data-based platform, the XGBoost algorithm can be carried out using certain training samples within a specific period of time. Though there have been approaches for XGBoost to determine a suggested number of trees, a fixed number 500 has been adopted for simplicity in generating the decision trees in the case study. Using the derived training model by XGBoost, the statistical results of different faults and the corresponding feature importance data enable us to construct or update the knowledge graph with respect to the faults need to be concerned in maintenance.

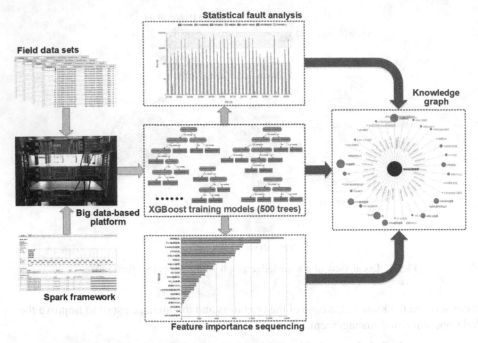

Fig. 3. Realization of big data platform and knowledge graph derivation.

4.2 Results of a Case Study

A case study is performed using the field data sets of 200H equipments from the January to June in 2017. The size of the adopted training set exceeds 131GB. It took a long time to carry out the XGBoost-based model training jobs. Figure 4 and Fig. 5 show the results of feature importance corresponding to the controlling fault mode.

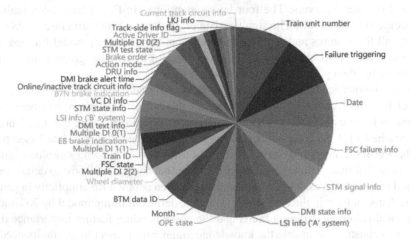

Fig. 4. Importance distribution of 33 major controlling-fault-related features.

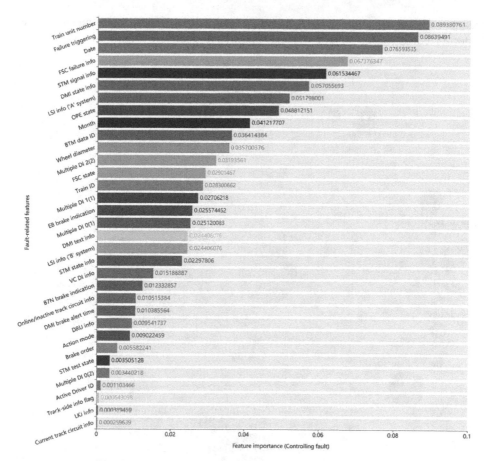

Fig. 5. Feature importance sequence of the controlling fault.

It can be found that not all the features are covered in the presented importance sequencing result. Based on the significance principle, only 33 major features from the whole feature set are considered in the feature importance sequencing and distribution analysis, since they achieved a contribution of 97.30% to the target fault mode. Figure 4 clearly shows the distribution of importance by each individual feature in the subset. In addition, Fig. 5 illustrates the differences among the 33 major features according to the normalized value of feature importance.

Based on the results of feature importance sequencing, the knowledge graph for the controlling fault mode is derived using the 33 major features. Using the open-sourced ECharts visualization tool, 33 feature nodes are integrated into this knowledge graph around a central node with a label "controlling fault". In order to distinguish the contributions to the fault mode from different features according to the machine learning model, the size of each feature node is determined dynamically according to the feature importance value. Furthermore, three colors have been adopted with a piecewise defined principle. That means a feature with a normalized importance larger than 0.05

indicates a red node in the derived KG, and the blue and green nodes represent the feature importance intervals of (0.01, 0.05] and (0, 0.01], respectively (Fig. 6).

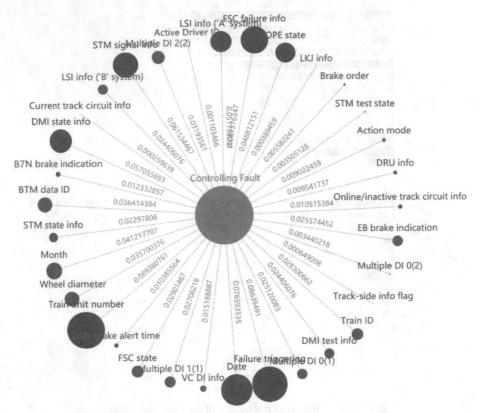

Fig. 6. Knowledge graph derived by the training model using the data set from 2017. (Color figure online)

We can find that there are 8 red nodes representing a higher importance. The other 16 blue nodes and 9 green nodes illustrate the moderate or lower influence to the fault mode by these features. The normalized importance values of each feature have been marked with the links. The knowledge graph clearly demonstrates a visualization interface to the users, which effectively reflects the inherence knowledge from a large data set. With the graph, we can use the central node "controlling fault" as the start to identify the features with significant effects to this fault mode according to the size, color and link value. The fault relevance information can be provided to specific engineers or staff to make decisions for adjusting maintenance plans. In addition, the prediction of fault probability can be achieved with new-coming feature data based on the trained model with respect to the knowledge graph, and that is a significant factor to enable the precise and effective condition-based maintenance. In general, the utilization of the XGBoost machine learning method based on a big data condition makes it possible of realizing the prognostics and health management of the specific on-board train control equipments based on the data-enabled knowledge of fault occurrence and progression over time during the life cycle.

It has to be noticed that only the "controlling fault" is involved in this case study. A complete knowledge graph corresponding to a whole on-board train control system level will cover all the defined fault modes. That means each feature will be connected with multiple sub-central nodes indicating the specific fault modes through several links. Thus, we will have to identify multiple attributes for a feature entity based on its contribution to different faults in constructing the knowledge graph and generating recommendations and assistance for the CBM purpose. Furthermore, only a fixed data set within half a year is adopted in the case study to demonstrate the knowledge graph constructing solution. Actually, this platform is capable of updating the derived models and knowledge graphs dynamically based on incremental data sets, which ensures the capability in life cycle monitoring and proactive maintenance of the on-board train control equipments in practical operations.

5 Conclusion and Future Works

This paper presents a data-driven framework for constructing the knowledge graph in pursuing the prognostics and health management of on-board train control system. A big data-based platform is designed and established to realize the storage and management of accumulative data files in the field operation. The XGBoost algorithm has been adopted to enable the model training with respect to specific fault modes, and it evaluates the importance of multiple feature entities. We also suggested principles of the knowledge graph with different nodes and links according to the derived feature importance. The design was realized with field data from real high-speed train control equipments. Results from a case study illustrate that the presented solution can determine the feature importance sequence and generate the knowledge graph with respect to specific fault modes, which reveals the relevance of the feature entities to the faults from a big-data-driven perspective.

In the future works, comparison analysis will be carried out based on multiple data sets within different time ranges, with which the effect of the incremental data condition will be further validated. Based on that, different training models will be used to perform fault probability prediction to realize a tight connection between models and decision making results for maintenance. Furthermore, more types of on-board train control equipment will be taken into account to enhance the coverage performance of the platform for assisting the practical operation and maintenance activities.

Acknowledgement. This research was funded by Beijing Natural Science Foundation (L191014), National Natural Science Foundation of China (61873023, U1934222), and Beijing Nova Program of Science and Technology (No. Z191100001119066).

The authors would like to thank Mei-hao Yang, Xin Han and Tian-tian Li for their assistance to the development and optimization of the big data-based platform and the cooperation with the operation maintenance department of the high-speed railway.

References

1. Saki, M., Abolhasan, M., Lipman, J.: A novel approach for big data classification and transportation in rail networks. IEEE Trans. Intell. Transp. Syst. **21**(3), 1239–1249 (2020)
2. Oneto, L., et al.: Train delay prediction systems: a big data analytics perspective. Big Data Res. **11**, 54–64 (2018)
3. Ghofrani, F., He, Q., Goverde, R., Liu, X.: Recent applications of big data analytics in railway transportation systems: a survey. Transp. Res. Part C: Emerg. Technol. **90**, 226–246 (2018)
4. Gulijk, C., Hughes, P., Figueres-Esteban, M.: Big data risk analysis for rail safety. In: Proceedings of 25th European Safety and Reliability Conference, Zurich, Netherlands, pp. 1–8 (2015)
5. Jiang, Z., Hsu, C., Zhang, D., Zou, X.: Evaluating rail transit timetable using big passengers' data. J. Comput. Syst. Sci. **82**, 144–155 (2016)
6. Fink, O., Wang, Q., Svensen, M., Dersin, P., Lee, W., Ducoffe, M.: Potential, challenges and future directions for deep learning in prognostics and health management applications. Eng. Appl. Artif. Intell. **92**, 1–15 (2020)
7. Chi, Z., Lin, J., Chen, R., Huang, S.: Data-driven approach to study the polygonization of high-speed railway train wheel-sets using field data of China's HSR train. Measurement **149**, 1–12 (2020)
8. Shahabinejad, M., Khabbazian, M., Ardakani, M.: An efficient binary locally repairable code for hadoop distributed file system. IEEE Commun. Lett. **18**(8), 1287–1290 (2014)
9. Bui, D., Hussain, S., Huh, E., Lee, S.: Adaptive replication management in HDFS based on supervised learning. IEEE Trans. Knowl. Data Eng. **28**(6), 1369–1382 (2016)
10. Yan, H., Yang, J., Wan, J.: KnowIME: a system to construct a knowledge graph for intelligent manufacturing equipment. IEEE Access **8**, 41805–41813 (2020)
11. Chen, T., Guestrin, C.: XGBoost: a scalable tree boosting system. In: Proceedings of the 22nd ACM SIGKDD International Conference on Knowledge Discovery and Data Mining, San Francisco, USA, pp. 785–794 (2016)
12. Song, K., Yan, F., Ding, T., Gao, L., Lu, S.: A steel property optimization model based on the XGBoost algorithm and improved PSO. Comput. Mater. Sci. **174**, 1–13 (2020)
13. Chen, W., Fu, K., Zuo, J., Zheng, X., Ren, W.: Radar emitter classification for large data set based on weighted-XGBoost. IET Radar Sonar Navig. **11**(8), 1203–1207 (2017)
14. Georganos, S., Grippa, T., Vanhuysse, S., Lennert, M., Shimoni, M., Wolff, E.: Very high resolution object-based land use-land cover urban classification using extreme gradient boosting. IEEE Geosci. Remote Sens. Lett. **15**(4), 607–611 (2018)
15. Friedman, J., Hastie, T., Tibshirani, R.: Additive logistic regression: a statistical view of boosting. Ann. Stat. **28**(2), 337–407 (2000)

Early Detecting the At-risk Students in Online Courses Based on Their Behavior Sequences

Shuai Yuan[1], Huan Huang[2(✉)], Tingting He[3], and Rui Hou[4]

[1] National Engineering Research Center for E-Learning, Central China Normal University, Wuhan, China

[2] School of Education, South-Central University for Nationalities, Wuhan, China
huanghuan@mail.scuec.edu.cn

[3] Hubei Provincial Key Laboratory of Artificial Intelligence and Smart Learning, School of Computer, National Language Resources Monitoring & Research Center for Network Media, Central China Normal University, Wuhan, China
tthe@mail.ccnu.edu.cn

[4] College of Computer Science, South-Central University for Nationalities, Wuhan, China

Abstract. Online learning has developed rapidly, but the participation of learners is very low. So it is of great significance to construct a prediction model of learning results, to identify students at risk in time and accurately. We select nine online learning behaviors from one course in Moodle, take one week as the basic unit and 5 weeks as the time node of learning behavior, and the aggregate data and sequence data of the first 5 weeks, the first 10 weeks, the first 15 weeks, the first 20 weeks, the first 25 weeks, the first 30 weeks, the first 35 weeks and the first 39 weeks are formed. Eight classic machine learning methods, i.e. Logistic Regression (LR), Naive Bayes (NB), Radom Forest (RF), K-Nearest Neighbors (KNN), Support Vector Machine (SVM), Iterative Dichotomiser3 (ID3), Classification and Regression Trees (CART), and Neural Network (NN), are used to predict the learning results in different time nodes based on aggregate data and sequence data. The experimental results show that sequence data is more effective than aggregate data to predict learning results. The prediction AUC of RF model on sequence data is 0.77 at the lowest and 0.83 at the highest, the prediction AUC of CART model on sequence data is 0.70 at the lowest and 0.83 at the highest, which are the best models of the eight classic prediction models. Then Radom Forest (RF) model, Classification and Regression Trees (CART) model, recurrent neural network (RNN) model and long short term memory (LSTM) model are used to predict learning results on sequence data; the experimental results show that long short term memory (LSTM) is a model with the highest value of AUC and stable growth based on sequence data, and it is the best model of all models for predicting learning results.

Keywords: Early detecting · The prediction of learning result · Long short term memory

Z. Deze et al. (Eds.): BDTA 2020/WiCON 2020, LNICST 371, pp. 17–33, 2021.
https://doi.org/10.1007/978-3-030-72802-1_2

1 Introduction

In the past decade, online learning has developed rapidly. Thousands of online learning systems have emerged, providing different online learning services for different kinds of learners. Compared with the traditional face-to-face teaching, online learning has many advantages undoubtedly. It breaks the limitation of learning time and space, expands the scale of learners, and effectively improves the autonomy of students. However, there are also some problems in online learning, one of which is that the participation of learners is low [1]. It leads many learners to faile in online courses. To solve this problem, many researchers recently suggest to using big data technology to identify at-risk learners timely and accurately, to provide adaptive learning intervention or support for them [2–4]. According to this, it is of great significance to find an effective learning result predicting method.

Based on the general process of data mining, the basic process of online learning result predicting is as follows: 1) collect learning process data in an all-round way to form a big dataset; 2) select or design some important predicting indicators of learning result based on the learning process data; 3) use a machine learning algorithm to build predicting model of learning result based on the indicators; 4) predict new ones' learning results based on their learning process data. It can be seen that predicting indicator and predicting algorithm are two key components of learning result predicting. For these two components, many scholars have carried out a lot of in-depth researches. In the aspect of predicting indicators, researchers have explored many behavior indicators, such as the total time of online learning, amount of resource views, test scores, and amount of forum posts [5–7]. In the aspect of predicting algorithm, researchers have explored many classic machine learning algorithms, such as Logical Regression (LR), Decision Tree (DT), K-Nearest Neighbor (KNN), Naïve Bayes (NB), Support Vector Machine (SVM), Random Forest (RF), and so on [8, 9]. However, nearly all the existing researches used aggregated data when extracting the predicting indicators, without considering the dynamic pattern of the predicting indicators. Some recent works have shown that some dynamic patterns of learning behavior may reflect the advanced cognitive characteristics of learners, which play an important role in online learning results. Accordingly, if these dynamic patterns are integrated into the predicting model of online learning results, the prediction effect should be improved to a certain extent.

To integrate the dynamic pattern of learning behavior into predicting model and improve predicting accuracy, this paper proposes an online learning result predicting method based on long short term memory (LSTM) neural network. LSTM is an outstanding representative of the recurrent neural network (RNN). RNN is a kind of neural network used to process and predict sequence data. It can mine the hidden dependent relationship or sequential pattern from a large number of sequence data, to achieve accurate predicting of sequential data. LSTM further solves the problem of long-term dependence in sequential data. At present, LSTM has achieved good results in speech recognition, machine translation, and sequential analysis and other applications. Given the remarkable performance of LSTM in processing sequence data, this study tries to apply LSTM in online learning result predicting. Different from the existing predicting methods, this method extracts value sets of predicting indicators based on the online learning behavior data in different time periods and form a sequence data. Based on the sequence data, it further mines the sequential pattern and its relationship with the learning result by using LSTM.

2 Related Work

Although early warning system for online learning was emerged until recent years, it has been concerned by many researchers since it was put forward. In the past decade, a large number of researches have been carried out on the key issue – learning result predicting. According to the basic process of learning result predicting (collect data, design predicting indicators, develop predicting model, and predict learning result), the existing researches will be examined. In the aspect of data collection, the existing researches mainly used the learning behaviors and test scores recorded in the learning management system [5–7]. However, with the deepening of research in recent years, some researches also used some background information and psychological characteristics of learners through survey, which is also an important basis for learning result predicting. For example, based on the theory of self-regulated learning, Pardo et al. combined the self-regulated learning index and online learning behavior of learners to predict their learning results, among which the self-regulated learning index is obtained through a survey [10]. In addition, most of the researches are based on the data of one course to develop predicting model for a specific course. Still, few researches also use the data of multiple courses to explore the cross-course predicting model. For example, Gašević et al. constructed a cross-course predicting model based on the data of nine courses, and compared it with the predicting models of each specific course [11]. The results show that it should be prudent to integrate the data of multiple course data to develop a cross-course predicting model because learners' online learning behaviors are quite different in different courses [11].

In the aspect of predicting indicators, researchers have explored the impact of many indicators on the effect of learning result predicting from different perspectives. Recently Fan and Wang summarized three kinds of indicators used in learning result predicting through the in-depth analysis of 83 kinds of literature: human-computer interaction indicators, human-human interaction indicators and individual tendency indicators [12]. Human–computer interaction indicators reflect the interaction between learners and learning platform, such as the frequency of login, the total time of online learning, number of browsed resources, number of completed assignments, scores of the tests and so on. Human-human interaction indicators reflect the interaction between the learner and leaner, learner and teacher, mainly include the number of posts, replies, social network location and so on. Individual tendency indicators mainly include background and psychological characteristics reflecting individual differences of learners, such as gender, age, education level, prior knowledge, learning motivation, the level of self-regulated learning and so on. The early research of online learning result predicting mainly used human-computer interaction indicators and human-human interaction indicators, but in recent years more and more researches began to introduce some advanced psychological characteristics into learning result predicting model to further improve its accuracy and interpretability. Although researchers have conducted in-depth research on the predicting indicators, due to different research scenarios and research data, the results of these studies are not consist of. Recently, Conijn et al. extracted 23 predicting indicators which were commonly used from the log data of 17 courses, and compared the effect of each indicator on the predicting of learning result of different courses [13]. They found that in addition to the mid-term test score is significantly related to the final result in all courses, other indicators are only significantly related to the final result in some courses, and the correlation between the same indicator and the final result shows different effect in different courses [13]. This shows that it is difficult to find a set of general predicting indicators, so we should select appropriate predicting indicators for specific situations.

In the aspect of predicting model development, the predicting variable defined by most of the researches is a binary classification variable. That means the predicting result is whether the learner passed the course or not. However, some researches also defined prediction variable as a continuous numerical variable. That means the prediction variable is a continuous grade of a student. According to the different predicting variable defined, the researchers adopt different predicting algorithms to develop a predicting model. When the predicting variable is the final grade of the student, the most used predicting algorithm is Mmultiple Linear Regression (MLR) [13]. When the predicting variable is whether a student will pass the course or not, the predicting algorithms used by the researchers mainly include Logic Regression (LR), Decision Tree (DT), Naïve Bayes (NB), K-Nearest Neighbor (KNN), Support Vector Machine (SVM), Random Forest (RF) and so on [8, 9]. For example, Marbouti et al. defined the predicting variable as to whether a student will pass the course or not, and they developed different predicting models using LG, DT, NB, KNN, MLP, SVM respectively. However, the experimental results showed that no one model can achieve satisfactory results in all aspects [8]. Therefore, they further used the ensemble learning to develop a prediction model and optimized the model through feature selection and increasing training set. Finally, they found the ensemble model is the best one [8]. Howard et al. defined the predicting variable as the final score, and developed predicting models using RF, BART, SGBoost, PCR, SVM, NN, KNN, respectively [9]. The experimental results show that the sixth week is the best time to identify at-risk students, which not only has enough time to intervene the students, but also can ensure the accuracy of the predicting model. Furthermore, at this time, the model developed by BART gets the best performance [9]. From the existing researches, we can know that although the researchers have compared the effect of a variety of predicting algorithms in learning results predicting, which algorithm was best for learning result predicting has not reached a consistent conclusion. Also, the existing predicting algorithms are the traditional classic machine learning algorithms, and few kinds of research have explored the effect of the latest advanced machine learning algorithms on learning result predicting, such as deep learning algorithms [14].

Based on the research on predicting methods, some institutions have also developed early warning systems for online learning, such as "Course Signals" of Purdue University in the United States, and "OU Analysis" of Open University in the United Kingdom. Course Signals is an early warning system for online courses developed by Purdue University in 2007. It was originally developed for the freshmen of Purdue University to predict the academic performance of students and improve the success rate and retention rate [15]. Course Signals mainly uses four kinds of predicting indicators: test scores, effort levels, previous academic achievements and background information [15]. Based on the above indicators, Course Signals uses a specific student success algorithm (SSA) to predict the learning results of learners. According to the predicted results, students' learning states are divided into three states: red light (high risk), yellow light (early warning) and green light (good) [15]. The results of a three-year study show that the academic achievement of students using Course Signals is significantly higher than that of students not using the system, and the corresponding retention rate of students is significantly higher than that of students not using the system [15]. OU Analysis is an early warning system for online courses developed by UK Open University. Its goal is to identify at-risk learners as early as possible, to give effective intervention to improve the retention rate of learners. To achieve this goal, OU Analysis selects some background information and online learning behavior of learners as predicting indicators, trains four predicting models using NB, KNN and CART respectively, and finally determines whether students are at risk or not using voting mechanism [16]. OU Analysis provides two views: course view and learner view. The course view shows an overview of all learners' online learning behavior, the predicted results of whether each learner will participate in the next test, and the predicted results of each learner's final score. The learner view shows an overview of a learner's online learning behavior, actual scores and predicted results of each test, as well as recommended learning activities and learning resources [16]. As of the summer of 2016, OU Analysis has been widely used in more than 40 courses of UK Open University.

3   Proposed LSTM-Based Framework

In order to integrate the dynamic pattern of learning behavior into the learning result predicting model, this paper proposes a learning result predicting method based on LSTM. The framework of this method is shown in Fig. 1, which includes two parts: predicting model development and learning result predicting. The basic process of the predicting model development is as follows: 1) aggregate each learner's scores according to the defined schema to generate the final scores, and further divide the learners into two or three categories, such as success, fail and withdraw; 2) select the appropriate predicting indicators based on the existing researches and the learning behavior data

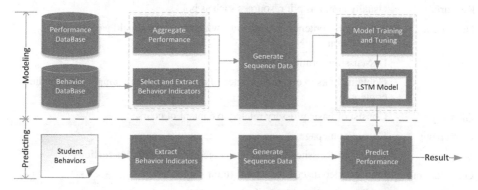

Fig. 1. The proposed framework for the detection of at-risk students

collected by the learning platform; 3) take one week as the period, extract the values of predicting indicators in each week from the raw learning behavior data, and generate a sequence data set; 4) train the LSTM-based predicting model using the back propagation algorithm and gradient descent algorithm. The basic process of learning result predicting is as follows: 1) extract the values of predicting indicators in each week from learners' raw learning behavior data to generate a sequence data; 2) input the sequence data into LSTM model to predict a learner's learning result.

3.1 Behavior Indicator Selection

From the previous literature review, we can see that researchers have explored many predicting indicators from many aspects. These predicting indicators mainly involve three aspects: first, the personal characteristics of learners, such as the gender, age, race, learning motivation, prior knowledge and so on; second, the results of process assessments, such as assignment scores, test scores, mid-term test scores and so on; third, the learning behaviors of learners, such as the frequency of login, number of browsed resources, number of posts and so on. As the goal of this study is to explore whether the dynamic pattern of learning behavior can be mined and improve the accuracy of learning result predicting, this study only considers the learning behavior indicators. It does not consider the personal characteristics and process assessment results.

In addition, because the data used in this study is from the Open University's Learning Analysis Dataset (OULAD) [8] when selecting the learning behavior indicators, we can only choose from the learning behaviors recorded in the dataset. OULAD is an open dataset produced by Kuzilek et al. of the Institute of Knowledge Media of the UK Open University, which records the detailed click behaviors and assessment scores of 22 courses [8]. All the 22 courses are deployed on the Moodle platform. However, the data in OULAD is not the raw Moodle log data, but the aggregate data. Kuzilek et al. divide the raw click behaviors of learners into 20 kinds of learning behaviors according

Table 1. Description of the nine behavior indicators

Activity type	Description
Resource	Usually contains pdf resources such as books
Oucontent	Represents content of assigments, which students should pass during presentation
Forumng	Disscussion forum
Url	Contains links to external or internal resources or for example video/audio content
Glossary	Consist of basic glossary related to content of course
Homepage	Course homepage
Subpage	Points to other sites in the course together with basic instructions
Oucollaborate	Online video discussion rooms (tutor - students)
Dataplus	Additional information/videos/audios/pdf

to the characteristics of the clicked objects [8]. OULAD recorded each learner's daily clicked objects, their frequency and the type of learning behaviors. Although OULAD contains 20 different types of learning behavior, not all courses contain these 20 types of learning behaviors. Because the course selected in this study only involves nine types of learning behaviors, these nine types of learning behaviors are selected as the predicting indicators. These nine learning behavior indicators mainly involve the use of learning resources, forums, assignments, glossary, homepage and other objects. See Table 1 for a detailed description.

3.2 Sequence Data Generation and Preprocessing

After selecting the predicting indicators, the value of each predicting indicator in a period can be calculated for training the predicting model. As mentioned above, most of the researches obtain values of predicting indicators from the accumulated data to train the predicting model. Different from these researches, this study calculates the value of each predicting indicator in different time periods, respectively, to generate the sequence data to train the LSTM model. Although every object clicked by each learner every day and its clicking frequency and learning behavior category are recorded in the OULAD, these data can't be directly used to train the LSTM model. They need to be transformed to generate the sequence data of each predicting indicator. The process of sequence data generation is shown in Fig. 2 below:

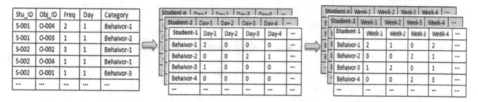

Fig. 2. Process of sequence data generation

Frist, according to the identification of learners, the behavior category, and the time when the clicking behavior occurs, we can calculate the frequency of every behavior indicator of every learner in every day. Second, these sequential data is further aggregated into the frequency of each behavior indicator of every learner in every week. The reason why the frequency of each behavior indicator is calculated by week is that there is a problem of data sparsity when calculating each behavior indicator by day. Some learning behaviors do not occur for several consecutive days while calculating by week can solve this problem to a certain extent.

After generating the sequence data of each behavior indicator, pre-processing is implemented. In OULAD, the learning results of learners are divided into four categories: pass, fail, withdraw and distinction. Because there are very few samples whose learning results are distinction, these samples are eliminated in the pre-processing stage. In this study, the final learning results of learners are divided into three categories: pass, fail and withdraw.

3.3 Prediction Modeling Based on LSTM

In order to use the dynamic characteristic of learning behavior to improve the accuracy of learning result predicting, we adopt the LSTM network to develop learning result predicting model. LSTM network is a special kind of RNN, which can make full use of not only the useful information close to the current position, but also the useful information far from the current position. The basic structure of the LSTM network is the same as that of the simple RNN, and the main difference is the internal structure of the recurrent unit. Different from the structure of the recurrent unit in simple RNN, the LSTM recurrent unit has a special structure with three "gates", which are usually called the input gate, forget gate and output gate. By these three gates, the LSTM selectively influences the state of the recurrent neural network in every moment. The structure of the recurrent unit in LSTM network is shown in Fig. 3:

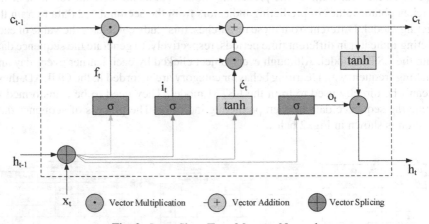

Fig. 3. Long Short Term Memory Network

In the above figure, c_t is the current state of the neural network, c_{t-1} is the state of the neural network last time, h_{t-1} is the output of neural network last time, $\acute{c}_t$ is the candidate state obtained by nonlinear function, x_t is the input of the current time, i_t is the input gate of the recurrent unit, $i_t \in [0, 1]^D$; f_t is the forget gate of the recurrent unit, $f_t \in [0, 1]^D$; o_t is the output gate of the recurrent unit, $o_t \in [0, 1]^D$. Forget gate f_t decides how much information of the state of last time c_{t-1} needs to be forgot. Input gate i_t decides how much information about the candidate state at the current time $\acute{c}_t$ needs to be saved. Output gate o_t decides how much information of the current state c_t needs to be passed to the output of current time h_t. When $f_t = 0$, $i_t = 1$, the recurrent unit clears the history information, and the candidate state vector $\acute{c}_t$ is written, the state of the neural network c_t is still related to the historical information of the previous moment. When $f_t = 1$, $i_t = 0$, the recurrent unit will copy the contents of the previous time without writing any new information.

LSTM calculates the state at the current time c_t and output h_t as follows:

1) Using the output of previous time h_{t-1} and the input at the current time x_t, three gates i_t, f_t, o_t are calculated. The calculation methods are shown in Formula 1, 2 and 3 respectively:

$$i_t = \sigma(W_i x_i + U_i h_{t-1} + b_i) \qquad (1)$$

$$f_t = \sigma(W_f x_i + U_f h_{t-1} + b_f) \qquad (2)$$

$$o_t = \sigma(W_o x_i + U_o h_{t-1} + b_o) \qquad (3)$$

2) Using forget gate f_t and input gate i_t to update the current state c_t. The update method is shown in formula 4:

$$c_t = f_t \odot c_{t-1} + i_t \odot \acute{c}_t \qquad (4)$$

By substituting Formula 1 and formula 2 into formula 4, we can further replace the calculation method of c_t, which is shown as formula 5:

$$c_t = \sigma(W_f x_i + U_f h_{t-1} + b_f) \odot c_{t-1} + \sigma(W_i x_i + U_i h_{t-1} + b_i) \odot \acute{c}_t \qquad (5)$$

3) Combined output gate o_t, pass information of internal state to external state h_t, h_t is calculated as follows:

$$h_t = o_t \odot \tanh c_t \qquad (6)$$

Substituting formula 3 into formula 6, h_t can be further expressed as:

$$h_t = \sigma(W_o x_i + U_o h_{t-1} + b_o) \odot \tanh c_t \qquad (7)$$

According to the forward propagation process of LSTM network, this study takes the sequence data of behavior indicators from the first week to the n-th week as the input of the LSTM network. It uses the back propagation algorithm and the gradient descent algorithm to train the LSTM network. To dynamically predict learners' learning results and identify at-risk leaners, we should train an LSTM model for every week.

4 Experiment and Result

4.1 Dataset and Data Preprocessing

The data of this study comes from Open University (OU), which is one of the largest distance learning institutions in Europe. The OU modules are increasingly using the Virtual Learning Environment, Moodle, to provide learning materials, rather than the previous paper materials provided in the past. In 2017, Open University Learning Analytics Dataset (OULAD) was released. OULAD contains a subset of the OU student data from 2013 and 2014, including the information about 22 courses, 32,593 students, their assessment results, and logs of their interactions with the VLE represented by daily summaries of student clicks (10,655,280 entries). At present, there are two public datasets commonly used for learning behavior analysis and learning result prediction: KDD Cup

2010 dataset and KDD cup 2015 dataset, Compared with these two datasets, OULAD is quite different, which includes demographic data of learners and interaction data with the university's VLE.

In the experimental stage, this study selected the "AAA" course (code_module = "AAA") from October 2014 (code_presentation = "2014J"). The course lasts 269 days from the official start to the end (from date = 0 to date = 269), taking seven days as a week, 38 weeks and three days, plus four days(all kinds of behavior data are expressed as 0), a total of 39 weeks. During this period, the number of learners who chose to study this course was 365. Learning outcomes are divided into four categories, among which 299 are "Pass", 46 are "Fail", 66 are "Withdraw", and 24 are "Distinction". Because the number of "Distinction" is too small, the whole experimental data may be unbalanced, leading to the prediction effect. Excluding the category of "Distinction", the number of learners in experiment is 341, learning results are divided into three categories: Pass, Fail and Withdraw. There are 147653 learning records for 341 learners in the experiment. There are nine main behavior operations: dataplus, forumng, glossary, homepage, oucollaborate, oucontent, resource, subpage, url, the number of each operation is shown in Fig. 4.

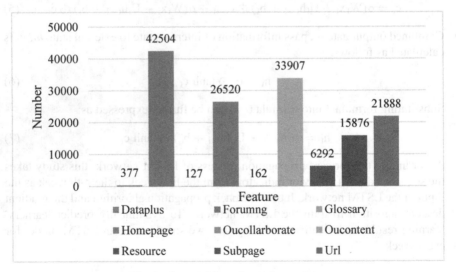

Fig. 4. Composition of experimental data

During the experiment, in order to ensure the validity of the experiment, the training set and test set are randomly assigned, according to 60% of the training set and 40% of the test set. Behavior data is processed in two ways: aggregate data and sequence data.

1) Aggregate data. The course contains 39 weeks, with five weeks as the time node, the first 5 weeks, the first 10 weeks, the first 15 weeks, the first 20 weeks, the first 25 weeks, the first 30 weeks, the first 35 weeks and the first 39 weeks as the units. The nine behavior categories in the time node segment are aggregated for statistics, and the data preprocessing results of each time node segment are 9 columns (categories).

Aggregate data is the aggregation statistics of 9 kinds of behavior data in a specified time period, reflecting the total number of each behavior operation in this time period.

2) Sequence data. Taking one week as the unit, the aggregation data of nine behaviors were counted. Then, the first 5 weeks, the first 10 weeks, the first 15 weeks, the first 20 weeks, the first 25 weeks, the first 30 weeks, the first 35 weeks and the first 39 weeks were taken as the time node, and the nine behaviors in the time node period were spliced and summarized by week. The data preprocessing results of each time node period were n * 9 columns (categories) (n = 5, 10, 15, ..., 35, 39). Sequence data not only reflects the total amount of each behavior in a specified time period, but also can compare the number of behavior changes in different time periods after splicing the behavior data of adjacent time periods.

4.2   Implementation Details

This paper mainly solves two problems: Which is the greater influence of on learning result prediction, sequence data or aggregate data? Which model is the best model to predict the learning results of sequence data? Aiming at these two problems, the following two experiments are designed.

4.2.1   Comparison of Prediction Models on Aggregate Data and Sequence Data

According to the prediction models of learning result used in related research, Logistic Regression (LR), Navie Bayes (NB), Radom Forest (RF), K-Nearest Neighbors (KNN), Support Vector Machine (SVM), Iterative Dichotomiser 3 (ID3), Classification and Regression Tress (CART), and Neural Network (NN) eight classic machine learning algorithms were selected, aggregate data and sequence data of the first 5 weeks, the first 10 weeks, the first 15 weeks, the first 20 weeks, the first 25 weeks, the first 30 weeks, the first 35 weeks and the first 39 weeks are respectively input into the models, the AUC of various prediction models were compared. LR model is generally used to solve the binary classification problem, because the learning results of this research are divided into pass, fail and withdraw, it belongs to multi classification problem, and one vs one (OVO) method is adopted, two categories are selected for comparison from the three categories, three comparisons are made, given a new sample, the probability corresponding to each category of the sample is calculated, and the prediction result of the new sample is the category with the highest probability; newton-cg algorithm is used to iteratively optimize the loss function by using the second derivative matrix of the loss function, i.e. Hessian matrix. NB model is based on GaussianNB classification algorithm, that is, the prior is Gaussian distribution of naive Bayes, the main parameter is prior probability, in the experiment, a priori probability $P = mk/m$, where m is the total number of training set samples, mk is the number of training set samples of the k class. RF model is a Meta estimator, which is composed of multiple decision trees, and each decision tree has no correlation. In the experiment, the number of decision trees in the forest is 10, and the entropy function of information gain is used to measure the performance of splitting quality. KNN model is a commonly used classification algorithm. If a sample is the most similar to K samples in the dataset, and most of the K samples belong to a certain category, the sample also belongs to a certain category. This model is related to the initial K. In our research, we set K = 3, 4, 5, 6, respectively, to compare the AUC of the model. Experimental results show that the AUC of the learning result prediction model is the highest when k = 5. And according to the sample data, it can automatically get the appropriate algorithm from the ball_tree﹑ kd_tree and brute algorithm. The SVM (SVC) classifier is selected, when the penalty parameter is set to 1.0, the penalty for mis-classification increases, the kernel function is rbf, radial basis function determines the classification boundary according to the distance from each support vector, which can be mapped to infinite dimensions. ID3 model and CART model are classic algorithms of DT. In the experiment, ID3 model uses information entropy as the standard of feature selection, CART model uses gini coefficient as the standard of feature selection, and both models set splitter as best, which require to find the optimal dividing point in all the dividing points of features. NN is a kind of artificial intelligence machine learning technology, which simulates the human brain. This experiment uses the most classic three-layer neural network, including input layer, hidden layer and output layer. When using aggregate data to predict learning results, the input layer is 9, the bath_size is 30, the activation function is relu; the hidden layer is 6, the activation function is relu; the output layer is 3, and the activation function is softmax. When using sequence data to predict learning results, the input layer is 9 * n (n = 5, 10, 15, 20, 25, 30, 35, 39), the bath_size is 30, the activation function is relu; when the hidden layer is 6, the activation function is relu; when the output layer is 3, the activation function is softmax. The optimizer selects Adam, which is an adaptive learning rate method. It dynamically adjusts the learning rate of each parameter by using the first-order moment estimation and the second-order moment estimation of gradient. Each iterative learning rate has a clear range, which makes the parameter change very stable. The loss function was categorical_crossentropy, and the evaluation standard was accuracy. The number of iterations is determined by the current experimental model. According to experience, the number of iterations may be different when the input data changes weekly. Since the test set and training set are randomly assigned, the values of AUC predicted by each model may be different. Therefore, each model on the aggregate data and sequence data in different weeks are experimented for ten times, and the average value of predicted AUC is taken as the final prediction result on aggregate data or sequence data in this period of the model.

4.2.2 Prediction Model of Learning Results Based on Sequence Data

The best prediction models of learning results selected from the last experiment are compared with RNN model and LSTM model on sequence data, and the best prediction model of learning results is selected.

RNN is mainly used for the prediction on sequence data. The experimental data in this research is sequence data. Through experiments, RNN is compared with the best model in the previous experiment. The Keras framework is used in the experiment. The RNN model is constructed in three layers. The input layer is a three-dimensional vector: input_size × time_steps × cell_size, input_size is the length of data in each time period, that is, the number of features. In our research, input_size is the nine features extracted in the earlier stage; time_steps is the number of weeks, i.e. time_steps = 5, 10, 15, 20, 25, 30, 35, 39; cell_size is the number of neurons, which is set as 351 in the experiment; If the data input model of the first 15 weeks is used for prediction, the input three-dimensional vector of the input layer is: $9 \times 15 \times 351$, the activation is relu; the units of the hidden layer are 351, the activation is relu; the output layer is output three classification, and the activation function is softmax. The model optimizer is Adam, corresponding to softmax classifier, and the model loss function is set to categorical_crossentropy, which is the logarithmic loss function of the multi classification. The criteria for model evaluation is accuracy. The same to the NN model, the number of iterations is determined by the current experimental model. The number of iterations may be different when the number of input data changes. According to the sequence data of different weeks, the model also tests ten times in each time period, and the average value of prediction AUC value is the ten times AUC values predicted by the learning results of the model.

RNN has a great advantage in processing sequence data. It can use the previous information to carry out corresponding operations on the current task, but if the location is far away, it can't be directly operated. LSTM is a special RNN model, which can solve the problem of "long dependence". In the experiment, a three-layer LSTM model is built by using Keras framework. The input layer of LSTM model is also a three-dimensional vector: input_size $\times$ time_steps $\times$ cell_size, the meaning and set of parameters in each dimension are the same as RNN model. Input_size is the length of data in each time period, that is, the number of features. Input_size is the nine features extracted in the earlier stage; time_steps is the number of weeks, including several weeks. In our research, five weeks is a time node, so time_steps $= 5, 10, 15, 20, 25, 30, 35, 39$; cell_size is the number of neurons, which is set as 351; the units in the hidden layer are 351, and activation is relu; the output layer is output three classification, and the activation function is softmax. The model optimizer is Adam, corresponding to softmax classifier, and the model loss function is set to categorical_crossentropy, which is the logarithmic loss function of the multi classification. The criteria for model evaluation is accuracy. Like RNN and NN models, the AUC value of LSTM model is also the average value of 10 times prediction results on sequence data in each time period.

4.3 Result and Discussion

4.3.1 Prediction of Learning Results on Accumulated Data and Sequence Data

Eight classic machine learning models, LR, NB, RF, KNN, SVM, ID3, CART and NN, are used to predict the learning results on aggregate data and sequence data, respectively. The prediction results are shown in Fig. 5. Where (a) represents aggregate data and (s) represents sequence data. For example, the prediction effect of LR model on aggregate data and sequence data are LR (a) and LR (s). It can be seen from the AUC of each learning result prediction model, the prediction AUC of LR model on aggregate data is 0.74 at the lowest and 0.80 at the highest, while that on sequence data is 0.68 at the lowest and 0.74 at the highest. KNN, SVM and LR are the same, the prediction results on aggregate data are better than that on sequence data. The prediction AUC of RF model on aggregate data is 0.76 at the lowest and 0.78 at the highest, while that on sequence data is 0.77 at the lowest and 0.83 at the highest. The prediction effect of RF on sequence data is better than that on aggregate data. The prediction AUC of NB, CART, ID3 and NN models on sequence data is higher than that on aggregate data. The experimental results show that the prediction effect on sequence data is better than that on aggregate data, the RF model and CART model are better than other models.

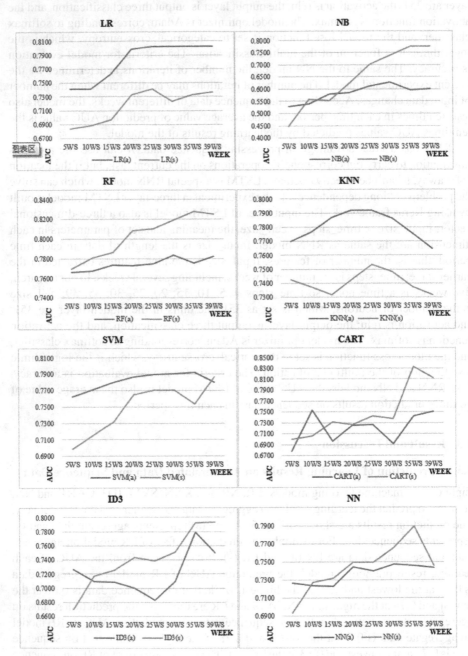

Fig. 5. Comparison of models in prediction of learning results

4.3.2   Prediction of Learning Results on Sequence Data

The experiment in the previous section proves that the prediction results on sequence data are much better than those on aggregate data. RF model and CART model with the highest average AUC value in each time period is selected as the representatives of machine learning models, and compared with RNN model and LSTM model; the results are shown in Fig. 6. The prediction results show that CART model is the worst of the four models. RF model based on the behavior data of the first ten weeks and the first 20 weeks is better than RNN model in the same time period, in other time periods, the RNN model is better. The prediction result of RNN model based on the behavior data of the first 35 weeks reaches the highest value of 0.85 of the four models. LSTM model has the best prediction effect of the four models, with the lowest AUC of 0.78 and the highest of 0.84. Generally speaking, the AUC values of the four models show a stable growth trend with the increase of the number of sequence data weeks until the first 35 weeks, and the predicted AUC based on the behavior data of the first 39 weeks shows a flat or even decline.

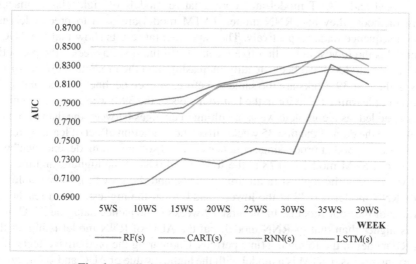

Fig. 6. Prediction of learning results of sequence data

5   Conclusion and Discussion

According to the related research of learning result prediction and the module of the learning platform, this paper divides the learning behaviors that affect learning results into three categories: human-computer interaction indicators, human-human interaction indicators and individual tendency indicators. A course of the Moodle platform is selected, and the nine most relevant learning behaviors are extracted. Taking one week as the basic unit and five weeks as the time node of learning behavior, the aggregate data and sequence data of the first 5 weeks, the first 10 weeks, the first 15 weeks, the first 20 weeks, the first 25 weeks, the first 30 weeks, the first 35 weeks and the first 39 weeks are formed. Eight classic machine learning methods, i.e. LR, NB, KNN, RF, SVC, CART, ID3 and NN, are selected to predict the learning results in different time nodes based on aggregate data and sequence data. The experimental results show that the prediction effect of the NB model, RF model, CART model, ID3 model and NN model on sequence data is better than that on aggregate data on the whole, and the prediction effect of the LR model, KNN model and SVM model on aggregate data are better than that on sequence data. Generally speaking, sequence data is more effective for the prediction of learning results than aggregate data. Sequence data is not only the aggregation of behavior data in a fixed time period, but also the splicing of behavior data between adjacent time periods. It not only reflects the amount of behavior data between different time periods, but also reflects the change of the amount of row data, which is also the implicit indicator of learning results. The prediction AUC of RF model on sequence data is 0.77 at the lowest and 0.83 at the highest; the AUC of the CART model on sequence data is 0.70 at the lowest and 0.83 at the highest. RF model and CART model are the best models of the eight prediction models on sequence data.

RF model and CART model are representative models of eight classic machine learning methods, they and RNN model, LSTM model are used to predict learning results on sequence data, respectively. The experimental results show that the AUC of each model is the lowest in the first five weeks. Until the first 35 weeks, the prediction effects of four models have been steadily increasing, and the prediction effects of four models in the first 39 weeks are the same as before, or even decline. It is estimated that the number of learning behavior in the last four days of the 39th week are all 0, which is artificially added, as a complete week, resulting in changes between the data of the first 39 weeks and the data of the first 35 weeks affect the prediction effect of learning results. LSTM model is good at processing sequence data and solving "long dependence" well. The AUC of LSTM model is 0.78 at the lowest and 0.84 at the highest, and the AUC of LSTM model is the highest in all time periods, and the growth is very stable. The AUC of RNN model is 0.78 at the lowest, and 0.85 at the highest, which reaches the peak value of the four models. In the first 20 weeks of sequence data, the AUC of RF model is higher than that of RNN model, but the AUC of RNN model is higher than that of RF model in the following time periods. Comparing the predictive effects of the four learning results, LSTM is a model with the highest value of AUC and stable growth based on sequence data, and it is also the best model for predicting learning results in existing experiments.

In future research, we will mine the sequence of learning behavior types based on sequence data, and constantly improve the deep learning model of learning result prediction, to predict the learning result early and accurately.

Acknowledgements. This work is supported by the Fundamental Research Funds for Central Universi-ties (CCNU18JCK05), the National Science Foundation of China (No. 61532008; No. 61572223), the National Key Research and Development Program of China (No. 2017YFC0909502), and the Ministry of Education of Humanities and Social Science project (No. 20YJCZH046).

References

1. Deng, R.Q., Benckendorff, P., Gannaway, D.: Progress and new directions for teaching and learning in MOOCs. Comput. Educ. **129**, 48–60 (2019)
2. Jayaprakash, S.M., Moody, E.W., Lauría, J.M., Regan, R., Baron, J.D.: Early alert of academically at-risk students: an open source analytics initiative. J. Learn. Anal. **1**(1), 6–47 (2014)
3. Hu, Y.H., Lo, C.L., Shih, S.P.: Developing early warning systems to predict students' online learning performance. Comput. Hum. Behav. **36**, 469–478 (2014)
4. Chen, W.Y., Brinton, C.G., Cao, D., Mason-Singh, A., Lu, C., Chiang, M.: Early detection prediction of learning outcomes in online short-courses via learning behaviors. IEEE Trans. Learn. Technol. **12**(1), 44–58 (2018)
5. Tempelaara, D.T., Rienties, B., Giesbers, B.: In search for the most informative data for feedback generation: learning analytics in a data-rich context. Comput. Hum. Behav. **47**, 157–167 (2015)
6. Zacharis, N.Z.: A multivariate approach to predicting student outcomes in web-enabled blended learning courses. Internet High. Educ. **27**, 44–53 (2015)
7. You, J.W.: Identifying significant indicators using LMS data to predict course achievement in online learning. Internet High. Educ. **29**, 23–30 (2016)
8. Marbouti, F., Diefes-Dux, H.A., Madhavan, K.: Models for early prediction of at-risk students in a course using standards-based grading. Comput. Educ. **103**, 1–15 (2016)
9. Howarda, E., Meehana, M., Parnell, A.: Contrasting prediction methods for early warning systems at undergraduate level. Internet High. Educ. **37**, 66–75 (2018)
10. Pardo, A., Han, F., Ellis, R.A.: Combining university student self-regulated learning indicators and engagement with online learning events to predict academic performance. IEEE Trans. Learn. Technol. **10**(1), 82–92 (2017)
11. Gašević, D., Dawson, S., Rogersb, T., Gasevic, D.: Learning analytics should not promote one size fits all: the effects of instructional conditions in predicting academic success. Internet High. Educ. **28**, 68–84 (2016)
12. Fan, Y.Z., Wang, Q.: Prediction of academic performance and risk: a review of literature on predicative indicators in learning analytics. Distance Educ. China **1**, 05–15+44+79 (2018). (in Chinese)
13. Conijn, R., Snijders, C., Kleingeld, A., Matzat, U.: Predicting student performance from LMS data: a comparison of 17 blended courses using Moodle LMS. IEEE Trans. Learn. Technol. **10**(1), 17–29 (2017)
14. Moreno-Marcos, P.M., Alario-Hoyos, C., Muñoz-Merino, P.J., Kloos, C.D.: Prediction in MOOCs: a review and future research directions. IEEE Trans. Learn. Technol. **12**(3), 384–401 (2019)
15. Arnold, K.E., Hall, Y., Street, S.G., Lafayette, W., Pistilli, M.D.: Course signals at Purdue: using learning analytics to increase student success. In: Proceedings of the 2nd International Conference on Learning Analytics and Knowledge, pp. 267–270 (2012)
16. Kuzilek, J., Hlosta, M., Herrmannova, D., Zdrahal, Z., Wolf, A.: OU analyse: analysing at-risk students at The Open University. Learning Analytics Review, LAK15–1, 1–16 (2015)

Do College Students Adapt to Personal Learning Environment (PLE)? A Single-Group Study

Changsheng Chen[1], Xiangzeng Meng[2(✉)], Junxiao Liu[2], and Zhi Liu[3]

[1] Shandong Youth University of Political Science, Jinan 250103, China
[2] Shandong Normal University, Jinan 250014, China
mxz@sdnu.edu.cn
[3] Central China Normal University, Wuhan 430079, China

Abstract. Home-based online learning is a typical application of personal learning environment. Understanding the adaptability and characteristics of college students in the personal learning environment (PLE) can effectively tap the potential of online courses and provide valuable references for learners' online and lifelong learning. In this single-group study, 80 college students received a 90-min self-regulated learning training. In pre- and post-class evaluations, media multi-tasking self-efficacy, perceived attention problems, self-regulation strategies and learning satisfaction are used as key variables in online learning to assess their personal learning environment adaptability and characteristics. Using descriptive statistics and one-dimensional intra-group variance to analyze the data, it was found that: Learners have a moderate degree of attention deficit in their personal learning environment, which is manifested in three aspects: perceived attention discontinuity, lingering thought, social media notification.; Under simple training or natural conditions, students have poor adaptability in the personal learning environment, and their behavior perception and behavior adjustment levels have improved, but they have not yet reached expectations; Participation in online learning has significantly increased the application of learners' self-regulation strategies, especially the application of behavior strategies.

Keywords: Personal Learning Environment (PLE) · Online learning · Self-regulated learning · Single-group design · Attention deficit

1 Introduction

In order to actively respond to the negative impact of the new crown epidemic on education, the Ministry of Education of China has issued a response to "No suspension of classes", effectively solving the problem of "No suspension of classes" for college students. The biggest impact of the epidemic on students is the transition from studying at school to online learning at home. Adapting to the home online learning environment is the key to ensuring the quality of learning. Personal learning environment (PLE) is a combination of tools created under the concepts of openness, interoperability, and learner control (Siemens 2008). Since the new semester, under the guidance of teachers, many

Z. Deze et al. (Eds.): BDTA 2020/WiCON 2020, LNICST 371, pp. 34–47, 2021.
https://doi.org/10.1007/978-3-030-72802-1_3

Chinese college students have built a personal learning environment with online learning platforms, social software, cognitive tools and home environment as key components. As an educational emergency, whether students can effectively construct and adapt to their personal learning environment and provide students with high-quality learning resources is a concern of the whole society. Studies have shown that live teaching in online learning at home is full of conditions, and students' low efficiency has caused various doubts and complaints (Song et al. 2020).

Online learning opens the door to lifelong learners, who tend to use online learning to satisfy personal or professional interests (Alonso-Mencía et al. 2019). Home-based e-learning is the epitome of lifelong Learning, which learners experience knowledge acquisition and construction in a personal learning environment. The development of technology has enhanced the accessibility of lifelong education. Martínez-Martínez et al. (2019) believe that guiding students to use Web 2.0 for lifelong learning can make it easier for them to build personal learning spaces, access and update their learning materials, and reduce the difficulty of current and future lifelong learning. Alonso-Mencía et al. (2019) believe that the importance and complexity of self-regulation is essential to online learning, and it is related to tapping the potential of online courses and supporting participants to develop lifelong learning. Therefore, how to enable students to better participate in online learning at home is a problem related to the long-term perspective of lifelong learning. Research on the adaptation status and basic characteristics of the personal learning environment of college students during the epidemic, and discover the influencing factors that hinder their participation in online learning, is a problem for self-directed learning. Ability training and future lifelong learning service design have forward-looking value.

2 Related Work

2.1 Research on the Connotation of Personal Learning Environment

At the level of connotation characteristics, scholars have put forward the concept, connotation and application value of personal learning environment. The idea of personal learning environment was brewed on the basis of the development of ubiquitous computing and social software. The concept was originally derived from the discussion of Virtual Learning Environment (VLE). Scott Wilson (2005) first adopted the Future VLE chart. Describes a preliminary model of the personal learning environment. At present, there still does not have a precise definition of the concept of personal learning environment. Existing studies mostly regard the personal learning environment as a collection of learning tools (Siemens 2008), individual perception of environmental forms (Downes 2005), and learning philosophy (Graham Attwell 2006) and the integration of applications and services (Graham Attwell 2007).

Kompen et al. (2019) proposed the reorganization and reconstruction of learning models and learning resources based on PLE, which is considered as a potential means to realize personalized learning. Learners use appropriate learning tools for self-directed and personalized learning. The integration of social media facilitates learning interaction and informal communication between students (Gillet 2013; Kop and Fournier 2014). Recent studies have shown that as a concept and an emerging practice, the personal learning environment is not only a technology-driven and student-centered learning innovation, but also a challenge and subversion to the concept of traditional knowledge (Castañeda et al. 2019). From the perspective of application value, the personal learning environment is a paradigm that supports digital learning, enabling learners to define, develop and configure learning spaces and experiences by themselves, and provides a choice for community members to choose learning scenarios.

2.2 Research on the Model and Framework of Personal Learning Environment

At the level of model and framework, scholars have proposed personal learning environment models and integrated frameworks from multiple perspectives in order to achieve the goal of technology enhanced learning (TEL). In the dimension of building the personal learning environment model, Scott Wilson (2005) regards the personal learning environment as the coordinator of various services and agents, and pioneered the Future VLE reference model. Afterwards, researchers studied the connotation of personal learning environment from the perspectives of tools, methods, concepts, and scenarios, and successively proposed multiple reference models such as "Ray's PLE", "Reference PLE", and Symbaloo EDU (Downes 2006; Markvan Harmelen 2006; Graham Attwell 2006; Siemens 2008). The proposal and application of these models have enhanced people's understanding of the characteristics and utility of the learning environment, and promoted the development of online learning.

Patterson et al. (2017) proposed that an effective personal learning environment should be a combination of technology, learning mode, and other teaching factors based on a comprehensive analysis of existing personal learning environment models. Bassani et al. (2018) analyzed the advantages of web2.0 to support the construction of learning environment, and constructed a personal learning environment model based on social applications from two levels of tool technical characteristics and tool applicability. In terms of the integration of personal learning environment, researchers believe that it is necessary to adopt a personalized and diversified learning framework based on self-direction and self-management to strengthen the role and responsibility of individuals in organizing, customizing, and reshaping the learning environment (Asuncionet et al. 2010; Johnson et al. 2011; Fiedler et al. 2011). The above models mostly take the "teacher center" as the perspective, emphasizing the integration and integration of learning resources, tools, and services, reflecting the importance of the interaction between learners and the learning environment.

2.3   Applied Research on Personal Learning Environment

At the level of teaching application, scholars pay attention to the preconditions of personal learning environment application, namely, teaching preparation and learning preparation. In the dimension of teaching preparation, the personal learning environment provides rich scenarios for teaching model innovation and evaluation. For example, as Fiedler (2011) pointed out, the personal learning environment may play a role in the transformation of a single, centralized system that dominates and still dominates formal education, and the personal learning environment can not only be used by allowing the use of new methods and methods, and it can help prepare learners for a smooth transition to a changing workplace. Learning theory also believes that the relationship between learners and the environment is the most important medium for creating the teaching and learning process. This process requires the use of traditional and virtual spaces at the same time, and is composed of tools, information sources and activities used by each student for their training to determine the relationship between them (Tomé et al. 2019).

In the dimension of study preparation, the personal learning environment puts forward new requirements for students' study preparation. For example, Kuhn (2017) believes that in order to achieve digital fluency and allow students to benefit from being active in the digital field, students should have an attitude toward technology, an understanding of technical capabilities in an academic context, and the skills to effectively use technology for learning. Jobs. Posner et al. (2012) believe that attention precedes cognitive information processing, and how learners maintain focus and engagement is the basis for cognitive activities. This reminds us that learners realize and intentionally regulate their attention is the key to achieving concentration. In response to this, a survey of 696 Taiwanese students found that the relationship between students' perception of attention problems, self-regulation strategies, and academic performance in a personal learning environment (Wu et al. 2015); and students' academic performance is negatively correlated with perceived attention problems, and positively correlated with self-regulation strategies in the personal learning environment (Wu et al. 2019). In addition, a study by Espinosa et al. (2019) on Spanish college students found that although they have digital abilities when studying college students, they still play a more traditional role. The above research analyzes the opportunities and challenges faced by teachers and students in adapting to the personal learning environment, which provides a theoretical basis for the construction and application of a personal learning environment from the perspective of omni-media ecology.

The personal learning environment is the natural form of autonomous learning. Perception, behavior, evaluation and feedback based on the personal learning environment are important indicators of learners' autonomous learning ability. However, current research focuses on the construction and application of personal learning environment. The focus is on the effectiveness of the autonomous learning model, but little attention is paid to the performance and dynamic changes of individual learners in adapting to the personal learning environment, which makes it difficult to achieve true personality improved learning and learning literacy. Especially for the future lifelong learning that everyone must face, it is more necessary to provide forward-looking and instructive learning strategies. This study adopted a single-group design method to ensure the reliability of the subject experiment (Gay and Airasian 2003) through the use of reliable scales, repeated measures, and detailed descriptions of experimental conditions (eg., measurement conditions and treatment properties). The study of adaptive performance and dynamic characteristics of individual learning environment will provide more operational suggestions for current online learning and future lifelong learning.

3   Method

3.1   Design and Setting

This research was conducted on undergraduates from Shandong Youth University of Political Science (www.sdyu.edu.cn) from February to June 2020. It is a single-group study. After confirming their participation in the research, the students received a 90 min training session. In order to give students time to experience and reflect on their online learning, the training is arranged in the fourth week after the start of the course. The evaluation will be conducted at the follow-up time points at the beginning of the course and the end of the course (Interval of 4 months).

3.2   Participants

Participants are sophomores majoring in hotel management. Affected by COVID-19, participants continued to participate in home-based e-learning for 4 months. The planned class hours during the semester were 128 h), So for the first time they experienced a long period of online learning, after excluding external factors such as work pressure, it is closer to the scene of lifelong learning or on-the-job learning. In addition, students also conducted long-term information retrieval around the course needs. The training is mainly conducted by distance teaching, with a total training duration of 90 min. All participants gave their written informed consent after receiving a complete description of the study.

The demographic characteristics of the participants are shown in Table 1. The majority of participants are female (77.5%), rural college students (72.5%), students are less involved in online before COVID-19, 90% of students have less than 10 courses experience, and 92.5% of them study online for less than 15 h per week, but during the epidemic period, the weekly online study hours of students have increased significantly, with 25% of students saying that the weekly online study time exceeds 15 h. It can be seen that the epidemic has forced students to be exposed to the personal learning environment and generated more online learning experiences.

Table 1. Baseline characteristics of participants (n = 80).

Variable	Value
Age, mean (SD)	21.31(0 .773)
Sex, n (%)	
Male	18(22.5%)
Famale	62(77.5%)
Registered permanent residenc, n (%)	
Rural	58(72.5%)
City	22(27.5%)
Background, n (%)	
Online learning experiences before coVID-19	
None	1(1.3)
[1–3]	31(38.8%)
[4–6]	29(36.3%)
[7–10]	11(13.8%)
>10	8(10%)
Weekly online learning hours before coVID-19	
[1–5]	39(48.8%)
[6–10]	20(25%)
[11–15]	15(18.8%)
>15	6(7.5%)
Weekly online learning hours after coVID-19	
[1–5]	7(8.8%)
[6–10]	26(32.5%)
[11–15]	27(33.8%)
>15	20(25%)

3.3 Self-directed Learning Training

See Table 2 for an overview of the training program. The training content mainly includes the basic concepts of Self-directed learning, habitual behaviors, the relationship between attention and learning, as well as self-regulation methods and time management skills. In addition, teachers also guided students to conduct attributional training for attention problems and learning effects (Weiner 1985; Wu et al. 2017), so that students can consciously associate the success or failure of attention monitoring with self-esteem.

Participants are encouraged to practice the training content outside of class and complete related homework. Before the follow-up evaluation after the training, participants were asked to submit their completed assignments and also received feedback from the researchers. The training program is conducted through video conferences. The training is taught by a PhD in educational technology. He has received learning and skills training in professional courses such as educational psychology, learning science and technology, and has more than 10 years of experience online teaching experience. Moreover, his research field are digital learning environment and learning behavior analysis.

Table 2. Overview of brief self-directed learning training.

Session	Agenda	Content
1	Introduction	Introduce the purpose and main content of the training
	What is self-directed learning?	The concept and elements of self-directed learning The difference self-directed learning and traditional learning
	The impact of attention and habitual behavior on online learning	Distracting and inappropriate habitual behavior Effects of distraction and habitual behavior on learning engagement
2	Methods of self-regulation	The way and method of self-regulation in learning; Schedule setting, self-rewarding and punishing, online interaction and learning community
	Attribution of learning outcomes	The relationship between Learning expectations and outcomes; The basic skills of negative emotion regulation and positive emotion maintenance
	Review and design action plans	Reviewing and summarizing the day's session; Setting an action plan (homework)

3.4 Instruments

This research mainly evaluated the learning behaviors and results of students' media multitasking, metacognitive skills and learning satisfaction after receiving training during online learning at home. The research tool for media multitasking self-efficacy was the MMSE scale proposed by Wu et al., which had 5 questions. Sample questions included "I can learn and do non-learning activities at the same time, and learn effectively". And "I can talk with my friends by video or audio while learning (such as QQ, WeChat), and I can also study effectively". Responses were rated on a 6-point Likert scale with 1 indicating not confident at all, and 6 very confident. Factor loadings ranged from 0.705 to 0.838 with internal consistency of 0.848.

The learning satisfaction research tool used a scale developed by Alqurashi (2018). Learning satisfaction was measured by four items. Sample questions included "Generally, I am very satisfied with my online learning experience." and "Generally, online learning has deepened my understanding of my learning style." Responses were rated on a Likert scale with 1 indicating extreme disagreement and 5 extreme agreement. Factor loadings ranged from 0.770 to 0.914 with internal consistency of 0.866.

The research tool for meta-attention skills was the OL-MARS scale proposed by Wu et al. (Wu et al. 2015, 2019). All questions on the scale were prepared for college students participating in online learning. In view of the cultural background differences between Taiwanese students and mainland students, the relevant expressions of the OL-MARS scale and the MMSE scale had been revised. For example, the social software such as Facebook mentioned in the original scale had been unified to WeChat and QQ. Then confirm with the team of professor Wu, the scale developer, to improve the reliability and validity of the measured items. Finally, OL-MARS scale included perceived attention problems (PAP) (15) and self-regulation strategies (SRS) (9), responses were rated on a Likert scale with 1 indicating extreme disagreement and 5 extreme agreement. Among them, PAP scale includes perceived attention discontinuity (PAD) (8), lingering thought (LT) (4) and social media notification (SMN) (3). Specifically, PAP subscale was measured by eight items. Sample questions included "I will open QQ or WeChat when I have to do my homework." and "While I was studying, I would unconsciously maintain the software or application system of the computer".

LT subscale was measured by four items. Sample questions included "When I use the Internet for my projects or studies, I unconsciously pay attention to what is happening at home." and "When I study online, I play my phone unconsciously." SMN subscale was measured by three items. Sample questions included "When I see or hear notifications from social media, I can't wait to check them." and "When studying, I can immediately notice the information from instant messaging software (e.g., WeChat or QQ)." Factor loadings of PAD scale ranged from 0.532 to 0.789 with internal consistency of 0.784.

SRS scale included behavioral strategies (BS) (6) and outcome appraisal (OA) (3), responses were rated on a Likert scale with 1 indicating extreme disagreement and 5 extreme agreement. Specifically, BS subscale was measured by six items. Sample questions included "When I use a computer to study, I use some strategies to help me focus on my work." and "While studying, I logged out of my social media account or shut down instant messaging software (e.g., WeChat and QQ)". OA subscale was measured by three items. Sample questions included "If I focus on what I should be doing when I use a computer (e.g., writing a paper, studying or searching for information), I will feel happy and proud." and "When I use the computer to study, I will feel guilty if I delay what I should do". Factor loadings of SRS scale ranged from 0.499 to 0.874 with internal consistency of 0.783.

3.5 Analysis

According to the research design of Yoshinaga et al. (2018), In this study, one dimensional intra-group analysis of variance (ANOVA) corrected by Greenhouse-Geisser was used to analyze the scores of adaptability index (MMSE PAD SRS SAT) before and after class. If the analysis of variance shows that there is a significant change, a paired

Bonferronicorrected t test is used for post-hoc testing. In order to further explain the data, in addition to the significance test of the null hypothesis, η^2 is used as the effect size of the independent variable in the analysis of variance, which is used to express the percentage of the variance of the dependent variable explained by the independent variable. According to Cohen (1988), the small, medium, and large effect sizes are 0.01, 0.06, and 0.14, respectively. Due to the small sample size in this study, all statistical tests are two-tailed tests, and α values less than 0.1 are considered statistically significant. Statistical analysis is mainly performed using SPSS 22 (Table 3).

Table 3. Changes in primary and secondary outcomes (n = 80)

	pre		post		F	p	η^2
	M	SD	M	SD			
MMSE	2.805	1.0487	2.71	0.95	0.72	0.399	0.009
PAD	2.77	0.50	2.86	0.55	1.27	0.26	0.02
PAP	2.77	0.43	2.85	0.45	2.10	0.15	0.03
LT	2.98	0.50	3.03	0.53	0.55	0.46	0.01
SMN	2.55	0.65	2.66	0.65	2.12	0.15	0.03
SRS	3.00	0.52	3.13	0.56	3.34	0.07	0.04
BS	2.83	0.50	2.95	0.61	2.87	0.09	0.04
OA	3.18	0.68	3.31	0.61	2.33	0.13	0.03
SAT	3.33	0.75	3.42	0.72	0.91	0.34	0.01

From the descriptive statistics of measurement indicators, students have many types of attention deficit behaviors in their personal learning environment. The frequency from high to low is lingering thought (M = 2.98, SD = 0.5) and perceived attention discontinuity (M = 2.98, SD = 0.5). = 2.77, SD = 0.43) and social media notification (M = 2.55, SD = 0.65). From the perspective of the source of attention deficit, lingering thought is the learner's attention to changes in the state of their favorite media or matters of concern during learning. It represents the learner's implicit attention deficit, and it has no obvious behavior performance, but it can always affect the state of online learning; perceived attention discontinuity and social media notification are learners' self-awareness of factors and behaviors that may interfere with attention in the learning environment, which is relatively obvious in online learning. According to Wu (2015), perceptual attention dispersion is related to the learner's executive control system, and is the learner's consciousness of choosing and processing things that are not related to learning.

In order to deeply understand learners' adaptability differences and dynamic changes, we will continue to conduct a comparative analysis of their self-efficacy, perceived attention problems, and self-regulation strategies before and after class. In addition to the decrease in self-efficacy of media multi-tasking self-efficacy, perceived attention problems (eg., PAD, LT, SMN) and Outcome appraisal have shown a certain degree of improvement. However, the one-dimensional analysis of variance within the group showed that time did not have a statistically significant effect on the above variables. It is worth noting that time has a significant impact on self-regulation strategies ($p < 0.1$), and its subsidiary index behavioral strategies is significantly higher than the outcome appraisal, and has reached statistical significance ($p < 0.1$). As an important dimension for evaluating online learning results, this study found that the post-test (M = 3.42, SD = 0.72) of student learning satisfaction is higher than the pre-test (M = 3.33, SD = 0.75), which indicates that the duration of online participation can be increased satisfactory, but unfortunately it did not reach statistical significance ($p = 0.34$).

From the perspective of the effect of independent variables, the effect size (0.04) of the influence of time on self-regulation strategies is close to the medium effect, which shows that learning time can only explain 4% of the differences in students' self-regulation strategies. The underlying factors are worth digging deeper. Time has a small effect on other variables, and follow-up research should explore the mechanism of action between variables based on structural relationships.

4 Discussion

4.1 Learners Have a Moderate Degree of Attention Deficit in Their Personal Learning Environment, Which is Manifested in Three Aspects: Perceived Attention Discontinuity, Lingering Thought, Social Media Notification

This conclusion is another verification of Wu's (2017) meta-attention theory. According to the research of Frasson and Chalfoun (2010), cognitive processes related to learning include attention, memory and reasoning, and positive emotions contribute to the improvement of these cognitive processes. If students are unable to concentrate during online learning, it will damage their learning engagement and advanced thinking ability. According to the process model of emotion regulation (Gross 1998), attention distribution or redirection of a person's attention in the process of emotion regulation can affect his/her emotions, which is a key factor to ensure high learning participation and high efficiency. Regarding emotion regulation strategies, Burić et al. (2016) believe that shifting attention from the event that caused unpleasant emotions to another object or topic can achieve self-regulation of learning emotions. In the practical application of teaching, some research on teaching design shows that when teachers design gamified activities to challenge students and keep them in the flow (high concentration) area, students will keep their participation throughout the course (eg., Zhu et al. 2017; Antonaci et al. 2018).

4.2 Under Simple Training or Natural Conditions, Students Have Poor Adaptability in the Personal Learning Environment, and Their Behavior Perception and Behavior Adjustment Levels Have Improved, but They Have not yet Reached Expectations

Participants in this study are sophomore students. They grow up in a digital environment. Before the study, we assumed that the research subjects have good online self-directed learning ability. After no or a small amount of training, they should learn from online learning, gaining similar effects, but failed to achieve what we wanted. The research conclusions of Aagaard (2015) may provide us with a reliable explanation. He believes that students are attracted to social media mainly through habitual distraction, and thus are seduced by the media and visit social media. The above research shows the widespread use of social media by college students and their vulnerability to such interference. However, as the personal learning environment is becoming a necessary space for college students or lifelong learners to continue their learning, how to promote them to better adapt to and integrate into the personal learning environment is urgent, and this should be the necessary digital literacy for future learners. Moghimi et al. (2020) believe that statistics on interruptions and delays in learning and their negative effects on academic performance require action-regulation strategies that students can use to manage their academic performance and happiness. Their research shows that the action-regulated SOC model can help explain college students' performance and learning satisfaction. Through self-efficacy beliefs, there is a positive indirect relationship between optimization (rather than selective choice) and good learning outcomes. In terms of the explanatory power of the research model, corresponding to the meta-analysis of Wiradhany and Koerts (2019), this study found that a large part of the difference in media multitasking behavior is still unexplained, and it also found a high degree of heterogeneity in the topic of attention regulation.

4.3 Participation in Online Learning has Significantly Increased the Application of Learners' Self-regulation Strategies, Especially the Application of Behavior Strategies

In early research, Weiner (1985) believed that there are two basic paradigms for self-regulation: behavioral strategies and Outcome appraisal. The former is the behavioral effort taken by learners to reduce the distraction that may be caused by external factors, and the latter is a class of typical psychological strategies of learners, which can associate the perceived success or failure of learning with positive or negative emotions, thereby affecting learning behavior. According to the analysis of meta-attention by Wu et al. (2019), learners control the perceived online learning behavior and results, which are usually divided into two ways: explicit and implicit. Among them, the explicit strategy is a behavioral strategy, which is characterized by behavioral control of network usage, such as denying website access and deleting equipment used for network connection; implicit strategy is psychological strategy, which is to achieve success or avoid feelings of guilt. Obviously, the latter has a strong concealment, and behavior adjustment as a direct reflection of past behavior and results, we can predict students' study efforts and goal expectations based on this.

5   Conclusions and Limitations

In the work, we explored the adaptability and dynamic characteristics of college students' online learning through a single-group design. Although they have been trained once in the research cycle, the results are not ideal. Continuous research on the adaptability and laws of lifelong learners' personal learning environment appears to be very necessary.

The limitations of this article are: on the one hand, the research cycle is short and the amount of collected data is not rich enough. This study lasted only 4 months, which has a certain impact on the systematic and in-depth insight into the dynamics of students' adaptation. On the other hand, this study only uses descriptive statistics and intra-group analysis of variance, and does not reveal the relationship and comprehensive effects between the research variables. Therefore, the conclusions drawn by the study are relatively basic. Subsequent research can strengthen the research on this topic by optimizing training design, increasing evaluation frequency and multiple analysis methods, enhancing the digital learning resilience of university online learners and lifelong learners, and making pleasant and effective learning a part of a happy life.

Acknowledgements. This work is funded by the National Natural Science Foundation of China [Grant No. 62077017, Grant No. 62007020], Shandong Social Science Planning Project of China [Grant No. 18DJYJ07] and Shandong Province Higher Educational Research Program of China [Grant No. J18RA144].

References

Alqurashi, E.: Predicting student satisfaction and perceived learning within online learning environments. Dist. Educ. **40**(1), 133–148 (2019)

Alonso-Mencía, M.E., Alario-Hoyos, C., Maldonado-Mahauad, J., Estévez-Ayres, I., Pérez-Sanagustín, M., Delgado Kloos, C.: Self-regulated learning in MOOCs: lessons learned from a literature review. Educ. Rev. 1–27 (2019)

Antonaci, A., Klemke, R., Kreijns, K., Specht, M.: Get gamification of MOOC right! How to embed the individual and social aspects of MOOCs in gamification design. Int. J. Serious Games **5**, 61–78 (2018)

Asuncion, J.L.R., Lee, M., Rommel, M., Feria, P.: Design and implementation of a cloud-based personal learning environment (2010). https://pleconference.citilab.eu/cas/wp-content/uploads/2010/09/ple2010_-submission_23.

Attwell, G.: Personal Learning Environments-the future of eLearning. Elearn. Pap. **2**(1), 1–8 (2007)

Attwell, G.: Evaluating E-learning: a guide to the evaluation of E-learning. Eval. Eur. Handb. Ser. **2**, 1610–875 (2006)

Burić, I., Sorić, I., Penezić, Z.: Emotion regulation in academic domain: development and validation of the academic emotion regulation questionnaire (AERQ). Pers. Individ. Differ. **96**, 138–147 (2016)

Bassani, P.B.S., Barbosa, D.N.F.: Experiences with web 2.0 in school settings: a framework to foster educational practices based on a personal learning environment perspective. Educ. Rev. **34** (2018)

Castañeda, L., Tur, G., Torres-Kompen, R.: Impacto del concepto PLE en la literatura sobre educación: la última década. Rev. Iberoamericana Educ. Dist. **22**(1), 221–241 (2019)

Cerezo, R., Sánchez-Santillán, M., Paule-Ruiz, M.P., Núñez, J.C.: Students' LMS interaction patterns and their relationship with achievement: a case study in higher education. Comput. Educ. **96**, 42–54 (2016)

Downes, S.: Learning networks: theory and practice. In International Conference on Methods and Technologies for Learning (2005)

Environments Questionnaire (PLE) and Social Integration of Unaccompanied Foreign Minors (MENA). Sustainability **11**(10), 2903

Espinosa, M.P.P., García, M.R., Calatayud, V.G.: How university students use technologies to learn: a survey about PLE in Spain. Educ. Knowl. Soc. **20**, 1–2 (2019)

Fiedler, S.H., Väljataga, T.: Personal learning environments: Concept or technology? Int. J. Virtual Pers. Learn. Environ. (IJVPLE) **2**(4), 1–11 (2011)

Frasson, C., Chalfoun, P.: Managing learner's affective states in intelligent tutoring systems. In: Nkambou, R., Bourdeau, J., Mizoguchi, R. (eds.) Advances in Intelligent Tutoring Systems, vol. 308, pp. 339–358. Springer, Heidelberg (2010). https://doi.org/10.1007/978-3-642-14363-2_17

Gillet, D., de Jong, T., Sotirou, S., Salzmann, C.: Personalised learning spaces and federated online labs for stem education at school. In: 2013 IEEE Global Engineering Education Conference (EDUCON), pp. 769–773. IEEE, March 2013

Gross, J.J.: The emerging field of emotion regulation: an integrative review. Rev. Gener. Psychol. **2**(3), 271–299 (1998)

Review of General Psychology **2**, 271–299. https://doi.org/10.1037/1089-2680.2.3.2.

Johnson, L., Adams, S., Haywood, K.: The NMC horizon report: 2011 K-12 edition[R/OL]. TheNew Media Consortium, Austin (2011).https://www.nmc.org/pdf/2011-Horizon-Report-K12.pdf. Accessed 26 Nov 2012

Kompen, R. T., Edirisingha, P., Mobbs, R.: Putting the pieces together: Conceptual frameworks for building PLEs with Web 2.0 tools. Dist. E-Learn. Transit. 783–808 (2013)

Kompen, R.T., Edirisingha, P., Canaleta, X., Alsina, M., Monguet, J.M.: Personal learning environments based on Web 2.0 services in higher education. Telemat. Inform. **38**, 194–206 (2019)

Kop, R., Fournier, H.: Developing a framework for research on Personal Learning Environments. E-Learn. Eur. J. **35**, 13–17 (2014)

Kuhn, C.: Are students ready to (re)-design their personal learning environment? The case of the e-dynamic. Space. J. New Approach. Educ. Res. **6** (2017)

Martínez-Martínez, A., Olmos-Gómez, M.D.C., Tomé-Fernández, M., Olmedo-Moreno, E.M.: Analysis of psychometric properties and validation of the personal learning environments questionnaire (PLE) and social integration of unaccompanied foreign minors (MENA). Sustainability **11**(10), 2903 (2019)

Moghimi, D., Van Yperen, N. W., Sense, F., Zacher, H., Scheibe, S.: Using the selection, optimization, and compensation model of action-regulation to explain college students' grades and study satisfaction. J. Educ. Psychol. 1–53 (2020)

Moghimi, J.: Drawn to distraction: a qualitative study of off-task use of educational technology. Comput. Educ. **87**, 90–97 (2015)

Patterson, C., Stephens, M., Chiang, V., Price, A.M., Work, F., Snelgrove-Clarke, E.: The significance of personal learning environments (PLEs) in nursing education: extending current conceptualizations. Nurse Educ. Today **48**, 99–105 (2017)

Posner, M.I., Rothbart, M.K., Sheese, B.E., Voelker, P.: Control networks and neuromodulators of early development. Dev. Psychol. **48**(3), 827 (2012)

Sáiz-Manzanares, M.C., Marticorena-Sánchez, R., García-Osorio, C.I., Llamazares, M.D.C.E., Queiruga-Dios, M.Á.: Conductas de aprendizaje en LMS: SRL y feedback efectivo en B-learning

Sáiz Manzanares, M.C., Queiruga Dios, M.Á.: Evaluación de estrategias metacognitivas: aplicación de métodos online. Rev. Psicol. Educ. **13**(1), 23–35 (2018)

Song, L.Q., Xu, L., Li, Y.X.: Accurate online teaching + home learning model: a way to improve students' learning quality in the epidemic period. China Educ. Technol. **03**, 114–122 (2020)

Tomé, M., Herrera, L., Lozano, S.: Teachers' opinions on the use of personal learning environments for intercultural competence. Sustainability **11**(16), 4475 (2019)

Van Harmelen, M.: Personal learning environments. In: Sixth IEEE International Conference on Advanced Learning Technologies (ICALT 2006), pp. 815–816. IEEE, July 2006

Weiner, B.: An attributional theory of achievement motivation and emotion. Psychol. Rev. **92**(4), 548 (1985)

Wilson, S.: Future VLE—the visual version (2005). https://zope.cetis.ac.uk/members/scott/blogview

Wiradhany, W., Koerts, J.: Everyday functioning-related cognitive correlates of media multitasking: a mini meta-analysis. Media Psychol. 1–28 (2019)

Wu, J.Y.: The indirect relationship of media multitasking self-efficacy on learning performance within the personal learning environment: implications from the mechanism of perceived attention problems and self-regulation strategies. Comput. Educ. **106**(MAR.), 56–72 (2017)

Wu, J.Y., Cheng, T.: Who is better adapted in learning online within the personal learning environment? relating gender differences in cognitive attention networks to digital distraction. Comput. Educ. **128**(JAN.), 312–329 (2019)

Wu, J.Y.: University students' motivated attention and use of regulation strategies on social media. Comput. Educ. **89**, 75–90 (2015)

Yoshinaga, N., Nakamura, Y., Tanoue, H., MacLiam, F., Aoishi, K., Shiraishi, Y.: Is modified brief assertiveness training for nurses effective? A single-group study with long-term follow-up. J. Nurs. Manag. **26**(1), 59–65 (2018)

Zhu, Y., Pei, L., Shang, J.: Improving video engagement by gamification: A proposed design of MOOC videos. In: Cheung, S.K.S., Kwok, L., Ma, W.W.K., Lee, L.-K., Yang, H. (eds.) ICBL 2017. LNCS, vol. 10309, pp. 433–444. Springer, Cham (2017). https://doi.org/10.1007/978-3-319-59360-9_38

A Big Data Intelligence Marketplace and Secure Analytics Experimentation Platform for the Aviation Industry

Dimitrios Miltiadou[1]([⊠]) [iD], Stamatis Pitsios[1] [iD], Dimitrios Spyropoulos[1] [iD],
Dimitrios Alexandrou[1] [iD], Fenareti Lampathaki[2] [iD], Domenico Messina[3] [iD],
and Konstantinos Perakis[1] [iD]

[1] UBITECH, Thessalias 8 & Etolias, 15231 Chalandri, Greece
dmiltiadou@ubitech.eu
[2] SUITE5, Alexandreias 2, Bridge Tower, 3013 Limassol, Cyprus
[3] ENGINEERING Ingegneria Informatica S.P.A., Piazzale dell Agricoltura 24,
00144 Rome, Italy

Abstract. Over the last years, the impacts of the evolution of information integration, increased automation and new forms of information management are also evident in the aviation industry that is disrupted also by the latest advances in sensor technologies, IoT devices and cyber-physical systems and their adoption in aircrafts and other aviation-related products or services. The unprecedented volume, diversity and richness of aviation data that can be acquired, generated, stored, and managed provides unique capabilities for the aviation-related industries and pertains value that remains to be unlocked with the adoption of the innovative Big Data Analytics technologies. The big data technologies are focused on the data acquisition, the data storage and the data analytics phases of the big data lifecycle by employing a series of innovative techniques and tools that are constantly evolving with additional sophisticated features, while also new techniques and tools are frequently introduced as a result of the undergoing research activities. Nevertheless, despite the large efforts and investments on research and innovation, the Big Data technologies introduce also a number of challenges to its adopters. Besides the effective storage and access to the underlying big data, efficient data integration and data interoperability should be considered, while at the same time multiple data sources should be effectively combined by performing data exchange and data sharing between the different stakeholders that own the respective data. However, this reveals additional challenges related to the crucial preservation of the information security of the collected data, the trusted and secure data exchange and data sharing, as well as the robust access control on top of these data. The current paper aims to introduce the ICARUS big data-enabled platform that aims provide a multi-sided platform that offers a novel aviation data and intelligence marketplace accompanied by a trusted and secure "sandboxed" analytics workspace. It holistically handles the complete big data lifecycle from the data collection, data curation and data exploration to the data integration and data analysis of data originating from heterogeneous data sources with different velocity, variety and volume in a trusted and secure manner.

Z. Deze et al. (Eds.): BDTA 2020/WiCON 2020, LNICST 371, pp. 48–62, 2021.
https://doi.org/10.1007/978-3-030-72802-1_4

Keywords: Big data · Data analytics · Data sharing · Data driven intelligence

1 Introduction

The Aviation industry encompasses a wide range of activities and industries directly linked to aircrafts' development, production and operation, as well as an extensive list of interrelated products and services that support the aircrafts' overall operations. Despite the fact that the aviation industry has successfully been raised into a leading and critical industry of the global economy, the various sectors of the industry operate on a fragmented manner. Over the last years, the impacts of the evolution of information integration, increased automation and new forms of information management are also evident in the aviation industry that is disrupted also by the latest advances in sensor technologies, IoT devices and cyber-physical systems and their adoption in aircrafts and other aviation-related products or services. It is also now acknowledged in the aviation industry that the aircraft owners have now huge amount of data and information about their aircrafts, which are critical and have real value impact on their aircrafts so they are in need to maximize the use of technology [1]. This is also obvious from the latest estimations reporting the generation of between 500 and 1,000 gigabytes of data on an average flight level [2], while on a global fleet level the generation of up to 98,000,000 terabytes of data by 2026 [3]. To this direction, the unprecedented volume, diversity and richness of aviation data that can be acquired, generated, stored, and managed provides unique capabilities for the aviation-related industries and pertains value that remains to be unlocked with the adoption of the innovative Big Data Analytics technologies.

In the Big Data era, a tremendous amount of information is generated in an increasing immeasurably magnitude from of a plethora of sources that should be effectively collected and harnessed in order to be properly processed towards the extraction of valuable knowledge and added value, the reveal of trends and hidden patterns or correlations that will facilitate the prediction and decision making [4, 5]. To accomplish this, a new generation of technologies that are referred as Big Data technologies have been arising, which are capable of extracting added value from an enormous volume of data with rich diversity towards the effective and efficient high-velocity capture, discovery, and analysis [6]. In this sense, the big data technologies are focused on the data acquisition, the data storage and the data analytics phases of the big data lifecycle by employing a series of innovative techniques and tools that are constantly evolving with additional sophisticated features, while also new techniques and tools are frequently introduced as a result of the undergoing research activities. Nevertheless, despite the large efforts and investments on research and innovation, the Big Data technologies introduce also a number of challenges to its adopters. Besides ensuring the employment of effective storage and access mechanisms, the crucial aspects of offering efficient mechanisms that enable data integration and data interoperability should be considered. Furthermore, in order to be able to execute data analytics that would generate valuable insights and information it is imperative that multiple data sources should be effectively combined. As a consequence, this usually implies that exchange and sharing of data is performed between the different stakeholders that own the respective data. However, this reveals additional challenges related to the crucial preservation of the information security of the collected data, the trusted and secure data exchange and data sharing, as well as the robust access control on top of these data.

The current paper aims to introduce the ICARUS big data-enabled platform which aims to provide a multi-sided platform that offers a novel aviation data and intelligence marketplace accompanied by a trusted and secure "sandboxed" analytics workspace. To this end, the platform holistically handles the complete big data lifecycle from the data collection, data curation and data exploration to the data integration and data analysis of data originating from heterogeneous data sources with different velocity, variety and volume in a trusted and secure manner. The platform exploits methods such as big data analytics, deep learning, data enrichment, and blockchain powered data sharing, in order to properly address the critical barriers for the adoption of Big Data in the aviation industry, facilitating the design and execution of big data scenarios from the stakeholders of the aviation industry.

2 Materials and Methods

Despite the embracement of the big data technologies in different domains and their advancements, it is proven that several challenges have not been yet addressed since the majority of the described big data technologies are still in their early stages. It is acknowledged that the crucial challenge in any big data platform is to gather, store, search, share, transfer, analyze and present data while ensuring that compliance to the identified requirements is maintained [7]. At the moment, the efforts are focused on effectively storing and accessing large data that are originating from heterogeneous and diverse data sources and are created in multiple (structured, semi-structured, unstructured) formats, while other aspects such as the data integration and data interoperability are often neglected. Furthermore, while big data analytics tools are constantly evolving and empowered with new features, less effort is spent in supporting seamless and effortless analytics on top of cross-origin data by the developed analytics tools. In the same context, the effective handling of information security while storing and managing of this vast amount of data from heterogeneous data sources remains a crucial challenge. The extraction of valuable knowledge and intelligence unavoidably requires the dynamic data exchange and data sharing between the various stakeholders of an industry or across different industries in a trusted, regulated and secure manner. Furthermore, data access control on top of these collected massive and rapidly evolving data must be properly addressed. Hence, it is also acknowledged that despite the constantly growing number of available technologies and techniques that have emerged, there is a real challenge on finding the proper balance between the effectiveness and performance of the dynamic analysis on diverse large data sets and the requirements for data integrity, data governance, data security and privacy [8].

Nevertheless, a promising opportunity arises from the latest developments and compelling features of the big data technologies to design and build a big data platform that capitalizes on these emerging offerings in order to build a novel data value chain in the aviation-related sectors. This platform will enable data-driven innovation and collaboration across currently diversified and fragmented industry players, by effectively addressing the challenges imposed by the nature of big data and the requirements of the aviation industry's stakeholders for a trusted and secure data sharing and data analysis environment.

2.1 The ICARUS Technical Solution

With a view to fulfil these objectives and address the challenges mentioned in the previous section, a thorough analysis of the collected requirements from the aviation stakeholders was performed towards the design and development of a big data-enabled platform that aspires to provide an intuitive aviation data and intelligence marketplace that provides a trusted and secure "sandboxed" analytics workspace.

The main objectives of the ICAURS platform [9] is to provide an innovative and intelligent big data-enabled environment that enables the aviation sector's data providers and data consumers to effectively and securely the complete big data lifecycle that includes initially the data preparation and upload as a first step, the data exploration, sharing and brokerage as a second step towards the final step of the data analysis and data visualization. In this context, the platform incorporates at its core advanced data management and data value enrichment methods that span over the axes of data collection, data curation, data safeguarding, data sharing and data analytics in order to effectively and efficiently cover all the aviation industry's needs, requirements and peculiarities with regards to big data, as well as to knowledge and insight extractions from these data.

To this end, we are developing an integrated big data-enabled platform that is composed by a set of key components which are designed and implemented by exploiting well-established and state-of-the-art big data infrastructure, technologies and tools. The architecture of the platform is a **modular architecture**, composed by **22 components** in total, that is designed aiming to offer the maximum flexibility and extensibility, enabling the smooth integration and effective operation of the various components that are implemented as distinct software modules. The designed software modules are exploiting and combining multiple technologies and tools towards the aim of accomplishing the aspired offerings of the platform.

During the design process, the major focus was on the functional decomposition, the strict separation of concerns, the dependencies identification and especially the data flow realization. To this end, each component has been designed in order to operate under a clear context, with distinct features and functionalities and a clearly defined scope within the architecture. The elicited technical requirements and functional specifications were carefully analyzed and facilitated the evolution of a mature concept architecture design that is aiming to address the ambition of delivering a novel big data platform for the aviation data value chain.

Towards this aim, the design of the platform ensures the offering of a scalable and flexible environment that will enable the interoperability of the various components that facilitate the execution of big data analytics and sharing of data through secure, transparent and advanced functionalities and features. The designed architecture incorporates all the entire lifecycle of the platform that spans from data preparation and data upload, to data exploration, data sharing, data brokerage and data analysis. To cope with the security and privacy constraints of the aviation sector, the platform adopts a security and privacy by-design approach that covers all the data confidentially, data privacy and data safeguarding aspects of the platform. The main axes of this approach is the end-to-end encryption of all the datasets that are available in the platform with a symmetric encryption key and the design and employment of a sophisticated secure decryption process with a decryption key in the form of key pair for each dataset per data consumer to facilitate the secure data sharing of the datasets across all the platform.

The platform architecture is conceptually divided in three main tiers, namely the **On-Premise Environment**, the **Core Platform** and the **Secure and Private Space**, and each tier is composed by a set of components, from the total list of 22 components, that are combined towards the realization of the functionalities of each specific tier in the underlying execution environment (see Fig. 1).

The On-Premise Environment is responsible for the execution of the data preparation and data uploading functionalities and features of the ICARUS platform, based on the instructions that are provided by the Core Platform in accordance with the preferences of the data provider. The On-Premise Environment is composed by multiple components that are running on the data provider's environment which are utilized towards the preparation and uploading of the data provider's private or confidential datasets to the Core Platform.

The Core Platform constitutes the main tier of the platform which undertakes the execution of all the core operations of the platform and the formulation and propagation of instructions to the On-Premise Environment and the Secure and Private Space tiers for local execution. In this context, in the Core Platform multiple components are integrated and combined in the platform's cloud infrastructure in order to execute all the data exploration, sharing and brokerage operations, as well as the design of the data preparation, data uploading and data analysis operations which will be executed by the On-Premise Environment and the Secure and Private Space respectively. Furthermore, the Core Platform is offering the user interface of the platform through which the users perform all these operations.

The Secure and Private Space constitutes the advanced analytics execution environment of the platform in which all the data analytics processing is executed in an isolated, secure and trusted way. The Secure and Private Space is composed by a set of components that formulate a trusted and secure sandboxed analytics workspace in which the data analysis executed in accordance with the analytics workflow that is designed by the user within the Core Platform. Hence, the Secure and Private Space is offering a rich stack of analytics tools and features whose management and orchestration is performed through the Core Platform and whose operation is performed by adhering the strict and rigorous security and privacy needs of the aviation sector.

In the following paragraphs, the three tiers of the ICARUS platform are presented, focusing in the components that compose each tier as well as the interactions between them.

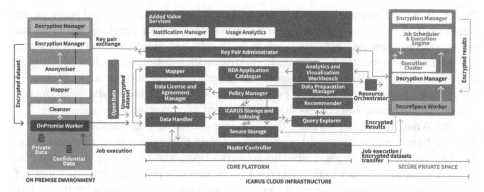

Fig. 1. The ICARUS platform conceptual architecture

On-Premise Environment. The scope of the On-Premise Environment is to provide the required services that will perform all the data preparation and data uploading steps as instructed by the Core Platform and is composed by the On-Premise Worker, the Cleanser, the Mapper, the Anonymiser, the Encryption Manager and the Decryption Manager.

The scope of the **On-Premise Worker** is to execute the jobs or tasks, according to the instructions provided by the Master Controller component of the Core platform, utilizing the available components on the On-Premise Environment. Hence, the On-Premise Worker interprets and executes the instructions for the job or task execution and provides the execution status of the requested jobs/tasks back to the Master Controller. Finally it supports the uploading of the prepared encrypted datasets from the On-Premise Environment to the Core Platform, as well as the downloading of the datasets to the local environment via the interaction with the Data Handler component of the Core Platform. The On-Premise Worker provides the user interface of the On-Premise Environment through which the user is able to perform all the described operations.

The **Cleanser** is the component undertaking the responsibility of the data cleansing functionalities of the platform. The Cleanser supports a set of techniques for performing simple and more advanced cleansing operations over datasets that contain erroneous or "dirty" data by detecting or correcting corrupted, incomplete, incorrect and inaccurate records from datasets with a variety of rules and constraints. For this purpose, the Cleanser employs a set of validation, cleansing and missing value handling rules based on the user input. Additionally, it provides the logging mechanism that monitors and stores all the identified errors, the actions performed and the corresponding results.

The **Mapper** is responsible for the harmonization process of the dataset by enabling the user to define the mapping of the fields of the dataset to the common aviation model employed in the platform in a semi-automatic way. Moreover, the Mapper enables the exploration of the common aviation model from the user in order to provide suggestions for possible extensions of the model. The Mapper has a dual presence in the architecture: a) it provides a graphical user interface as part of the Core Platform that facilitates the definition of the mapping between the dataset fields and the common aviation model and b) a backend mapping service operating on the On-Premise Environment that executes the actual defined mapping from the user's data to the common data model based on the user's input from the user interface. In a nutshell, the Mapper generates the proposed mapping from a new dataset to the common data model and allows the users to review and update it based on their knowledge and expertise on their datasets. The defined mapping is provided in the form of instructions to the backend mapping service that resides in the On-Premise Environment through the Master Controller and the On-Premise Worker. The defined mapping can be also stored and reused as a mapping template.

The **Anonymiser** is providing the data anonymization functionalities in order to filter or hide the private, sensitive or personal data that cannot be disclosed outside the data provider's premises, corporate network or personal filesystem. It provides the means to deal with privacy issues and protection of sensitive information with a variety of anonymization techniques. It employs a privacy and anonymization toolset with a variety of privacy models such as the K-anonymity, the L-diversity and T-closeness models and anonymization techniques such as the Generalization, Masking, Micro-aggregation and Clustering and Micro-aggregation in order to handle the incoming datasets and provide the anonymized datasets.

The **Encryption Manager** is undertaking all essential encryption processes with regard to encryption of the data provider's dataset. It provides the encryption cipher mechanism that generates the symmetric encryption key and the encrypted dataset by performing on-demand column-based encryption of a dataset. Moreover, it facilitates the dataset sharing, upon the agreement of the data provider and the data consumer, with the generation of the appropriate decryption keys, in the form of key pairs, one per dataset per data consumer. It undertakes the storage and management of the generated decryption keys and the secure transmission of the corresponding decryption key from the data provider to the data consumer. Finally, it maintains a local key store where the generated decryption keys and all relevant information are stored and handles the revocation requests in case access to an encrypted dataset is revoked for a specific data consumer.

The **Decryption Manager** is enabling the decryption of the dataset on the On-Premise Environment when an encrypted dataset is downloaded locally, provided that a valid smart contract, handled by the Data License and Agreement Manager of the Core Platform, exists permitting the downloading of the specific dataset locally. The Decryption Manager provides the mechanisms to verify the identity of the data consumer via a certificate or public key, to request for the decryption key from the data provider and the decryption mechanism in order to temporarily reproduce the encryption key in order to decrypt the dataset. It interacts with the Key Pair Administrator residing on the Core Platform to initiate the request for a dataset that will trigger the generation of the decryption key from the data provider and facilitates the establishment of the secure connection with the data provider for decryption key transmission.

Core Platform. The scope of the Core Platform is to provide all the required components for the execution of the core operations of the platform, as well as compilation of the instructions that are executed by the On-Premise Environment and the Secure and Private Space. The Core Platform is composed by the core data components, namely the Master Controller, the Data Handler, the Data License and Agreement Manager, the Policy Manager, the Storage and Indexing, the Query Explorer, the Recommender, the

Key Pair Administrator, the Resource Orchestrator, the Secure Storage, the Data Preparation Manager, the Analytics and Visualisation Workbench and the BDA Application Catalogue, as well as the added value components, namely the Notification Manager and the Usage Analytics.

The **Master Controller** is the component responsible for compiling a set of instructions for the execution of specific jobs or tasks, as provided by the components of the Core platform, and for providing this set of instructions for local execution to the workers running on the On-Premise Environment and the Secure and Private Space, namely the On-Premise Worker and the Secure-Space Worker. Additionally it monitors the execution status of requested jobs or tasks. Furthermore, it transfers the list of selected encrypted datasets to the Secure Storage and supports the uploading of the encrypted analysis results from the Secure and Private Space to the Secure Storage.

The **Data Handler** component encapsulates the various services responsible for the tasks related to making the data available from and to the platform, as well as among different platform components. It serves as the "data gateway" in the architecture, as it supports the complete workflow of uploading proprietary and open datasets to the platform in order to be stored in the platform's storage, downloading datasets from the platform to the end user's On-Premise Environment and/or to the Secure Storage in order to be utilized by the Secure and Private Space, and finally the uploading of data generated in a Secure and Private Space back into the Secure Storage. The Data Handler interacts with the Master Controller in order to perform the data upload or download operations.

The **Data License and Agreement Manager** is the component responsible for handling all processes related to the data licenses and IPR attributes, as well as the drafting, signing, and enforcement of the smart data contracts that correspond to data sharing agreements between platform users. It allows the users to define IPR related attributes, pricing terms and policies, as well as the license for the datasets they own in the platform. Furthermore, it implements the blockchain functionalities of the platform which hosts a local blockchain node and enables the users to create, edit, review, negotiate, update and decline or sign data sharing agreements that are translated into smart data contracts in the blockchain. Finally, it provides, checks or updates the status of a smart data contract.

The **Policy Manager** is the component providing the authorization engine that implements the access control mechanisms within the platform. The purpose of the Policy Manager is to provide the logical access control that prevents the unauthorized access of any type of resource of the platform such as data, services, tools, any kind of system resources, as well as all other relevant objects. Hence, the Policy Manager is responsible for the implementation of the authorization engine that is be based on the ABAC model and incorporates the required authorization XACML-based policies. The purpose of this authorization engine is the provide the access control decision that will either grant or deny the access to the requestor by enforcing the formulated authorization policies. Additionally, the Policy Manager enables the definition, storage, reuse, update and disposal of the authorization policies in order to allow the data providers to effectively define and manage the protection and sharing aspects of their datasets.

The **Storage and Indexing** is the component that enables the storage and indexing capabilities of the platform. This component is responsible for the effective and efficient storage and maintenance of large, complex and unrelated datasets within the platform, as well as the flexible and high-performance indexing of the stored datasets. It handles all the requests for storage or data retrieval from the various components of the platform, as well as the indexing of the incoming datasets, simple or geospatial query execution and full-text search on top of the stored datasets.

The **Query Explorer** is the component that offers dataset exploration and discoverability functionalities to the platform users. Query Explorer has two main offerings: (a) a graphical interface for users to search for datasets and view the search results and (b) a service that translates each search to a query that can be processed by the storage and indexing component. As such, the Query Explorer constitutes the main facilitator of the data marketplace functionalities and the main interaction point from the user's perspective. It enables the users to define search criteria, which includes selecting fields from the data model, define and apply filters based on the metadata or the actual unencrypted data of the datasets in order to discover potentially interesting datasets in the platform. Furthermore, it stores the query history of each user in order to be re-executed and provides dataset suggestions to the user upon interacting with the Recommender component.

The **Recommender** is providing the enhanced recommendation functionalities that enable the dataset exploration and discoverability. In particular, this component is responsible for recommending and suggesting the users additional related datasets during the search and query process using a combination of collaborative filtering and content-based filtering. Furthermore, the Recommender provides recommendations based on the users' preferences and history of searches, requests and purchases.

The **Key-Pair Administrator** is the component that is facilitating the exchange of the decryption keys between the data consumer and the data provider in order to enable the end-to-end data encryption and secure sharing of the encrypted datasets. In this context, the Key-Pair Administrator performs the signaling operations between the data consumer and the data provider in order to achieve the establishment of a secure connection between these parties, by performing the identity verification of each party and the successful handshake between them. Moreover, it maintains the list of data providers that have provided encrypted datasets so as to facilitate the key exchange process, as well as the mechanism for the revocation of the decryption keys upon needs.

The **Resource Orchestrator** is enabling the provisioning and management of the Secure and Private Space in the form of a scalable isolated environment running on virtualized infrastructure. More specifically, the Resource Orchestrator is exploiting the concept of isolated containerized execution environments with easy monitoring, autoscaling and orchestration of applications utilizing the Docker container technology. The Resource Orchestrator is utilizing the well-established open source platform of Kubernetes for container orchestration that facilitates the deployment of the Secure and Private Space components in the form of containerized applications with extensive support of features like service discovery, load balancing, storage orchestration, automated rollouts and rollbacks, health monitoring and self-healing processes, while at the same time ensuring the required isolation and security features of the Secure and Private Space tier.

The **Secure Storage** is providing the secure and trusted storage of the Secure and Private Space with a two-fold purpose: i) to enable the effective and secure storage of the data provider's datasets, that includes the owned private and confidential datasets as well as the ones purchased through the marketplace of the platform, in order to be exploited by the Secure and Private Space in the context of data analysis and b) to provide the trusted and secure storage for the produced results of the executed data analysis. To meet its goals, the Secure Storage is formulated by a stack of big data-enabled state-of-the-art technologies towards the assurance of high availability and high performance for the computationally-intense data analysis operations with: a) the Hadoop Distributed File System (HDFS) that is provisioned and monitored by the Apache Ambari in the first layer for actual storage of both the datasets and the analysis results, b) the Apache Hive operating on top of the HDFS as a second layer, acting as a data warehouse software, offering an abstraction layer on top of the datasets residing in HDFS, while at the same time enabling the effective data lifecycle management of the underlying datasets and results with data query and analysis functionalities and c) the Presto high-performance query engine that offers the required fast parallel analytics query support against data of any size that are residing in Hive and consequently HDFS.

The **Data Preparation Manager** is enabling the data manipulation and data preparation operations on top of the datasets or results residing on the Secure Storage in order to be utilized by the Analytics and Visualisation Workbench. In this sense, the Data Preparation Manager facilitates the user to employ multiple data preparation operations in the form of sequential steps on his/her datasets in accordance to his/her needs for the data analysis or data visualization. The data preparation operations spans from column creation (timestamp-related, math-related, aggregation related, shift and conditional operations), column drop and column renaming, row filtering to dataset merging, data completion and compute aggregations operations. Under the hood, the Data Preparation Manager is exploiting the Presto functionalities in order to create new versions of the dataset(s) within the Secure Storage in order to address the needs of the user for data analysis preparation.

The **Analytics and Visualisation Workbench** is providing the graphical environment where the users of the platform are able to design, execute and monitor the data analytics workflows and also where the visualization and dashboards are displayed. The Analytics and Visualisation Workbench offers a large list of analytics algorithms and their customization with a list of options per algorithm. Furthermore, it offers a variety of visualization types that can be customized based on the user's needs. The Analytics and Visualisation Workbench decouples the design of the data analytics workflow from its actual execution. It offers a novel interactive canvas-based graphical user interface to the users in order to compose their desired data analytics workflows in the Core Platform while orchestrating and managing the actual execution of the analysis is that performed within the Secure and Private Space with the use of the Master Controller, the Secure Storage and the Secure-Space Worker that utilizes the rest of the services of the Secure and Private Space in order to perform the actual data analysis execution. Furthermore, through the Analytics and Visualisation Workbench the advanced visualization capabilities of the platform are offered through a modern data visualization suite of charts and visualizations that span from basic charts to advanced multilevel visualizations which can be combined in order to form dynamic dashboards upon the user needs. In this context, the user is able to create an application, which contains the list of datasets that were selected for analysis, the selected algorithm, as well as the selected visualization type, along with the corresponding parameters, and store it in the BDA Application Catalogue for later reuse.

The **BDA Application Catalogue** implements a repository of the applications created by the users of the platform. As such, the applications can be stored, retrieved, modified and loaded in the Analytics and Visualisation Workbench by the users at any time. The purpose of the BDA Application Catalogue is to enable the reuse of the designed data analytics workflows from the users, as well as the sharing of these workflows among the users through a defined license in order to further empower the analytical capabilities of the platform.

The **Notifications Manager** is responsible for providing the updated information to the users with regards to the datasets or the scheduled analytics jobs. More specifically, the Notifications Manager provides notifications to the users related to the availability of new datasets according to their configured preferences or any possible updates on the datasets that the users are entitled to use, as well as any updates on the execution status of the scheduled analytics jobs.

The **Usage Analytics** component is responsible for providing the tools that collect, analyze and visualize the usage of the various services and assets of the platform in order to extract useful insights and statistics. The Usage Analytics monitors the user's behavior in various levels such as the usage and adoption of specific features or services and the usage of each dataset or algorithm towards the aim of providing usage information to both the users and the platform administrator.

Secure and Private Space. The scope of the Secure and Private Space is to provide all the required components for the formulation of the trusted and secure advanced analytics execution environment of the platform. The Secure and Private Space is composed by the Secure-Space Worker, the Job Scheduler and Execution Engine and the Execution Cluster, as well as running instances of the Encryption Manager and the Decryption Manager.

The **Secure-Space Worker** is the component residing at the Secure and Private Space that undertakes the responsibility of the executing the actual data analysis on the Secure and Private Space by interpreting the instructions provided by the Core Platform. The Secure-Space Worker is interacting with the Master Controller component towards the realization of the Master/Worker paradigm that is adopted in the ICARUS platform architecture in order to locally execute the designed in the Core Platform data analysis jobs utilizing the local services of the Secure and Private Space. Hence, the Secure-Space Worker is performing the following main operations based on the received instructions: a) transfer the selected encrypted datasets that will be utilized in the data analysis in the Secure Storage, b) decrypt the encrypted datasets with the help of the Decryption Manage, c) execute the data analysis job with the help of the Jobs Scheduler and Execution Engine, d) the encrypt the produced results with the help of the Encryption Manager and store them in the Secure Storage.

The **Jobs Scheduler and Execution Engine** undertakes the execution of the analytics jobs as provided by the Analytics and Visualisation Workbench by managing the execution on its complete lifecycle. In this sense, the Job Scheduler and Execution Engine performs the deployment of the Execution Cluster that will perform the data analysis in an isolated and secure environment with the help of the Resource Orchestrator. The Job Scheduler and Execution Engine initiates the immediate or scheduled execution on the Execution Cluster constantly monitoring the whole operation. Furthermore, it supports all the data handling aspect of the job execution by ensuring the access and storage of the required datasets or produced results by interacting with the Secure Storage. The Jobs Scheduler and Execution Engine is performing all the cluster management operations by interacting with the Kubernetes in order to effectively monitor and allocate the required resources, manage the job execution and report the status back the Analytics and Visualisation Workbench.

The **Execution Cluster** is the actual cluster-computing framework of the platform that is deployed within the isolate environment spawned by Kubernetes and is managed by the Jobs Scheduler and Execution Engine. In this sense, the Execution Cluster is exploited by the Jobs Scheduler and Execution Engine in order to perform the data analysis within a secure and isolated private instance of the cluster-computing framework. Under the hood, the dominant Apache Spark framework is utilized, exploiting the rich set of features offered by Spark, the offered powerful processing engine that supports the execution of an extended list of data analysis algorithms that span from simple statistical analysis to more advance and complex machine learning and deep learning algorithms.

Within the Secure and Private Space, running instances of the **Encryption Manager** and the **Decryption Manager** are also deployed. As described above, the role of the Encryption Manager in this tier is to encrypt the results of the analysis before they are securely transmitted and stored in the Core platform. On the other hand, the role of the Decryption Manager in this tier is the decryption of the dataset on the data consumer side in order to be used in the data analysis in the same manner as it is performed for the download and decryption of a dataset within the On-Premise Environment.

3 Results

The ICARUS platform aims to provide a novel big data-enabled platform with sophisticated and valuable platform features and offerings for the aviation data value chain. The development of the ICARUS platform followed the design specifications that were presented in the previous section, adopting an iterative approach of incremental releases based on the Agile development methodology. However, as the implementation of the ICARUS platform was recently completed no scientific results have yet been made available. Nevertheless, the ICARUS platform will be thoroughly verified and evaluated by **four core use cases** of the aviation data value chain in order to ensure the added value of the implemented platform and to showcase its unique innovation potential in the aviation industry. The following sections briefly present these use cases, focusing on the description of the context of each use case and the expected added value from the utilization of the ICARUS platform.

3.1 Extra-Aviation Services in an Integrated Airport Environment

Airports maintain a crucial role across the aviation industry as they constitute the indispensable connection to all the aviation-related activities, companies and organizations that are directly or indirectly linked to aviation. One crucial parameter of their operation is the capacity of the airport infrastructure (stands, gates vs planned aircraft arrivals) and its efficient planning. The main goal of the airport capacity planning is to ensure that the capacity of the airport infrastructure is sufficiently meeting the demand of the airport's stakeholders even during busy periods when the demand increases due to unforeseen reasons (i.e. difficult weather conditions) or due to increased incoming or outgoing traffic (i.e. high season travel periods).

The scope of the specific use case is to facilitate the effective capacity enhancement decisions that will enable the sustained increase in throughput performance and will increase capacity in all weather conditions. In this use case, the variety of the descriptive and predictive analytics algorithms offered by the ICARUS platform will be exploited towards the following main axes of the airport capacity planning: a) the Capacity Modelling, b) the Airport Traffic Forecasting, c) the Flight Delay Prediction and d) the Position and Slot Allocation/Scheduling. Through the ICARUS platform, the expected added value is the enhancement of the Airport Airside Capacity with the resource usage optimization of the airport airside infrastructure and the enhancement of the runway Operations Capacity. In the initial phase of the use case execution, the focus will be on the following aspects of the Capacity Modelling and Forecasting: i) the enhanced planning of flight schedules per season, ii) the optimized coordination of ground services and iii) the enhancement of the airport operation services.

3.2 Routes Analysis for Fuel Consumption Optimization and Pollution Awareness

Airlines are constantly addressing the challenge of reducing the fuel expenses in order to reduce their operational expenses but also to adhere the imposed regulations for reducing the environmental impact of the airline activities. However, this requires extensive and flexible analysis of various parameters in order to be in position to correctly assess the viability of route network extensions or modifications from an economic perspective that is dependent on the prediction of key operational metrics such as block time, block fuel and payload capacity.

The scope of the specific use case is to enable the optimized analysis of pollution data and aircraft emissions by performing advanced modelling of pollution data towards the prediction of aircraft performance in conjunction with the environmental impact. Furthermore, within this use case the analysis will be taken one step further by scaling this analysis from a single route into a massive route network on the second phase of the use case execution, by modelling aircraft payload capacity scenarios, taking also into consideration the weather conditions, towards the prediction of the aircraft performance in relation with a massive route network. For this specific use case, an external tool capable of performing route analysis, aircraft performance and economic investigations will be exploited in order to perform the required pre-processing calculations that will be used as input in the data analysis process that will conducted within the ICARUS platform that will allow the extraction of insights for aircraft fuel burn and carbon emissions for defined flight legs or a massive route network through the proper visualizations.

3.3 Aviation-Related Disease Spreading

The global spreading of epidemics requires the design and utilization of the advanced and complex mathematical models. The scope of this mathematical tools is to provide additional insights on the various parameters of the spreading of epidemic and most importantly the useful analysis and forecasting of the evolution of each epidemic towards the effective policy making from the corresponding health authorities. To this end, a model associated to meta-population has been developed in order to exploit the available real data as collected during any epidemic outbreak.

The scope of the specific use case to introduce the required non-incremental improvements on this meta-population model by leveraging the aviation-related data, and especially airline traffic data, in order to further model the relationship between the human mobility and the spread of an infectious disease. The use case will firstly leverage the aviation-related data in order to further optimize the existing model, as well as to perform a both qualitative and quantitative assessment of the model, utilizing also historical and current epidemic forecasts. To this end, the use case will exploit the offering of the ICARUS platform for data exploration and data exchange, as well as data preparation in term of pre-processing, anonymization and cleaning in order to produce the updated model version that will be holistically evaluated. On the second phase of the use execution, more passenger demographical data will be leveraged and combined with population-related and airline data in formulate the modelling framework that will enable the full coupling between human mobility and intra-population interactions.

3.4 Enhancing Passenger Experience with ICARUS Data

A major ongoing challenge of all the service providers on the aviation industry is the enhancement of the passenger experience with the optimization of the provided services and offerings to the passenger from the moment they arrive at the airport till the moment that they arrive at their destination. Hence, the specific use case will demonstrator the added value obtained by the ICARUS platform towards this aim by focusing on two different axes, firstly the prediction of on-board sales and the optimization of the tray loading towards the reduce of cabin food waste and the increase of revenue and secondly the prediction of profitable discounts and offers towards the increase of inflight sales.

The scope of the specific use case is to demonstrate the added value that can be obtained through the predictive algorithms and methods offered by the ICARUS platform for the prediction of the optimal loading weight of the duty-free and catering trays on board that can be exploited by both catering services and airlines prior to each flight in order to reduce cabin food waste and optimize their profits. Furthermore, the specific use case will demonstrate how the utilization of the predictive algorithms and methods offered by the ICARUS platform can provide added value to airlines and catering service companies by predicting valuable discounts and offers on products and bundles that will increase in-flight sales while at the same time increase passenger experience.

4   Conclusions

The scope of the current paper is to introduce the ICARUS big data-enabled platform that aims to provide a multi-sided platform which offers a novel aviation data and intelligence marketplace accompanied by a trusted and secure "sandboxed" analytics workspace. The ICARUS platform holistically handles the complete big data lifecycle from the data collection, data curation and data exploration to the data integration and data analysis of data originating from heterogeneous data sources with different velocity, variety and volume in a trusted and secure manner. The platform exploits methods such as big data analytics, deep learning, data enrichment, and blockchain powered data sharing, in order to properly address critical barriers for the adoption of Big Data in the aviation industry facilitating the design and execution of big data scenarios from the stakeholders of the aviation industry. In order to verify, validate and evaluate the ICARUS concept, approach and technical solution the four core representative use cases of the overall aviation's value chain, as briefly presented, will be performed.

Acknowledgement. ICARUS project is being funded by the European Commission under the Horizon 2020 Programme (Grant Agreement No. 780792).

References

1. The Aviation Industry Leaders Report 2019: Tackling headwinds. KPMG (2019)
2. Wholey, T.J., Deabler, G., Whitfield, M.M.: Commercial aviation and aerospace: big data analytics for advantage, differentiation and dollars. Tech. No. GBW03316- USEN-00. IBM Global Business Services, Somers, NY (2014)
3. Cooper, T., Smiley, J., Porter, C., Precourt, C.: Global Fleet & MRO market forecast summary. Oliver Wyman Assessment Report (2016)
4. Golchha, N.: Big data-the information revolution. Int. J. Adv. Res. 1(12), 791–794 (2015)
5. Tsai, C.-W.: Big data analytics: a survey. J. Big Data 2(1), 1–32 (2015)
6. Gantzand, J., Reinsel, D.: The digital universe in 2020: big data, bigger digital shadows, and biggest growth in the far east. In: IDC iView: IDC Big Data in 2020, Technical report (2012)
7. Chidambararajan, B., Kumar, M.S., Susee, M.S.: Big data privacy and security challenges in industries. Int. Res. J. Eng. Technol. 6(4), 1991 (2019)
8. Benjelloun, F.Z., Lahcen, A.A.: Big data security: challenges, recommendations and solutions. In: Web Services: Concepts, Methodologies, Tools, and Applications, pp. 25–38. IGI Global (2019)
9. ICARUS EC H2020 project Homepage. https://www.icarus2020.aero/. Accessed 15 June 2020

A Multi-valued Logic Assessment of Organizational Performance via Workforce Social Networking

José Neves[1,2(✉)] ⓘ, Florentino Fdez-Riverola[3] ⓘ, Vitor Alves[3] ⓘ, Filipa Ferraz[1] ⓘ,
Lia Sousa[2] ⓘ, António Costa[1] ⓘ, Jorge Ribeiro[4] ⓘ, and Henrique Vicente[1,5] ⓘ

[1] Centro Algoritmi, Universidade do Minho, Braga, Portugal
{jneves,costa}@di.uminho.pt, filipatferraz@gmail.com
[2] Instituto Politécnico de Saúde do Norte, CESPU, Gandra, Portugal
lia.sousa@ipsn.cespu.pt
[3] Departamento de Informática, ESEI – Escuela Superior de Ingeniería Informática,
Universidad de Vigo, Campus Universitario As Lagoas, Ourense, Spain
riverola@uvigo.es, vitoralves@estg.ipvc.pt
[4] Instituto Politécnico de Viana do Castelo, Rua da Escola Industrial e Comercial de
Nun'Álvares, 4900-347 Viana do Castelo, Portugal
jribeiro@estg.ipvc.pt
[5] Departamento de Química, Escola de Ciências e Tecnologia, REQUIMTE/LAQV,
Universidade de Évora, Évora, Portugal
hvicente@uevora.pt

Abstract. *Social Media* have changed the conditions and rules of *Social Networking* (*SNet*) where it comes from people intermingling with each other, i.e., *SNet* is to be understood as a process that works on the principle of many-to-many; any individual can create and share content. It is intended to explore explore the complex dynamics between *SNet*, *Logic Programming* (*LP*), and the *Laws of Thermodynamic* (*LoT*) in terms of entropy by drawing attention to how *Multi-Value Logic* (*MVL*) intertwines with *SNet*, *LP* and *LoT*, i.e., its norms, strategies, mechanisms, and methods for problem solving that underpin its dynamics when looks to programmability, connectivity, and organizational performance. Indeed, one's focus is on the tactics and strategies of *MVL* to evaluate the issues under which social practices unfold and to assess their impact on organizational performance.

Keywords: Social media · Social science and networking · Philosophy · Logic programming · Entropy · Multi-valued logic · Organizational performance · Artificial neural networks

1 Introduction

Social Norms (*SN*), the informal rules that govern behavior in groups and societies and underlie behavioral comparisons, may come from society as a whole and/or from individuals that are not only intimate but go on acknowledged, such as group members (being

Z. Deze et al. (Eds.): BDTA 2020/WiCON 2020, LNICST 371, pp. 63–77, 2021.
https://doi.org/10.1007/978-3-030-72802-1_5

a group viewed as a social unit or ecosystem) formed by one or more people with the expectation of mutual affection, responsibility and pro term duration, and characterized by commitment, shared decisions and common goals [1–3]. With a few exceptions, the *Social Science (SS)* literature conceives of norms as exogenous variables. Since norms are mainly seen as constraining behavior, some of the key differences between moral, social, and legal norms as well as differences between norms and conventions have been vague [4].

Philosophers have taken a different approach to norms. In the writing on norms and conventions, they are viewed as factor in a causal model or system whose value is determined by the states of the variables in the system, i.e., as the product of individual interactions [5–7]. Beliefs, expectations, group knowledge and general knowledge have therefore become central concepts in the development of a philosophical view of *SN* and as such supported by a collection of self-fulfilling expectations that will be addressed in terms of a *Theory of Declarative Knowledge*, based on an entropic perspective for *Knowledge Representation and Reasoning (KRR)* that will help to differentiate among *SN, Conventions* and *Descriptive Norms* [8]. This essential distinction is often overlooked in *SS* reports, but it is critical if one needs to diagnose the type of behavior pattern in organizational performance in order to intervene and express preferences, allowing for the construction of scenarios of the form *X and optionally Y* or *X or otherwise Y* based only on the empowered logic values that the alternatives may present and that range in the interval *0...1* [8, 9]. Indeed, in this article are identified four implicit roles on *Social Networking (SNet)*, namely physical, emotional, mental and spiritual. Integrates human beings daily life chores into their *Social Interactions*, which leads to new questions as well as to a reinterpretation of some currently accepted roles in the position of men [10], and to investigate the possibility of using the underlying *MVL* to express more general preferred enquiries, viz.

- *Do you use social networks to socialize?*
- *Do you use social networks to get job-related information?*
- *Do you use social networks to create your social identity?*
- *Do you use social networks to reduce academic and organizational stress?*
- *Do you use social networks for collaborative learning?*
- *Do you use social networks to watch the funny sharing?*

It was also assumed that there is a significant correlation between the networking scale and the measures that may be considered given the people answers to questionnaires like *Entertainment, Constraints, Academic and Organizational Strain*, and *Socialization*. This study was carried out in in northern Portugal. A total of 30 (thirty) workers took part in this study. The ages ranged from 20 to 60 years old, with 60% women and 40% men. The questionnaires were divided into two sections, the first containing general questions (e.g., age, gender, and academic and organizational qualifications), while the second included statements on working conditions, interpersonal relationships and emotional feelings.

The article is divided into five sections. Following the introduction, a new section is presented that examines the basics used in this work, namely the concept of *Entropy* and how it potentiates the use of *LP* for *KRR* [8, 9, 11, 12]. Section 3 presents the methods followed in this work and address the thematic of a thermodynamics approach to *SN* and introduces the computational models to assess organizational performance. Then conclusions are drawn, and future work outlined.

2 Preliminaries

2.1 Entropy vs. Knowledge Representation and Reasoning

The problem-solving method presented in this article is based on the *Laws of Thermodynamics* and aims to describe the practices of *Knowledge Representation and Reasoning* (*KRR*) as a process of energy degradation. This means that energy can be converted in a system but cannot be created or destroyed. It is measured in terms of entropy, a property that quantifies the ordered state of a system and its evolution, whose universe of discourse is expressed here as logic theories or logic programs [9].

On the other hand, it is undeniable that expressing *KRR* practices as logic theories as logic programs has become more natural and general as the field of *Logic Programming* (*LP*) matured and other arenas began to use its tools and results. Theories are typically uttered as a series of patterns (rules) and facts that make it possible to infer non-logical consequences using logical inference. In writing such rules and facts, both explicit (strong) negation or negation by failure and explicit declarations may be used to reinforce knowledge. Since the most common situation in the real world is incomplete and updateable, any system that makes serious attempts to deal with real-world situations must cope with such complexities [13].

Therefore, and in order to collect information about a *MVL* assessment of *SN* in the workplace it was considered the questionnaires *Entertainment Questionnaire Four-Item (EQ-4), Constraints Questionnaire Four-Item (CQ – 4), Academic and Organizational Strain Questionnaire-Six-Item (TQ – 6)*, and *Socialization Questionnaire-Four-Item (SQ – 4)*. The former one encompasses the statements, viz.

E1 – I use social networking sites for sharing pictures;
E2 – I use social networking sites to look at funny sharing;
E3 –I use social networking sites for watching movies; and.
E4 – I use social networking sites to get relief from academic and organizational stress.

They denote all possible occurrences in the discourse universe, the purpose of which is to evaluate the general feelings of the workforce about their behavioral relationships in the workplace. To make the process understandable, it is shown graphically. The scale used was based on an extension of the Likert scales expanded to cover the concept of entropy, viz.

always agree (4), sometimes agree (3), rarely agree (2), never agree (1), rarely agree (2), sometimes agree (3), always agree (4)

Moreover, it is included a neutral term, *neither agree* nor *disagree*, which stands for *uncertain* or *vague*. The reason for the individual's answers is in relation to the query, viz.

As a member of an organization, how much would you agree with each one of EQ – 4 referred to above?
leading to Table 1.

Table 1. A workforce member answers to *EQ – 4*.

Questions	Scale							
	(4)	(3)	(2)	(1)	(2)	(3)	(4)	*Vagueness*
E1		×	×					
E2								×
E3				×				
E4					×			

Leading to → Table 2 ← Leading to

Once the input for *E1* closely matches *(3)* → *(2)*, meaning that the system tends to deteriorate; i.e., the input for *E1 (3)* → *(2)* indicates that there is a tendency for system degradation. The inputs are read from *left* to *right* (e.g., from *(4)* → *(1)* (with increasing entropy) or from *(1)* → *(4)* (with decreasing entropy)). The markings on the axis correspond to one of the possible scaling options that can be used from *bottom* → *top* (i.e. from *(4)* → *(1)*), which indicates that the performance of the system decreases as the entropy increases, or becomes from *top* → *bottom* (i.e. from *(1)* → *(4)*), which indicates that the performance of the system increases with decreasing entropy. It is now possible to have an evaluation of the entropic state of the system according to the individual answers of a person to the above questionnaire for the *Best* and *Worst* scenarios [8] (Table 2).

Table 2. The extent of the *eq − 4's relation* in terms of an individual answer to the *EQ − 4* questionnaire. The corresponding logical program for the *Best-case scenario* is now given as *Program 1*, below.

EX BCS	VA BCS	AN BCS	SNA BCS	QoI BCS	EX WCS	VA WCS	AN WCS	SNA WCS	QoI WCS
0.45	0.33	0.30	0.89	0.55	0.78	0	0.22	0.63	0.22

Leading to   Leading to
→ **Program 1** ←

- The *SNA*, in general, is given as $\sqrt{1 - (EX + VA)^2}$; it stands for the sum of social, emotional and cognitive skills that enable the workforce to face the challenges of and to adapt to the demands of the organization (i.e., a *MVL* value that ranges in the interval *0… 1* (Fig. 1)), viz.

$$SNA_{BCS} = \sqrt{1 - EX^2} = \sqrt{1 - (0.45)^2} = 0.89$$

$$SNA_{WCS} = \sqrt{1 - (EX + VA)^2} = \sqrt{1 - (0.78 + 0)^2} = 0.63$$

- *QoI values are* evaluated, in general, in the form, viz.

$$QoI\ values = 1 - (EX + VA)/Interval\ Lenght\ (IL)$$

that stand for the *SNA's* sustainability degrees, i.e., it shows how the workforce was identified and adapted to the organizational environment, i.e., an *MVL* value that ranges in the interval *0 ... 1*, viz.

$$QoIvalues_{BCS} = 1 - (EX + VA)/1 = 1 - (0.45 + 0) = 0.55$$

$$QoIvalues_{WCS} = 1 - (EX + VA)/1 = 1 - (0.45 + 0.33) = 0.22$$

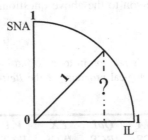

Fig. 1. *SNA* evaluation.

```
{


    ¬ eq – 4 (EX, VA, AN,  SNA,  QoI)

                              ← not eq – 4 (EX, VA, AN,  SNA,  QoI),

                        not exception_{eq-4} (EX, VA, AN,  SNA,  QoI)

    eq – 4 (0.45, 0.33,  0.30, 0.89, 0.55).

}
```

Program 1. The extent of the relation *eq – 4* for the *Best-case scenario*.

On the other hand, by looking at Table 1, it is possible not only to adjust but also to quantify the tendency for system deterioration and / or system improvement. In fact, the partition originating from (4) $\rightarrow$ (1) tends to set the system deterioration tendency, while the partition originating from (1) $\rightarrow$ (4) determines the system improvement. Looking now at Table 2 it is possible to measure the entropy associated with each partition. For the *Best-case scenario* one may have, viz.

$$entropy_{(4)\rightarrow(1)} = E_1 + E_2 + E_3 + E_4 = 0.06 + 0 + 0.25 + 0 = 0.31$$

$$entropy_{(1)\rightarrow(4)} = E_1 + E_2 + E_3 + E_4 = 0 + 0.25 + 0.25 + 0.14 = 0.64$$

Therefore, and once $0.31 < 0.64$, the system tends to develop positively. To evaluate the *Worst-case scenario,* the following procedures are similar.

3 A Declarative Knowledge Theory for Evaluating Organizational Performance Using Workforce Social Networking

A social unit consists of one or more people who live in a community or prefer to live rather than alone. It is characterized by commitment, joint decision-making and goal achievement. Looking at society in this way, one can take into account different attitudes and arrangements that exist in humanity today. Indeed, understanding its structure, function and process is of paramount importance in characterizing it and how it can contribute to the good of the individual or group. This understanding is addressed here in the form of questionnaires to assess entertainment, limitations, academic and organizational burdens, and the socialization practices referred to above.

3.1 Constraints

Today, time and cognitive constraints put an upper limit on the number of social relationships an individual can maintain at a given level of intensity. Similar restrictions may have worked throughout hominin evolution, affecting the size and structure of social networks. In order to decide in which extension this is the case, one can answer questions such as, viz.

C1– I face difficulty in finding exact information for academic via social networking sites;
C2 – Compulsive usage of social networking sites is a problematic issue;
C3 – I usually postpone my academic task for spending more time on the social networking sites; and
C4 – While using social networking sites it is difficult for me to concentrate on my studies.

once it is of the utmost importance to obtain as much information on the subject as possible. They represent the *Constraints Questionnaire Four Item (CQ – 4)*, whose answers in terms of qualitative and quantitative values of consumed energy are shown in Tables 3 and 4, respectively.

3.2 Academic and Organizational Strain

Academic and organizational social networks enhance the ability to share knowledge and this can be the final stepping stone to scientific research and organizational practices at both levels. Given their target audience and the product they offer, it is worth taking a closer look at the mission of social networks in an academic and organizational context and their most common uses, their effects on intellectual and organizational performance and their benefits. The value of this communication model also lies in its role as a strong emotional resource, as it creates a special atmosphere in the academic and organizational community by modeling groups of people with similar interests who are ultimately supposed to develop a sense of belonging and differentiation, therefore serving as a channel for creativity in the educational and organizational sectors. In consequence, to know if someone is feeling happier, more relaxed, or healthier, answer questions like, viz.

A1 – I use social networking sites to solve my academic, research and organizational problems;
A2 – I use social networking sites for online academic and organizational group discussion;
A3 – I communicate with my friends via social networking sites for preparation of group work;
A4 – I use social networking sites for collaborative learning and organizational practices;
A5 – I use social networking sites to learn about my curricular aspect; and
A6 – I use social networking sites to seek help from my peers and colleagues.

which stand for the *Academic and Organizational Strain Questionnaire-Six-Item (AOSQ – 6)*, whose answer by a worker is given in terms of its qualitative and quantitative values in Tables 3 and 4, respectively.

3.3 Socialization

Socialization is a process that introduces people to social norms and customs, i.e., a person learns to become a member of a group, community or society. To know how people feel about this process, answer questions such as, viz.

S1 – I use social networking sites to become more sociable;
S2 – I use social networking sites to create my social identity;
S3 – I prefer using social networking sites to attending social gathering; and
S4 – I used social networking sites for strengthening interpersonal relationships.

that make the *Socialization Questionnaire-Four-Item* (*SQ* – 4), whose answers in terms of qualitative and quantitative values are shown in Tables 3 and 4, respectively.

Table 3. An individual answers to the *CQ* – *4*, *AOSQ* – *6* and *SQ* – *4* questionnaires.

Questionnaires	Questions	Scale							Vagueness
		(4)	(3)	(2)	(1)	(2)	(3)	(4)	
	Q1				×		×		
CQ – 4	Q2		×						
	Q3								×
	Q4						×		
	A1						×	×	
	A2					×			
AOSQ – 6	A3		×		×				
	A4						×		
	A5								×
	A6		×		×				
	S1		×		×				
SQ – 4	S2								×
	S3	×		×					
	S4					×		×	

Leading to ⟶ Table 4 ⟵ Leading to

Table 4. The extent of relations *eq* – *4*, *cq* – *4*, *aosq* – *6* and *sq* – *4* stand for an individual answers to the questionnaires *EQ* – *4*, *CQ* – *4*, *AOSQ* – *6* and *SQ* – *4* for the *Best* and *Worst-case scenarios*.

Questionnaires	EX BCS	VA BCS	AN BCS	SNA BCS	QoI BCS	EX WCS	VA WCS	AN WCS	SNA WCS	QoI WCS
EQ – 4	0.45	0.33	0.30	0.89	0.55	0.78	0	0.22	0.63	0.22
CQ – 4	0.27	0.36	0.48	0.96	0.73	0.63	0	0.37	0.78	0.37
AOSQ – 6	0.23	0.30	0.60	0.97	0.77	0.53	0	0.47	0.85	0.47
SQ – 4	0.10	0.50	0.66	0.99	0.90	0.59	0	0.41	0.81	0.41

Leading to ⟶ Program 2 ⟵ Leading to

3.4   A Computational Make-Up

The computational framework forms the basis for a symbolic rating of the level of *Social Networking* (*SNA*) for an individual or group of people, measured by the *Quality-of-Information* used in their rating, which in relation to *MVL* stands for a set of truth values that lie in the interval $0...1$. The corresponding logical program for the *Best-case scenario* is given as Program 2 [8], viz.

{

/* The extent of eq – 4, cq – 4, aosq – 6 and sq – 4 predicates for the Best-case scenario */

¬ eq − 4 (EX, VA, AN, SNA, QoI truth values)

← not eq − 4 (EX, VA, AN, SNA, QoI),

not abducible$_{eq-4}$ (EX, VA, AN, SNA, QoI).

eq − 4 (0.45, 0.33, 0.30, 0.89, 0.55).

¬ cq − 4 (EX, VA, AN, SNA, QoI)

← not cq − 4 (EX, VA, AN, SNA, QoI),

not abducible$_{cq-4}$ (EX, VA, AN, SNA, QoI).

cq − 4 (0.27, 0.36, 0.48, 0.96, 0.73).

¬ aosq − 6 (EX, VA, AN, SNA, QoI)

← not aosq − 6 (EX, VA, AN, SNA, QoI),

not abducible$_{aosq-6}$ (EX, VA, AN, SNA, QoI).

aosq − 6 (0.23, 0.30, 0.60, 0.97, 0.77).

¬ sq − 4 (EX, VA, AN, SNA, QoI)

← not sq − 4 (EX, VA, AN, SNA, QoI),

not abducible$_{sq-4}$ (EX, VA, AN, SNA, QoI)

sq − 4 (0.10, 0.50, 0.66, 0.99, 0.90).

}

Program 2. A Formal Description of the Universe of Discourse for the *Best-case scenario*.

It is now possible to generate the data sets in order to train an *ANN* (Fig. 2) which, for the *Best-case scenario*, may be obtained by proving the theorem [14, 15], viz.

$$\forall \, (EX_1, VA_1, AN_1, SNA_1, QoI_1, \cdots, EX_4, VA_4, AN_4, SNA_4, QoI_4),$$

$$(eq\text{-}4 \, (EX_1, VA_1, AN_1, SNA_1, QoI_1)),$$

$$? \; (cq\text{-}4 \, (EX_2, VA_2, AN_2, SNA_2, QoI_2)),$$

$$aosq\text{-}6 \, (EX_3, VA_3, AN_3, SNA_3, QoI_3),$$

$$sq\text{-}4 \, (EX_4, VA_4, AN_4, SNA_4, QoI_4))$$

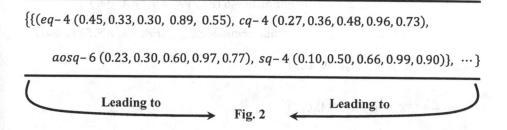

Leading to   →   **Table 5**   ←   Leading to

i.e., generate in all conceivable ways the sequences that combine the extent of predicates $eq-4$, $cq-4$, $aosq-6$, and $sq-4$ [14, 15] (where the symbols "$\forall$" and "?" stands for "for all" and "*falsity*", respectively), leading to Table 5.

Table 5. ANN's inputs for the *Best-case scenario*.

$\{\{(eq\text{-}4 \, (0.45, 0.33, 0.30, \; 0.89, \; 0.55),\; cq\text{-}4 \, (0.27, 0.36, 0.48, 0.96, 0.73),$

$aosq\text{-}6 \, (0.23, 0.30, 0.60, 0.97, 0.77),\; sq\text{-}4 \, (0.10, 0.50, 0.66, 0.99, 0.90)\}, \cdots\}$

Leading to   →   **Fig. 2**   ←   Leading to

For the *Worst-case scenario* the procedure is analogous. The corresponding logical program is given as Program 3 [8], viz.

{

/ The extent of eq – 4, cq – 4, aosq – 6 and sq – 4 predicates for the Worst-case scenario */*

¬ eq − 4 (*EX, VA, AN, SNA, QoI truth values*)

← not eq − 4 (*EX, VA, AN, SNA, QoI*),

not abducible$_{eq-4}$ (*EX, VA, AN, SNA, QoI*).

eq − 4 (0.78, 0, 0.22, 0.63, 0.22).

¬ cq − 4 (*EX, VA, AN, SNA, QoI*)

← not cq − 4 (*EX, VA, AN, SNA, QoI*),

not abducible$_{cq-4}$ (*EX, VA, AN, SNA, QoI*).

cq − 4 (0.63, 0, 0.37, 0.78, 0.37).

¬ aosq − 6 (*EX, VA, AN, SNA, QoI*)

← not aosq − 6 (*EX, VA, AN, SNA, QoI*),

not abducible$_{aosq-6}$ (*EX, VA, AN, SNA, QoI*).

aosq − 6 (0.53, 0, 0.47, 0.85, 0.47).

¬ sq − 4 (*EX, VA, AN, SNA, QoI*)

← not sq − 4 (*EX, VA, AN, SNA, QoI*),

not abducible$_{sq-4}$ (*EX, VA, AN, SNA, QoI*)

sq − 4 (0.59, 0, 0.41, 0.81, 0.41).

}

Program 3. A Formal Description of the Universe of Discourse for the *Worst-case scenario*.

It is now possible to generate the data sets in order to train an *ANN* (Fig. 3) which, for the *Worst-case scenario*, may be obtained by proving the theorem [14, 15], viz.

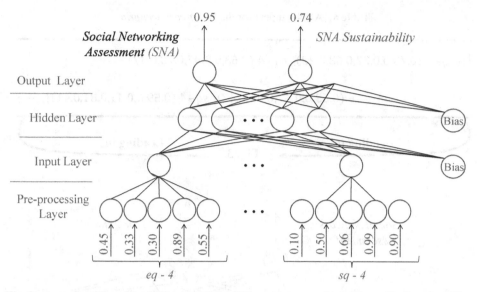

Fig. 2. A creative view of the *ANN* topology for *SNA* assessment and a measure of its *Sustainability* for the *Best-case scenario*.

$$\forall \, (EX_1, VA_1, AN_1, \, SNA_1, QoI_1, \, \cdots, \, EX_4, \, VA_4, \, AN_4, \, SNA_4, QoI_4),$$

$$(eq\text{-}4 \, (EX_1, VA_1, AN_1, \, SNA_1, QoI_1)),$$

$$?\ (cq\text{-}4 \, (EX_2, \, VA_2, \, AN_2, \, SNA_2, \, QoI_2),$$

$$aosq\text{-}6 \, (EX_3, \, VA_3, \, AN_3, \, SNA_3, QoI_3),$$

$$sq\text{-}4 \, (EX_4, \, VA_4, \, AN_4, \, SNA_4, QoI_4))$$

Leading to   **Leading to**

Table 6

leading to Table 6.

Table 6. ANN's inputs for the *Worst-case scenario*.

$\{\{(eq-4\ (0.78,0,0.22,0.63,0.22),\ cq-4\ (0.63,0,0.37,0.78,0.37),$

$aosq-6\ (0.53,0,0.47,0.85,0.47),\ sq-4\ (0.59,0,0.41,0.81,0.41)\},\ \cdots\}$

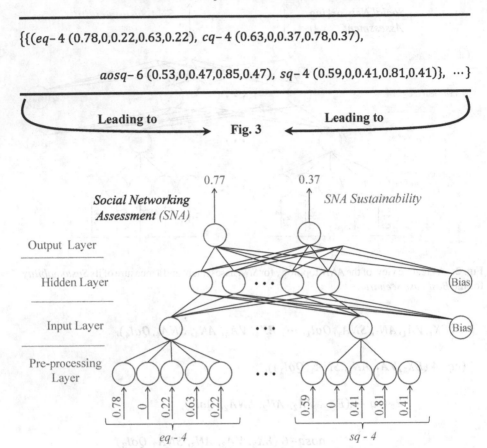

Fig. 3. A creative view of the *ANN* topology for *SNA* assessment and a measure of its *Sustainability* for the *Worst-case scenario*.

The output of the ANNs in Figs. 2 and 3 shows that the relationships between two people should not be viewed as dyadic ties, but rather as embedded in a larger network of relationships between network members; indeed $|SNA_{BCS}- SNA_{WCS}| = |0.95{-}0.77| = = 0.18\ (0.18 \neq 0)$, which shows that there are a greater number of relationships between network members, which emphasizes its impact on *Organizational Performance*.

4   Conclusions and Future Work

Social Networking according to the results so far obtained (Figs. 2 and 3) proves that relationships between two individuals should not be viewed as dyadic ties, but as embedded within a larger network of relations between network members. However, a network can act as a scaffold to the dyadic tie, reducing the time and cognitive costs of maintaining the relationship. Together with affairs based on empathy, this scaffolding will allow for larger groups to exist among hominins, what would not be possible if such networks were based purely on dyadic ties between individuals. These results show that one may have to change the way of living, accept new challenges, adapt to new experiences, develop new behavioral, cognitive, or emotional responses, a range of subjects that will be the subject of future work, matters for future work.

Acknowledgments. This work has been supported by FCT – Fundação para a Ciência e Tecnologia within the R&D Units Project Scope: UIDB/00319/2020.

References

1. Bicchieri, C.: The Grammar of Society – The Nature and Dynamics of Social Norms. Cambridge University Press, Cambridge
2. Bicchieri, C.: Norms in the Wild: How to Diagnose, Measure, and Change Social Norms. Oxford University Press, New York (2016)
3. Black, M.: The Social Theories of Talcott Parsons: A Critical Examination. Literary Licensing, LLC, Whitefish (2012)
4. van Dijck, J., Poell, T.: Understanding Social Media Logic. Media Commun. **1**, 2–14 (2013)
5. Lewis, D.: Convention: A Philosophical Study. Blackwell Publishing, Oxford (2002)
6. Ullmann-Margalit, E.: The Emergence of Norms. Oxford University Press, Oxford (2015)
7. Vanderschraaf, P.: Convention as correlated equilibrium. Erkenntnis **42**, 65–87 (1995)
8. Neves, J., et al.: Entropy and organizational performance. In: Pérez García, H., Sánchez González, L., Castejón Limas, M., Quintián Pardo, H., Corchado Rodríguez, E. (eds.) Hybrid Artificial Intelligent Systems. Lecture Notes in Computer Science, vol. 11734, pp. 206–217. Springer, Cham (2019). https://doi.org/10.1007/978-3-030-29859-3_18
9. Neves, J.: A logic interpreter to handle time and negation in logic databases. In: Muller, R., Pottmyer, J. (eds.) Proceedings of the 1984 Annual Conference of the ACM on the 5th Generation Challenge, pp. 50–54. ACM, New York (1984)
10. Burr, V.: Gender and Social Psychology. Routledge, London (1998)
11. Wenterodt, T., Herwig, H.: The entropic potential concept: a new way to look at energy transfer operations. Entropy **16**, 2071–2084 (2014)
12. Fernandes, B., Vicente, H., Ribeiro J., Capita, A., Analide, C., Neves, J.: Fully informed vulnerable road users – simpler, maybe better. In: Proceedings of the 21st International Conference on Information Integration and Web-based Applications & Services (iiWAS2019), pp. 600–604. Association for Computing Machinery, New York (2020)
13. Kakas, A., Kowalski, R., Toni, F.: The role of abduction in logic programming. In: Gabbay, D., Hogger, C., Robinson, I. (eds.) Handbook of Logic in Artificial Intelligence and Logic Programming, vol. 5, pp. 235–324. Oxford University Press, Oxford (1998)
14. Cortez, P., Rocha, M., Neves, J.: Evolving time series forecasting ARMA models. J. Heuristics **10**, 415–429 (2004)
15. Fernández-Delgado, M., Cernadas, E., Barro, S., Ribeiro, J., Neves, J.: Direct Kernel Perceptron (DKP): ultra-fast kernel ELM-based classification with non-iterative closed-form weight calculation. J. Neural Netw. **50**, 60–71 (2014)

Research on the Sharing and Application of TCM Digital Resources

Min Hu[1](✉) and Hao Li[2]

[1] Hubei University of Chinese Medicine, Wuhan 430065, China
[2] Central China Normal University, Wuhan 430079, China
lihao205@mail.ccnu.edu.cn

Abstract. With the vigorous development of online teaching and online learning, it has further increased the demand for digital resources, and further enhanced the feasibility of digital education, the necessity of digital resource construction and the importance of digital resource sharing in the information age. In this study, the status quo of TCM digital resources was studied from the aspects of literature research and resource construction, and a questionnaire survey was conducted among teachers and students in the major of TCM acupuncture in a TCM university. On this basis, suggestions on the application of digital resources in TCM acupuncture courses were proposed.

Keywords: Traditional Chinese Medicine · Digitalization · Learning resource · Resource sharing · Resource application

1 Introduction

Under the background of educational informatization, students' learning needs and learning styles have changed significantly, and the advantages of digital learning resources are fully reflected in the learning process. This new learning mode based on advanced educational technology can effectively promote the reform of teaching content presentation mode, teachers' teaching mode and students' learning mode, which not only puts forward higher requirements for teachers' personal quality, but also puts forward new challenges to learning resources. In October 2015, the Chinese medicine industry education cloud platform was officially launched, and the digitalization process of Chinese medicine industry education officially began.

Domestic scholars began to study teaching resource database in the early 21st century. In the past ten years, very important research achievements have been made. From the initial theoretical research to the application of various new theories and technologies at home and abroad to the construction of educational resources in recent years, relevant departments of the state have organized the nationwide development of digital resources in the form of engineering projects and built various national resource databases at all levels. Governments at all levels and schools of various types have also built a number of resource libraries of different sizes. At present, the well-known digital resource

Z. Deze et al. (Eds.): BDTA 2020/WiCON 2020, LNICST 371, pp. 78–89, 2021.
https://doi.org/10.1007/978-3-030-72802-1_6

construction platforms for medical science in China include: national excellent course resource network, Tsinghua University online school, medical vision world medical resource database, human health medical network, etc.

The research on digital learning resources in foreign countries is relatively early, especially in United States, Britain, Germany, France, Japan and other countries. The emphasis of digital teaching research in e-learning environment abroad is theory and technology. In Britain, United States and other western countries, the construction of learning resources has formed a set of very strict standards for resource development and related modes for implementation and management. Among these successful models, the representative resource portals in foreign countries mainly include: GEM project in United States, EdNA in Australia and CANCORE in Canada [1].

The implementation of national quality engineering represented by high-quality curriculum plays a significant role in promoting the construction of high-quality teaching resources, but the quality resources recognized by teachers and students in the practice process are still scarce. Experts and scholars are actively exploring the construction of digital resources, and TCM ancient books resources have been effectively developed [2–4]. Although China has always attached great importance to the construction of high-quality teaching resources, due to the lagging development of education and the complexity of the educational environment, the construction and application of high-quality teaching resources are still not optimistic. In particular, the systematic research and development of digital learning resources related to traditional Chinese medicine is less, and they are still in the stage of learning and absorbing achievements. How to construct high-quality digital teaching resources, network platform and high-quality digital education resources in the information technology environment is a problem to be further studied.

In the construction and application of digital resources, resource construction is the foundation and guarantee, resource application is the ultimate goal, and resource construction should serve resource application, which in turn promotes resource construction. As an indispensable element in the process of digitization of education, the construction and application of digitization resources are paid more and more attention. Digitalization of TCM can be realized to improve resource utilization and provide services for TCM teaching, scientific research and clinical application [5]. In order to better meet the learning and teaching needs of students major in traditional Chinese medicine, it is necessary to build high-quality digital educational resources for traditional Chinese medicine, constantly promote the co-construction and sharing of digital resource network platform, and gradually realize the network and digitalization of teaching and learning.

2   Analysis on the Current Situation of TCM Digital Resources

The analysis of the current situation of digital resources of traditional Chinese medicine is mainly carried out from two aspects: first, analyze the development and changes of literature research in recent years from literatures related to digital learning resources of traditional Chinese medicine, and the second, analyze the digital resources of TCM in each network resource platform.

2.1   Literatures Research Status

Database Selection
The databases selected for this study are CNKI, WANFANG DATA, and Chongqing VIP database.

Literatures Selection Criteria
The selection of paper follows the following criteria:

1) Papers should be published and be income to the academic papers database.
2) Papers retrieval periodicals should be limited to education, medical science and technology journals.
3) Papers should be published between January 2009 and August 2020.
4) When paper retrieval is carried out, "subject" is the limiting constraints.

Results and Analysis
The results retrieved from each database are shown in Fig. 1.

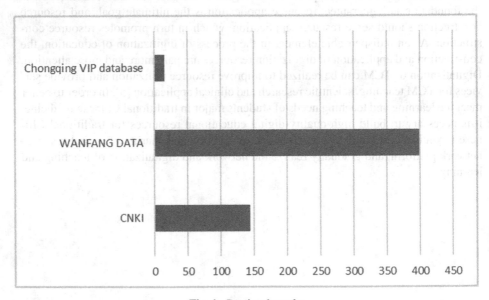

Fig. 1. Retrieval results.

Relevant retrieval indexes were set on CNKI and retrieved with the themes of "Traditional Chinese medicine digital resources" and the theme of "Traditional Chinese medicine Network platform construction" respectively. By August 2020, a total of 144 relevant literatures had been retrieved.

Relevant retrieval indexes were set on WANFANG DATA and retrieved with the themes of "Traditional Chinese medicine digital resources" and the theme of "Traditional Chinese medicine Network platform construction" respectively. By August 2020, a total of 399 relevant literatures had been retrieved.

Relevant retrieval indexes were set on Chongqing VIP database and retrieved with the themes of "Traditional Chinese medicine digital resources" and the theme of "Traditional Chinese medicine Network platform construction" respectively. By August 2020, a total of 15 relevant literatures had been retrieved.

Among the retrieved literatures, the literature with low relevance, such as advertisements, conferences, contribution invited and news, as well as repeated literatures were eliminated by manual screening, and finally 295 literatures related to digital resources of traditional Chinese medicine were selected.

Through the preliminary analysis of the literature content, in the era of rapid development of digital network, the development trend of TCM universities is to strengthen the construction of digital resources while maintaining the characteristics of TCM specialty. In addition, through the network resource platform, realizing the resource sharing and application can accelerate the construction of digital resources and create a digital resource construction road with the characteristics of traditional Chinese medicine.

2.2   Current Situation of Resource Construction

Excellent Courses

There are 23 traditional Chinese medicine universities in China, and each university had built a website of excellent courses. The constructions of excellent courses in each universities are shown in Table 1. Some universities cannot open the network of excellent courses normally, or we cannot obtain the data of excellent courses through other ways, so it is marked as "-" in Table 1. Due to the fact that some universities have not updated their websites of excellent courses in time, the statistical data cannot be guaranteed to be completely accurate, but it can also reflect the general situation of the construction of excellent courses in traditional Chinese medicine universities.

In addition to excellent courses, Beijing University of Chinese Medicine, Guangzhou University of Chinese Medicine, Fujian University of Traditional Chinese Medicine and Jiangxi University of Traditional Chinese Medicine have set up national bilingual teaching model courses. Zhejiang Chinese Medical University and Hubei University of Chinese Medicine have also set up resource-sharing courses, high-quality postgraduate courses and other curriculum resources.

Open Resource Platform

Influenced by foreign open courses and drawing lessons from the essence of online open course teaching mode, the national excellent course construction project came to an end. In 2011, the Ministry of Education launched the second round of undergraduate teaching project -- national excellent open course construction, including excellent video open

Table 1. The construction of excellent courses in universities of Chinese medicine.

No	Universities	National Excellent Courses	Provincial and Municipal Excellent Courses	University-level Excellent courses
1	Beijing University of Chinese Medicine	6	11	41
2	Guangzhou University of Chinese Medicine	3	–	–
3	Shanghai University of Traditional Chinese Medicine	7	17	17
4	Nanjing University of Chinese Medicine	6	–	23
5	Chengdu University of TCM	5	27	31
6	Shandong University of Traditional Chinese Medicine	7	33	–
7	Heilongjiang University of Chinese Medicine	8	22	52
8	Tianjin University of Traditional Chinese Medicine	6	10	–
9	Hunan University of Chinese Medicine	1	8	12
10	Liaoning University of Traditional Chinese Medicine	3	24	–
11	Hubei University of Chinese Medicine	1	11	–
12	Zhejiang Chinese Medical University	4	25	–
13	Changchun University of Chinese Medicine	3	23	–
14	Fujian University of Traditional Chinese Medicine	3	26	–

(*continued*)

Table 1. (*continued*)

No	Universities	National Excellent Courses	Provincial and Municipal Excellent Courses	University-level Excellent courses
15	Jiangxi University of Traditional Chinese Medicine	2	4	1
16	Henan University of Chinese Medicine	–	17	–
17	Shaanxi University of Chinese Medicine	–	20	20
18	Yunnan University of Chinese Medicine	–	17	–
19	Guangxi University of Chinese Medicine	–	14	–
20	Anhui University of Chinese Medicine	1	18	22
21	Gansu University of Chinese Medicine	–	9	39
22	Guizhou University of Traditional Chinese Medicine	–	13	–
23	Shanxi University of Chinese Medicine	–	11	

course and excellent resource sharing course [6, 7]. In this study, statistics on TCM related resources in open resource platforms were conducted, and the results are shown in Table 2.

Table 2. The number of TCM resources in each open resource platform.

No	Website	The number of TCM resources
1	https://open.163.com	18
2	https://www.icourses.cn/	149
3	https://www.xuetangx.com/	97
4	https://www.coursera.org/	14
5	https://www.edx.org/	8
6	https://www.cnmooc.org/home/index.mooc	62

Results and Analysis

As can be seen from Table 1 and Table 2, the number of digital resources related to TCM is not large. In domestic 23 excellent course websites of university of Chinese medicine, there are national excellent courses, including pharmaceutical, traditional Chinese medicine, nursing, basic medical, clinical medicine, such as Basic Theory of TCM by Xiazhen Guo from Beijing University of Chinese Medicine, Internal Medicine of TCM by Chunguang Xie from Chengdu University of TCM, Nursing of Chinese Mesicine by QiuHua Sun from Zhejiang Chinese Medical University, and Authentication of Chinese Medicines by Dekang Wu from Nanjing University of Chinese Medicine, etc.

As can be seen from Table 1, a small number of excellent courses are not updated in time, or the course resources website cannot be opened, or there is no open course resources. All these are detrimental to the construction, sharing and application of digital resources in TCM universities.

As can be seen from Table 2, among the open resource platforms, the number of TCM related open and shared resources is not large and the construction is insufficient. Students can use the resources in various open resource platforms for online learning at anytime and anywhere, free from time and space restrictions, and make full use of the fragmented time for learning. Therefore, TCM universities should actively build excellent open and share courses, give full play to the advantages of high-quality teaching resources, and improve the utilization rate of excellent teaching resources.

Different TCM universities have the same excellent courses, but also have different excellent courses. Even if it is the same excellent course, because of the different teaching style, teaching method and teaching means, students will have different experience and feelings while learning. Therefore, excellent courses of TCM universities can realize inter-school openness, exchange and sharing, enrich the quantity of excellent teaching resources of each university, make up for the shortage of excellent teaching resources, and encourage teachers and students to make full use of these excellent teaching resources for teaching and learning.

Combined with traditional Chinese medicine, by promoting the construction of digital resources and network platform, it can provide better and more practical digital learning resources to assist students' learning. It is a development trend in the future. With the passage of time and the development of information networks, more and more digital resources of different forms will be generated among Chinese medicine universities, and digital resources will be shared among them. If we make full use of excellent learning resources, we can improve the level of education and teaching, and then promote students' learning.

3   Application of Traditional Chinese Medicine Digital Learning Resources

To investigate the application of digital resources and the students' use of digital resources in the learning process, this study conducted a questionnaire survey for teachers and students major in acupuncture and moxibustion from a university of traditional Chinese medicine.

3.1 Questionnaire Design

Teachers should combine information technology, educational theory and subject curriculum together, and then combine their own teaching practice to achieve the purpose of teaching innovation and optimization [8]. To solve this problem, this study designed a questionnaire about teachers' use of information technology in teaching. In order to understand students' demand for digital teaching resources in the learning process, this study designed a questionnaire on the application of digital teaching resources.

3.2 Respondents

The respondents are divided into two categories: one is teachers from College of Acupuncture and Orthopedics in a University of Chinese Medical, and the other is students from the class of acupuncture and massage (Acupotomy) of 2018 in the same university.

3.3 Results and Analysis

Analysis of Results of the Information Technology Use Questionnaire (teacher)

A total of 10 questionnaires were distributed to teachers from college of Acupuncture and Orthopedics in a University of Traditional Chinese Medicine. Ten questionnaires were collected in this questionnaire survey, and the recovery rate was 100%. Among them, there were 10 valid questionnaires, and the questionnaire effectiveness was 100%.
Results analysis:

1) On the application of computer ability, for computer proficiency, 70% of respondents were more skilled, 30% of the respondents had average proficiency.
2) For information teaching ability, 70% of respondents did not deliberately use network resources, and 30% actively used network resources.

The results showed that it is feasible for teachers to use digital quality teaching resources in teaching.

Analysis of Results of the Digital Resource Application Questionnaire (students)

A total of 60 questionnaires were distributed to undergraduates from the class of acupuncture and massage (Acupotomy) in 2018 in a university of Traditional Chinese Medicine. A total of 60 questionnaires were collected and the questionnaire recovery rate was 100%. Among them, there were 60 valid questionnaires and the questionnaire effectiveness was 100%.
Results analysis:

1) When applying digital learning resources, the proportion of respondents choosing text, image, animation, audio and video was respectively 20%, 13%, 15%, 12%, 40%, and the proportion of respondents choosing media materials, questions and papers, courseware and cases, online courses, others was respectively 35%, 13%, 28%, 18%, 6%.

2) Theory class, the students thought video tutorials (34%), courseware (16%), knowledge map (26%) and reference books (16%) were helpful.
3) Practice class, three effective resources were video tutorials (36%), experiment guidbook (18%), animation or image resources (30%).
4) In question feedback, the main problems were: too many resources and not enough time to study (33%), lack of organization in resource integration (27%), and lack of guidelines for effective resource use (24%).

The results showed that students were more inclined to use video resources, text resources, media materials and courseware cases when using digital resources. Through the rational and effective application of digital resources, students will take the initiative to accept and show greater interest in learning, and change from passive learning to active learning.

3.4 Suggestions

Acupuncture and moxibustion as a traditional Chinese medical means, combines theory with practice, has its special nature and charm. Usually, the knowledge of acupuncture and moxibustion of TCM is taught through traditional teaching methods. In order to truly optimize the application effect of digital resources and improve the quality of digital teaching and learning, corresponding countermeasures should be taken [9].

Application of Digital Resources in Different Types of Courses
Application of Digital Resources in the Theoretical Basis of TCM Acupuncture and Moxibustion
Acupuncture and moxibustion is a course combining theory with practical operation. Theoretical knowledge in the early stage is difficult to understand, and practical operation is still needed in the later stage. For such a class of courses, the application of digital resources such as video, pictures and websites will be the key to solve the teaching problem. In the theoretical teaching of acupuncture and moxibustion in traditional Chinese medicine, the introduction of meridians and acupoints in the early stage is quite critical. It is not only necessary for students to clearly understand the composition and distribution of meridians, the location and function of acupoints, but also the location and circulation of fourteen meridians. These meridians and acupoints are relatively conceptual things, which cannot simply be explained clearly through words. Therefore, adding appropriate digital resources in the classroom will greatly improve the teaching quality.

Application of Digital Resources in Clinical Operation of TCM Acupuncture and Moxibustion
The application of digital resources in teaching enriches the teaching content to a large extent. For acupuncture and moxibustion major, which is highly operational and highly skilled, the traditional teaching methods imitated by students can no longer satisfy students' knowledge cognition only by teachers' on-site practice in class, leading to low teaching efficiency and effectiveness. If we make full use of network resources, multimedia technology, dynamic teaching AIDS and other modern teaching tools and means, we can impart more knowledge to students [10]. As a part of the clinical practice of

acupuncture and moxibustion, the former teaching mode is more about teachers practicing on the spot in the operation class and students following to strengthen the mastery of acupuncture and moxibustion skills. However, in order to further improve the teaching quality, we can add high-quality learning videos and high-quality teaching videos of acupuncture and moxibustion masters to the actual teaching process of acupuncture and moxibustion, so as to deepen the understanding and mastery of acupuncture and moxibustion skills. In this way, the application of high-quality digital teaching resources in traditional acupuncture and moxibustion teaching can greatly enhance learning, improve teaching quality and enrich teaching content.

Application of Digital Resources in Different Types of Teaching Content
Use Digital Resources in the Form of Thematic Projects
Through the understanding of the curriculum system of acupuncture and moxibustion, the learning knowledge can be divided into several sections, which are meridians, acupoints, acupuncture, and treatment. Through the teachers' understanding of several parts, it will be an effective way to strengthen the teaching quality to select the corresponding digital teaching resources in the teaching process, form the corresponding thematic learning mode, and display and absorb the knowledge in a precise, familiar, structured and systematic way.

The content of each project can be realized in the form of courseware, documents, pictures, videos, animations and other resources, which can greatly satisfy students' learning content and interest. Taking a thematic teaching as an example, the thorn moxibustion theory introduction (courseware and document), acupuncture point acquaintance (the human body acupuncture point diagram - picture), thorn moxibustion methods guidance (real acupuncture find video - video), such series of knowledge on collocation of thorn moxibustion series of high-quality digital resources, on the one hand, reduce teachers' burden, on the one hand, improve students' interest.

Applying Digital Resources in Task-Driven Form
Task-driven teaching and learning can provide students with situations of experiencing practice and perceiving problems, learning around tasks, testing and summarizing learning process by task completion results, etc., so as to change students' learning status and enable them to actively construct a learning system of exploring, practicing, thinking, applying and solving high wisdom.

1) Create a situation: Create a learning situation that is relevant to the current learning topic and as real as possible, and guide learners to enter the learning situation with real tasks. Aiming at the study of the theoretical operation of acupuncture and moxibustion, an acupuncture and moxibustion practice class is set up here, and a video of acupuncture and moxibustion (national excellent course) is selected.
2) Identify the problem: In the situation, select the real problems related to the current learning topic as the central content of learning, so that students need to be faced with a real problem that needs to be solved immediately. According to the video teaching, the teacher puts forward a series of operational problems, such as "How to fix acupoints? To what extent?"
3) Independent learning: Instead of telling students how to solve problems directly, students should collect problem-solving methods from the high-quality teaching

resources provided by teachers, so as to achieve the goal of self-directed learning. At the same time, students are encouraged to discuss and communicate with each other.

4) Effect evaluation: The evaluation of learning effect mainly includes two aspects: the first is the process and outcome evaluation of whether the student solves the problems, and the second is the evaluation of the student's independent learning ability. For example, whether the student has found the corresponding acupoint, and whether the student can complete acupuncture at a certain acupoint.

The application of digital resources has its convenience and flexibility, but there are also some shortcomings, which need to give full play to its essence when using. With the reform of traditional Chinese medicine teaching, the traditional teaching mode is changing, and information-based teaching methods, teaching tools and teaching means have been integrated into it. Under the background of education informatization, it is necessary to make full use of various tools and digital resources and apply them efficiently in the teaching classroom.

4 Conclusion

Through the research on the current situation of traditional Chinese medicine digital teaching resources, the progress of digital teaching is understood, and the necessity of digital education in the information age and the importance of digital resource construction are understood more clearly. Taking acupuncture and moxibustion for example, this study suggested that the use of digital resources in classroom teaching should be focused, concise and clear, and as much as possible to add some students easy to accept and understand the way of resource expression to highlight the intuitive teaching content, stimulate students' interest in learning, promote students' understanding of the teaching content, students' positive thinking.

The construction, sharing and application of TCM digital resources is a complex problem, and there are still some imperfections in this study, which need to be further studied.

1) In terms of the construction of digital teaching resources, in the context of China's vigorous development of "Internet + Traditional Chinese Medicine" and emphasis on "collect crowd funding, gather crowd strength", it is possible to make full use of the advantages of information technology, give full play to the initiative and creativity of network groups, and introduce public wisdom into the construction and sharing of traditional Chinese medicine digital resources.

2) In terms of the application of digital teaching resources, this study only proposes some Suggestions on the application of digital teaching resources in acupuncture and moxibustion, and the application strategies and effects need to be further studied.

Acknowledgement. The work was supported by MOE General Project of Humanities and Social Science (19YJC880032), National Natural Science Foundation of China (NSFC) (No.61807013) and Fundamental Research Funds for the Central Universities (CCNU20QN028).

References

1. Chen, W., Luo, C.Y., Wang, Y.X., Qin, W., Yuan, Z.Y.: The construction and application of digital teaching resources of Formulaology. Modern Traditional Chinese Med. **5**(35), 204–206 (2015)
2. Xiong, F., Song, G.Q.: Investigation on the construction status of digital resources of ancient Chinese medicine books in universities. Inner Mongolia Sci. Technol. Econ. **15**, 97–99 (2020)
3. Jiang, Y.J., Li, X., Sun, L., Guo, L.: Construction of digital resource platform for ancient ancient doctors and their medical books in Jingchu. China J. Traditional Chinese Med. Pharmacy **34**(8), 3808–3810 (2019)
4. Zhou, J.Y., Yang, P., Wang, S.W.: Current situation of digitization construction of TCM information resources in China. Chinese J. Med. Libr. Inf. Sci. **25**(7), 49–52 (2016)
5. Cao, H.Z.: On the digitization construction of TCM resources. Chinese Med. Modern Distance Educ. China **4**(10), 49–50 (2006)
6. Liu, K.N.: From the construction of excellent courses to the construction of high-quality open courses – the exploration of Chinese Mooc. Sci. Technol. **27**(007), 344 (2017)
7. Shen, L.Y., Zhao, A.J., Dong, R.: From national quality curriculum to the national quality open video class open education movement in China has entered a new period. Modern Educ. Technol. **22**(11), 62–67 (2012)
8. Zhao, Y.R., Han, P.L., Xiang, T.C.: Application status and Analysis of digital teaching resources in college teaching. Guangzhou Chemical Industry **39**(2), 144–146 (2011)
9. Yu, Q.C.: Research on the Strategies of classroom Teaching application of digital teaching resources in universities. Educ. Teach. Forum **43**, 73–75 (2013)
10. Ma, F.Y.: Primary exploration in figure teaching of ophthalmology of TCM. Guiding J. Traditional Chinese Med. Pharmacy **12**(1), 88–89 (2006)

Statistical Research on Macroeconomic Big Data: Using a Bayesian Stochastic Volatility Model

Minglei Shan[✉]

Shandong Youth University of Political Science, Jinan 250103, China

Abstract. The alternative variation of variance in Stochastic Volatility (SV) models provides a big data modelling solution that is more suitable for the fluctuation process in macroeconomics for de-scribing unobservable fluctuation features. The estimation method based on Monte Carlo simula-tion shows unique advantages in dealing with high-dimensional integration problems. The statis-tical research on macroeconomic big data based on Bayesian stochastic volatility model builds on the Markov Chain Monte Carlo estimation. The critical values of the statistics can be defined exactly, which is one of the drawbacks of traditional statistics. Most importantly, the model pro-vides an effective analysis tool for the expected variable generation behaviour caused by macroe-conomic big data statistics.

Keyword: Bayesian stochastic volatility models · Economic big data statistics · Monte Carlo simulation algorithms

Owing to the impact of the COVID-19 epidemic, China's macroeconomic performance is currently exhibit-ing more multi-dimensionality and heterogeneity. In this case, the lag and limitations in the application of tradi-tional statistical theories and research tools are more no-ticeable. Therefore, modeling application methods based on time-varying fluctuation processes are valued and men-tioned by academic scholars and government economics officials working in the area of macro-statistics. In view of the new charac-teristics of volatility clustering and nonlin-ear dynamic structure presented by the time series in the economic system during the epidemic period, the modeling analysis of the Bayesian stochastic volatility model grad-ually showed its advantages in fusion and algorithm.

1 Theoretical Basis and Research Significance

1.1 Related Concepts

The Bayesian algorithm, developed by the English mathematician Thomas Bayes in the 18th century, assumes the prior knowledge used to estimate the parameters are random variables, where unknown parameters are independent of the distribution. Based on

Z. Deze et al. (Eds.): BDTA 2020/WiCON 2020, LNICST 371, pp. 90–103, 2021.
https://doi.org/10.1007/978-3-030-72802-1_7

the probability rule, when the probability of the sample event is close to the overall probability, the posterior information of the parameter is obtained. The basic formula is:

$$p(\theta \,|X) = \frac{p(X \,|\theta)p(\theta)}{p(X)} \propto p(X \,|\theta)p(\theta),$$

In this formula, P(θ|X) represents the posterior probability density function of the parameter given for the sample X, P is a constant function of a relationship formed between the posterior probability of θ when X occurs, and x represents the prior probability density function of the parameter.

The stochastic volatility model, also known as the SV model in statistics, was proposed by the mathematicians Taylor and Shephard in the 1980s and 1990s. It was originally used to explain the autoregressive phenomenon of serial volatility in economics (performance conditional heteroscedasticity, also called the GARCH model). Random fluctuations focus on measuring the degree of random variation in a particular time series. Random volatility is defined as the standard deviation or covariance in a continuous difference model. Its model has the characteristics of dynamic fluctuations, assuming that the interference item is unobservable and follows the process of random fluctuations.

The Monte Carlo Method is used to construct a sample with a $\pi(x)$ stationary distribution through probability theory and statistical theory, and perform various statistical inferences based on these $\pi(x)$ samples. The core of the algorithm is to use the experimental mathematical method of digital simulation in order to construct or describe the probabilistic process by mastering the geometric quantity and geometric characteristics of the object motion. Based on the probability model, the simulated experimental sample is used as an approximate solution to find and establish an estimate quantity, and then perform statistical inference.

The nonlinear structure of macroeconomics. Nonlinear structure refers to the characteristics that a node may have multiple successors and several precursors. Random sampling and empirical research show that the linear expression of macroeconomics is not often the case and is mostly non-linear. The interaction of macroeconomic factors, the process of information internalization to form market prices, and the operation of economic fluctuations are all inherently non-linear. Research in these areas has inaugurated a new field for macroeconomics research and put forward higher requirements for most macroeconomic modeling.

1.2 Research Significance

Theoretical significance: The final goal of the development of SV Model modeling theory is to apply aggregate volatility observations, by also including unobservable implicit volatility variables. In the entire development process of the time-varying volatility model, various typical characteristics of the macroeconomic time series can be effectively portrayed and the similarity function can be accurately expressed, thus conforming to the driving force of actual modeling to the greatest extent. Owing to the limitation of the level of macroeconomic models, the volatility observation of the time-varying Monte Carlo estimation method is slower than that of the GARCH model. The SV Model modeling theory can describe more accurately the characteristics of volatility, and has more important significance in predicting the big data of uncertainty continuous coefficient change point fluctuation and volatility risk.

Practical significance: The COVID-19 epidemic has severely affected the economic and social operations, to such a degree that it caused large economic downturns and turmoil within a certain period of time and made the non-linear structure of the macro economy obvious. Moreover, the instability is expected to grow further, which overall shows a decline at the macroeconomic level. The trend has strengthened, economic growth momentum has weakened, and overall volatility has increased. For similar nonlinear states, the traditional Kalman filter method cannot perform a comprehensive analysis. It is necessary to consider the approximate filter method in the form of Bayesian estimation model for processing. The full use of the characteristics of prior information is beneficial to the actual situation and big data analysis and forecasting.

2 Purpose and Content

2.1 Main Research Purpose

This research aims to focus on a typical time-varying volatility model: SV Model, which introduces a new stochastic process with strong fitting ability and high estimation difficulty. Since the model contains unobservable latent wave variables, it is difficult to obtain an accurate expression of the likelihood function for its nonlinear structure. In addition, the extended form of nonlinear structure in macroeconomic big data is more complicated, making it difficult to estimate potential state variables and related parameters. Therefore, model estimation is traditionally presented as the focus and difficulty in the modeling process. The time-varying volatility model based on steady-state simulation is a frontier subject of modern econometrics research and has important theoretical value. Sequential Bayesian filtering technology has strong adaptability to macroeconomic fluctuation state filtering and parameter learning methods, and can better deal with the estimation of large-scale nonlinear non-Gaussian state space models. This model can effectively separate expected information, accurately carry out big data statistical prediction and analysis, and promote the development of big data algorithms in the field of volatility modeling. This kind of research has good adaptability to the expansion of various volatility models. Furthermore, in-depth discussion of its algorithm regarding the improvement and application of the nonlinear structure state of macroeconomic big data, as well as big data related modeling based on volatility model research field has high reference value.

In the entire development trajectory of the big data time-varying volatility model, we can effectively describe the various typical characteristics of the macroeconomic time series. This is the driving force for the continuous development and change of the model form. The basic goal of the Monte Carlo estimation method of the time-varying volatility model in the field of macroeconomic big data statistics is to describe more accurately the characteristics of various fluctuations, which are the risk management of the macroeconomic field. In addition, it has an important role in the prediction of macroeconomic risks and price fluctuations. Traditional statistical inference methods are based on the overall data, and pay more attention to the derivation of causality. This impedes them in meeting the requirements of big data operations in terms of calculation amount and sensitivity. The big data simulation technology recursively updates the estimated value, avoiding the storage and reprocessing of the previous observation data, and effectively reducing the actual calculation cost. Moreover, the introduction of big data simulation technology into the estimated value of the time-varying volatility model can effectively solve the problems of repeated calculation and time lag in parameter estimation and state prediction, and realize the time-varying sequential prediction effect of the online data intelligent volatility model.

With the development of modern econometrics and computer technology, the non-linear structural time-varying fluctuation process modeling method is provided as a powerful analysis tool for effective macroeconomic risk management, and its use has been partially applied to asset portfolios and macro capital flows field. It can be seen from the existing literature that the construction and estimation of time-varying volatility models have been rapidly developing. Especially in recent years, the application of statistical forecasting has gradually become a hot spot in the field of model design and academic research. In addition, the time series data of macroeconomic big data usually does not meet the independent repeated test conditions in classic statistics. Therefore, with the continuous development of macroeconomic big data statistical research, the observation and calculation techniques for the behavior of expected variables should not only change accordingly, but improve. In the Bayesian method, the model parameters are random variables, which have a specific statistical distribution form. This proves to be an effective tool for solving the macroeconomic nonlinear structure observation problem. Research in this area mainly focuses on the classical statistical modeling theory.

The distribution of parameter estimates and test statistics in the volatility models are unknown, so it is difficult to determine the level of accurate critical values. Owing to the complexity of the model form, it is difficult to obtain analytical expressions of model parameters. In an attempt to describe the volatility characteristics of the time series of big data more accurately and comprehensively, people have developed various extended forms of time-varying volatility models. The Monte Carlo model provides a set of effective estimation methods for various complex models, especially for those that are difficult to estimate. Owing to the high correlation between economic big data samples, traditional methods have slow convergence speed, which is not conducive to empirical analysis. However, the design of effective estimation methods for various extended time-varying volatility models and related application research still needs in-depth work. Since this model is a typical nonlinear and non-Gaussian state space model, it only has the analytical expression of the posterior distribution in concept, so it is necessary to find the approximate solution of Bayesian estimation. When new observations appear in this process, the posterior probability density of the Monte Carlo estimation method will be re-estimated based on the Markov chain mantissa algorithm. Further use of the estimation technology based on the Bayesian stochastic volatility model is used to convert the state of the complex system into the prior probability density of the simulated and predicted state. Following, the latest observations are used to make corrections to obtain the posterior probability density, and, finally, to obtain the best estimate of the state. In other words, it is not necessary to process all the data of the past time every time, but to estimate the current state vector based on the observation vector of the current time and the state vector of the previous one or more times. This technology can also be applied to online data analysis that is common in macroeconomic analysis.

2.2 Research Context and Technical Route

Based on the analysis of the research background and literature review, the research group used induction and simulation methods to sort out the theory of the Bayesian stochastic volatility model. A macroeconomic big data statistical program based on this model was further proposed, and an online reasoning method was explored. According to the current research status, the following main issues are discussed:

Under the classical statistical modeling theory system, research of improved algorithms and applications of regression are conditional on heteroscedasticity models and their respective extended models in the area of macroeconomics. Furthermore, they are dependent on the accurate critical values of parameter estimation and test statistical distribution in the volatility model. With the development of the macroeconomic system, time series data in this field no longer meet the independent repeated test conditions in classical statistics, and the behavior of expected variables will also change accordingly. The Bayesian model has a specific statistical distribution form, where the parameters present random variables. The framework of the Bayesian method is used to analyze the time-varying fluctuation model, which provides a broad exploration space for solving the above problems.

For the application of the Bayesian model in the non-linear structure of the macroeconomics, we focus on big data algorithms. First, in order to develop an extended form of the time-varying volatility model, we use the auxiliary particle filter algorithm corresponding to the Bayesian sequence to accurately and comprehensively describe the volatility characteristics of the macroeconomic time series. Owing to the complexity of the model form, it is difficult to obtain analytical formulas for model parameters. The Monte Carlo simulation method provides an effective calculation method for various complex models, especially the SV Model, which is difficult to estimate. Owing to the high correlation between data samples, the traditional Markov chain Monte Carlo (MCMC) method has a very slow test speed, which is not conducive to empirical analysis. Therefore, it proves to be a challenge to design effective MCMC estimation methods for various extended forms of time-varying volatility models and conduct related application research.

The MCMC sampling algorithm's estimation of the SV model will generate potential state variables of the simulated data. Therefore, the corresponding MCMC sampling method will generate multiple sampling chains. It can be seen from the data calculation of the sequence autocorrelation function of each sampling chain that there are two single steps. The state autocorrelation performance of the MCMC sampling method declines very slowly, while the state of the combined sampling method where the Bayesian model participates in the sample size autocorrelation performance declines quickly, and maintains a low level of correlation. This is mainly due to the joint sampling process, where the latent state variables are extracted as a whole, so that the Markov chain has a faster convergence speed. Besides the fact that the joint sampling method based on normal approximation has a large deviation from the state value, other methods have little difference in the estimation accuracy of state variables. In each algorithm, calculating the mean square error (MSE) between the estimated value of the state variable and the true value leads to obtaining a more accurate value.

2.3 The Main Content of the Research

Owing to the instability of the macroeconomic system, venture capital and macroeconomic control tools with volatility as their main component have received extensive research and attention. With the development of "descriptive economics", big data modeling and analysis of market price volatility under macroeconomic regulation have gradually become the focus of attention in both theoretical and practical circles. In view of the new characteristics of time series and changes in economic aggregates (quantity space) in the macro economy, the big data modeling method of time-varying fluctuations has been greatly developed. The SV Model in the time-varying volatility model has a strong fitting ability and a more challenging estimation difficulty.

SV Model contains unobservable latent wave variables, which makes it difficult to obtain an accurate expression of the likelihood function. Its various expansion forms are more complicated, and it is difficult to estimate potential state variables and parameters. Therefore, the estimation of big data models has always been the key issue in the modeling process. With the continuous development of computing technology, the estimation method based on the Monte Carlo simulation has shown its unique advantages in dealing with high-dimensional integration problems. Among them, the MCMC algorithm has become the fastest growing and most widely used model method among time-varying volatility model estimation methods. Combined with the application of background in macroeconomics, the research group made an effort to: improve the SV Model, study the Bayesian reasoning process, design the MCMC sampling algorithm based on the Bayesian model, and compare the effectiveness of various MCMC sampling algorithms in the SV Model. In the application field of big data models, two time-varying volatility models are used to study the dynamic relationship between the inflation level and the uncertainty persistence coefficient change point during the fluctuation period of the macroeconomic continuous coefficient change point, and under the influence of global epidemic conditions. The market trend of China can provide a useful reference for the application of this model in the current macroeconomic risk management and economic policy formulation. In this way, we follow the standard Bayesian conjugate prior to setting the model (Alston, Mengersen, and Pettitt, 2012), and select the hyper-parameters to correspond to the non-informative prior settings. This way the information contained in the data set corresponds to the appropriate covariance conditions, where weighting coefficients are assigned to the MCMC prior distribution:

$$p(\rho) = \text{Dir}\left(\rho; \alpha_1^{(0)}, \ldots, \alpha_K^{(0)}\right);$$

The prior distribution of the mean conditioned on the covariance matrix is an independent multivariate normal distribution:

$$p(\mu \mid T) = \prod_{j=1}^{K} N_d\left(\mu_j; m_j^{(0)}, \left(\beta_j^{(0)} T_j\right)^{-1}\right);$$

The prior of the exact matrix is given by the MCMC distribution:

$$p(T) = \prod_{j=1}^{K} W\left(T_j; v_j^{(0)}, \Sigma_j^{(0)}\right);$$

Therefore, the joint distribution will eventually be: $p(y, z, \theta) = p(y, z \mid \theta)p(\rho)p(\mu \mid T)$, where the number of $p(T)$ are all hyper-parameters.

In the MCMC estimation method, each time a new observation is obtained, the posterior probability density must be re-estimated, with all previous samples needing to be retained, which may take up a lot of the calculation. The Sequential Monte Carlo (SMC) technology uses the system transition model to predict the prior probability density of the state, and then uses the latest observation data to obtain the posterior probability density of the state, thereby calculating the optimal estimate of the state. Meaning, the technology can be used to analyze online data commonly found in macroeconomics and economic analysis.

The focus of the research is an SV MODEL and its extended SMC estimation method. A sequential Bayes filter parameter learning algorithm is proposed, building upon the existing parameter learning method based on artificial noise process. Following, various filtering algorithms are compared and analyzed. Finally, due to the impact of emergencies in the macroeconomic field, the fluctuations of big data time series are usually clustered at different levels. Establishing a model with variable structural fluctuation characteristics has important practical value for improving the accuracy of macroeconomic market fluctuation forecasts and avoiding macroeconomic investment risks. Therefore, the research team focused on the variable structure form of the SV MODEL. In particular, the spotlight was on the comparative analysis of the structure expansion form of the big data model and the sequential Monte Carlo algorithm, combined with the current domestic macroeconomic actual continuous coefficient change point shock situation. The model was used for the purposes of potential fluctuation prediction and its application in emergency detection showed good performance.

The research is based on the estimation of the time-varying volatility Bayesian model of Monte Carlo simulation method, including the focus on several topics:

The research group proposed a variety of standard MCMC sampling algorithms for SV MODEL based on an analysis of the research status and related background of time-varying wave models at home and abroad, as well as Monte Carlo simulation methods. The SV MODEL introduces random error terms into the wave equation to make the data modeling process more flexible and the estimation process more difficult. The method of the simulation analysis and comparison is used to systematically summarize the combined the design of the standard SV MODEL and MCMC algorithm, which further promotes the research progress of the SV MODEL and highlights its basic statistical characteristics. Based on several main estimation methods of the SV MODEL in recent years and by analyzing their respective advantages and disadvantages, the sampling algorithm of a standard SV MODEL is clarified.

Based on the background of macroeconomic applications, the existing SV MODEL has been expanded and improved. Namely, the improved MCMC sampling algorithm and several important extensions of the long memory SV MODEL are studied, as well as the Bayesian reasoning process. Furthermore, the design of the corresponding MCMC sampling and macroeconomic application background improves the model. In the category of multivariable SV MODEL, the Gibbs joint sampling algorithm is used to design the model by long memory in order to infer a special form of forecast distribution, and further determine the difference between the asymmetric mean of the SV MODEL, and the current macroeconomic level and uncertain fluctuations of the dynamic relationship. A Bayesian comprehensive national credit premium model based on multi-factor SV MODEL is established to distinguish the characteristics of average recovery rates of different scales. Moreover, a multi-step MCMC method based on mixed normal distribution is used to simulate credit premium index sequences for companies using different remaining payment conditions and perform applicability analysis. In view of the reasoning requirements of online data and the fact that SV MODEL and its extended form are nonlinear non-Gaussian state-space models, together with the time-varying and uncertainty of the current economic level, the known parameters of the sequential Monte Carlo model are systematically discussed using the SMC technology. The Monte Carlo model in SV MODEL performs big data simulation analysis. The specific calculation method is as follows:

The distribution q(θ, z) is chosen to minimize the Kullback-Leibler (KL) divergence between the approximate density q(θ, z) and the true joint density p(θ, z|y). For this reason, an attempt is made to obtain a relatively low lower limit of the marginal density p(y). In order for the maximization method to be used to estimate the parameters of the objective approximation function, the correlation density must be manipulated and re-expressed to allow for the introduction of a variational approximation function (McGrory and Titterington, 2007). From then on, the calculation model can be derived for a simulation analysis of parameters:

$$\log p(y) = \log \int \sum_{\{z\}} p(y, z, \theta) d\theta$$

$$= \log \int \sum_{\{z\}} q(\theta, z) \frac{p(y, z, \theta)}{q(\theta, z)} d\theta$$

$$\geq \int \sum_{\{z\}} \log \frac{p(y, z, \theta)}{q(\theta, z)} d\theta$$

Among them, the multi-step MCMC method of mixed normal distribution can analyze the compound state model through the Bayesian method. When q(θ, z) = p(θ, z|y), it is completely minimized, q(θ, z) is close to the true density, and Q(θ, z) is limited to the factorized form Q(θ, z) = q θ(θ)Ž(z).

In online data analysis, where the model parameters are unknown, the parameter learning method based on sequential Monte Carlo is further discussed. As a result, a sequential Bayes filter parameter learning method is processed by using artificial noise technology. After adopting a parameter learning method based on the SMC model and having sufficient statistical characteristics, the statistical model variables are fully considered. The filter density function is decomposed to employ the sequential Bayes filter parameter learning algorithm. On the one hand, the parameter learning method based on auxiliary particle filter and its improved algorithm are studied in the simulation analysis. On the other hand, the effectiveness of this algorithm is illustrated by comparing various filtering algorithms. Therefore, the simulation results of the sequential Bayes filter parameter learning algorithm can be further discussed and compared with the existing learning algorithm. It is found that the standard SV is a more practical and effective alternative method.

For the variable structure of an SV MODEL, the model contains some extreme cases that are of particular importance to risk management. The research group relies on the sequential Bayes filter parameters for simulation and empirical analysis of the learning algorithm. The results show that this algorithm can effectively describe the dynamic structural characteristics of macro-market fluctuations and can avoid the subjective bias of prior information. The use of the sequential Bayes filter parameter learning algorithm is threefold: 1) to conduct empirical research on China's macroeconomics, 2) to decompose the joint filter density function from another angle, 3) and to conduct empirical research on the variable structure characteristics of macroeconomic fluctuations. It can

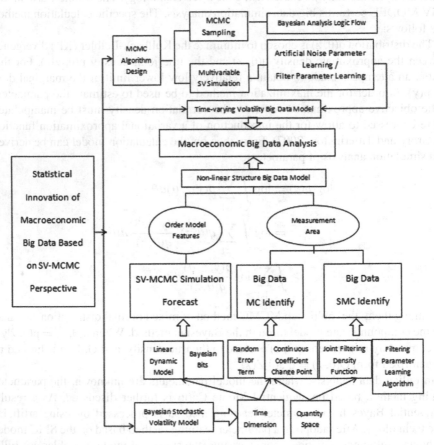

Fig. 1. Research on macroeconomic big data statistics using a Bayesian stochastic volatility model

be said that the use of the SV MODEL in the MCMC algorithm can lead to improvements in MC identification and calculation in terms of model prediction, and emergency detection estimation efficiency and accuracy under potential fluctuations.

The overall framework and specific steps of the research content are shown in Fig. 1:

3 Analysis

The Bayesian stochastic volatility model is used to identify and analyze the SMC of major macroeconomic big data indicators. At present, major foreign research institutions such as the National Bureau of Economic Analysis and the Oxford Institute for Economic Research are using the Bayesian method to make statistics on the macroeconomic situation. Compared with traditional volatility modeling and estimation methods, the Bayesian method has the advantage of maintaining effective estimation capabilities in situations where the affected continuous coefficient change point fluctuation is greater than the number of continuous fluctuations at the model stopping point. The research group draws on the Arch model measurement method proposed by the American scholar Engel, a Nobel Prize winner in economics, and relies on the metrological stochastic volatility model for processing and research. The unit of continuous volatility is set to (Yt), and the sum is calculated according to the MCMC sampling algorithm. The posterior distribution is:

$$Y_t = \left[\int_0^1 Y_{jt}^{\frac{1}{\lambda_{f,t}}} dj \right]^{\lambda_{f,t}}, \quad 1 \le \lambda_{f,t} \le \infty$$

The time is labelled as jt, the number of continuous wave points is presented as dj, and the function curvature caused by the wave is λf, t.

Since a single variable structure prediction method is suitable for different systems with limited measurement accuracy, the model should have different parameter selection mechanisms in order to be able to automatically select the best prediction parameters in the same system. In practice, the period of macroeconomic fluctuations is getting shorter and shorter, and the information response is becoming more and more sensitive, resulting in a large amount of online data. For time-varying market conditions, the MCMC sampling simulation technology has a great dependence on the model and parameter settings. Every operation in this estimation process is based on the overall data, which is abundant. From the perspective of variable diagnosis structure points, segmented modeling is a relatively simple method. Also, the maximum likelihood value of the estimation is obtained based on sequential Monte Carlo simulation. In these equations, Yt is replaced by ŷi, where ŷi corresponds to the weighted observation and is defined as follows:

$$\hat{y}_i = \frac{\gamma_i \times y_i}{\frac{1}{n} \sum_{i=1}^n \gamma_i}$$

The expected value required to update the expression remains unchanged. In specific, it keeps the same form adopted by the standard VB algorithm. This algorithm outlines the pseudo-code of the weighted VB algorithm, which we call Core Set Variation Bayes (CVB). The CVB algorithm input is expressed as:

$$C = \{(\gamma(\times 1), \times 1), (\gamma(\times 2), \times 2), \ldots, (\gamma(\times N), \times N)\}$$

In such way, it allows for a hierarchical structure of data points to be constructed and the weight of the multiplicity of the sampling points to be associated with the log likelihood. If the estimated log likelihood has the smallest variance, the weight is set to the optimum. This kind of structure of the sampling set helps to provide higher probability for observations that are far away from the initial cluster center. Furthermore, the sampling deviation can be fixed by adjusting the weights related to the sampling probability. This finally allows for a possibility to build an appropriate core set from the entire data set based on the weight.

In the process of time series modeling, the main purpose of the research is to extract the statistical characteristics rules from the observation data containing noise, with a final goal to make effective statistical inferences for MC identification. Compared with traditional time series models, the state-space big data modeling process can express the dynamic structure of observed variables and latent state variables, thus directly reflecting the movement of the data generation process. More importantly, in the framework of state space modeling, time series models (such as ARMA model and SV MODEL) can be integrated into a unified structure in such a way that estimation methods with general characteristics can be used for analysis. When compared with the MCMC, the standard SV method has higher calculation accuracy, although there may be cases where the analysis needs to be performed in a shorter time frame. For super large data, this would mean facing the problem of cumbersome calculations. A resolution to this can be proposed by reducing the amount of data that actually has to be processed in the first place. Deleting a part of the data set before analysis is a lot less incommoding when the data sets provide the same or very similar information. For example, consider trying to fit a mixed model to an image. We do not have to analyze all of the observed intensity levels present in the complete data set to get a good mean estimate for that particular cluster.

In addition to resolving the cumbersome calculation issue, the state space form of this big data model also provides a more effective way to simplify the maximum likelihood estimation and deal with missing values. Since the system identification of the state space model is based on the Bayesian principle, it mainly reflects to the approximate filtering of the state space model. In the field of frequency statistics, the sequential Monte Carlo is chosen for maximum likelihood estimation method. For the estimation of the linear Gaussian state space model, statistical inference and analysis can be completed through the iterative process of mean and variance. In a statistical sense, the Kalman filter can be used as the best estimation method. However, for the nonlinear non-Gaussian state-space models, the approximation results are very sensitive to the resampling process. This is mainly because the Bayesian estimation of the model is more complicated or has a high dimension, and therefore cannot be applied to online data estimation, nor can it be analyzed in a broad sense.

Consider using other optimization methods to solve the maximum likelihood estimation problem, such as approximate filtering methods or simulation-based filtering methods. Knowing the algorithm parameters, the regional metric distribution can be obtained through the following iterative process. The distribution formula is as follows:

$$P(x, |y'\theta) = p(x, Ix, \theta)p(y, Ix, \theta)$$

Once the distribution function $P(x,|y'\theta)$ in the model with known parameters is obtained, that is, θ is a constant factor, the problem is transformed into a filtering analysis of the model state variables. The joint posterior density function of the state variables I $= N$, with sampling the increase of the number N follows the core idea of a Monte Carlo estimation.

This formula cuts in from the mixed smooth distribution, combined with the filtering process, and proposes an algorithm for sequential Bayes filter parameter learning. In order to obtain the sampling form of direct filtering, we consider the filtering process and statistical marginal distribution of state variables. The basic idea of the approximate filtering method is to transform the nonlinear non-Gaussian state space model into a linear Gaussian model. The Kalman filter method is used to realize the system identification, and the recognition field is represented by the extended Kalman filter (EKF) and the Kalman filter. However, this method only plays a role in approximate sampling. In addition, Gaussian mixture distribution approximation is used to deal with the estimation problem of the state space model. In practical applications, not all models can be converted into a Gaussian linear form. The approximate filtering method with models is used to estimate state variables and parameters. In particular, these methods may have common problems. The integral approximation process is based on the approximation result, which in return drives the approximation error to be larger and larger, making the estimated value to deviate from the actual value. This method is shown in Fig. 2:

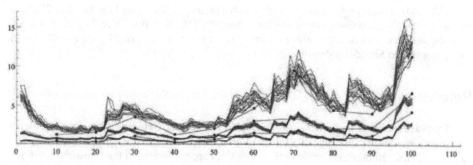

Fig. 2. Approximate filtering method used to estimate fluctuation characteristics of the SV model order model

In nonlinear and non-Gaussian state space big data models, simulation-based filtering methods provide a more general solution for the system identification problem. This method is based on Monte Carlo simulation, combined with sequential Bayesian filtering. It should be noted that the sampling distribution of the parameters is set in the form of a mixed normal distribution. When new data is received, changes in the model are reflected in time. Nevertheless, the effective information can be extracted to correct and estimate the model parameters. Compared with the MCMC method, this method has multiple advantages: high sensitivity, small calculation amount, high estimation accuracy, and higher practical significance. A combination of increasing number of observed variables, rapid growth of computing power and the continuous decrease of computing costs provides a broad development space for the convergence and complexity of the SMC method in the state space of the known parameter random fluctuation model.

4   Conclusion

In the field of macroeconomic risk research, the modelling and estimation of big data time series are undoubtedly of great significance. With the development of computer technology and Bayesian method, big data modelling overcomes the problem of difficulty to accurately determine the critical value of test statistics in the traditional statistical modelling process. In addition, with the continuous development of the economy and the macroeconomic system, Monte Carlo simulation can help solve the complex numerical calculation problems in the estimation of big data models, and the behaviour of expected variable generation will also change accordingly. The time-varying fluctuation model based on Monte Carlo simulation also provides an effective research tool for solving the above stated problems. Owing to the complexity of the time-varying wave model and its model in extended form, it is difficult to obtain analytical expressions of big data model parameters using only MCMC simulation method and SMC simulation method. The Monte Carlo simulation method provides a set of effective estimates for various models. The application of SV Model is expected to have more research and contributions in the future, especially in the field of macroeconomics that is characterised by many wave points and complex forms.

Fund Project.   Major project of statistical research project of Shandong Province in 2019: "statistical research on macro-economic big data based on Bayesian stochastic fluctuation model: from the perspective of Monte Carlo simulation" (No.: kt1907); supported by the growth plan of young teachers in Shandong Province.

References

1. Tanaka, M., Katayama, T.: Robust Kalman filter for linear discrete-time system with Gaussian sum noises. Int. J. Syst. Sci. **18**(9), 1721–1731 (2019)
2. Chow, H.K.: Robust estimation in time series: an approximation to the Gaussian sum filter. Commun. Stat. Theory Methods **23**(12), 3491–3505 (2014)
3. Kahn, H., Marshall, A.W.: Methods of reducing sample size in Monte Carlo computations. J. Oper. Res. Soc. Am. **1**(5), 263–271 (2013)
4. Kloek, T., van Dijk, H.K.: Bayesian estimations of equation system parameters: an application of Monte Carlo integration. Econometrica **46**(1), 1–20 (2018)
5. Shephard, N.M., Pitt, K.: Likelihood analysis of non-Gaussian measurement time series. Biometrika **84**(3), 653–667 (2007)
6. Richard, J.F., Zhang, W.: Efficient high-dimensional importance sampling. J. Econ. **141**(2), 1385–1411 (2017)
7. Liya, H.: Bayesian stochastic volatility model based on Monte Carlo simulation and its application research. Hunan University (2011)

8. Wang, J., Xiao, F., Chen, J., Yao, X.: Reliability analysis of pile foundation based on Bayesian theory and Monte Carlo simulation. J. Undergr. Space Eng. **13**(S1), 85–90 (2017)
9. Meng, L., Zhang, S.: Empirical eigenfunction method for parameter estimation of SV model. Syst. Eng. **22**(12), 92–95 (2004)
10. Su, W., Zhang, S.: Multiple long memory SV model and its application in Shanghai and Shenzhen stock markets. J. Manag. Sci. **7**(1), 38–44 (2004)
11. Xu, M., Zhang, S.: Research on estimation method of long memory stochastic volatility model based on wavelet transform. China Manag. Sci. **14**(1), 7–14 (2006)

Introducing and Benchmarking a One-Shot Learning Gesture Recognition Dataset

Panagiotis Kasnesis[✉][iD], Christos Chatzigeorgiou[iD],
Charalampos Z. Patrikakis[iD], and Maria Rangoussi[iD]

Department of Electrical and Electronics Engineering, University of West Attica,
Egaleo, Greece
{pkasnesis,chrihatz,bpatr,mariar}@uniwa.gr

Abstract. Deep learning techniques have been widely and successfully applied, over the last five years, to recognize the gestures and activities performed by users wearing electronic devices. However, the collected datasets are built in an old fashioned way, mostly comprised of subjects that perform many times few different gestures/activities. This paper addresses the lack of a wearable gesture recognition dataset for exploring one-shot learning techniques. The current dataset consists of 46 gestures performed by 35 subjects, wearing a smartwatch equipped with 3 motion sensors and is publicly available. Moreover, 3 one-shot learning classification approaches are benchmarked on the dataset, exploiting two different deep learning classifiers. The results of the benchmark depict the difficulty of the one-shot learning task, exposing new challenges for wearable gesture/activity recognition.

Keywords: Datasets · Deep learning · Wearable gesture recognition · One-shot learning

1 Introduction

Gestures are a very natural and intuitive way for humans both to interact with an electronic device (e.g., TV) and to control it [18]. As a result, gesture-based interfaces based on arm, hand or finger motions are becoming increasingly popular [9]. To this end, wrist-worn devices are widely used for recording motion data signals; they are effective and unobtrusive devices which have been used successfully in several domains, such as smart home environments [16], smart factory [26], physical security [11]. They are also exploited for effective gesture-based human-machine interaction [5,23,31].

In order to accurately recognize the body movements and translate the results into commands, after having established a one-to-one correspondence between gestures and commands to action, these gesture-based interfaces are based on machine learning algorithms [11]. In particular, Deep Learning (DL) algorithms, such as Convolutional Neural Networks (CNNs; ConvNets) and Long-Short Term

© ICST Institute for Computer Sciences, Social Informatics and Telecommunications Engineering 2021
Published by Springer Nature Switzerland AG 2021. All Rights Reserved
Z. Deze et al. (Eds.): BDTA 2020/WiCON 2020, LNICST 371, pp. 104–116, 2021.
https://doi.org/10.1007/978-3-030-72802-1_8

Memory (LSTM) have been efficiently applied to human gesture/activity recognition over the last five years [12,20,22,25]. However, these algorithms demand large datasets to be trained on; moreover, only few works have examined their knowledge transfer capabilities [1,21,29], especially when it comes to one-shot learning [8].

A disadvantage of existing approaches is that the algorithms have to be trained on large source datasets, such as those reported in [4,24], before evaluating their knowledge on the target dataset. On the other hand, although, there do exist publicly available small datasets [7,17] that contain dozens of different gestures, the wrist-worn devices used for gesture monitoring suffered from low sampling rate (i.e., 10 Hz) and time windows (i.e., 1 s), making it almost impossible to train a DL model on them. Moreover, the scientific interest in applying neural networks to small-data tasks has been increased the last two years [3,10], where new deep learning paradigms, such as Neural Tangent Kernel, have been proposed. As a results, a standard benchmark for learning from few examples, such as Omniglot [15], is therefore lacking in the human activity/gesture recognition domain.

In the present paper, we introduce a one-Shot lEaNning geSture rEcognition Dataset[1] (SENSED); it is a dataset consisting of 46 gestures, including existing English characters, numbers and symbols performed (hand-written on a surface) only once by 35 subjects, who are wearing a commercial smartwatch. SENSED has been deliberately designed to be small to avoid arbitrary downsampling of existing large datasets, and is split into train, validation and test sets to enable a fair comparison between the machine learning algorithms [2]. Moreover, SENSED is benchmarked by 3 one-shot learning classification approaches. In particular, the contribution and innovation of this work is summarized in the following:

1. To the best or our knowledge, SENSED is the first wearable-based gesture recognition dataset particularly built for one-shot learning.
2. Three deep learning approaches for one-shot learning were applied to SENSED with promising results.
3. The collected dataset is made publicly available, to be used as a benchmark for one-shot learning sensor-based gesture recognition.

The rest of this paper is organized as follows. Section 2 elaborates on the data collection procedure, while Sect. 3 describes in detail all the investigated one-shot learning network architectures. Section 4 describes the experimental setup for data processing and Sect. 5 presents and discusses the obtained results of our experiments. Finally, Sect. 6 concludes the paper and proposes future research steps.

2   Dataset Collection

The dataset is designed to contain a total of 46 characters. The first 26 are all the English capital letters, i.e., A to Z. The next ten include all the ten digits ranging

---

[1] https://github.com/ounospanas/sensed.

from 0 to 9. The last ten characters include some commonly used characters and math symbols: @, \$, #, €, ?, !, %, *, + and =. We selected these type of gestures to be included since character and digit recognition could be useful in several domains, such as producing short texts messages, converting dynamically handwritten texts to online documents, entering security passwords without the use of a physical interface and many others. The English capitals letters were used as the train set, the numbers were used for creating the validation set and the special characters were used as the test set. In total, 35 subjects participated in the creation of the dataset and performed the gestures only once. However, not all subjects performed all characters. 25 subjects wrote the English letters, 5 subjects wrote the digits and 5 subjects wrote the remaining special characters. The above information is summarized in Table 1.

The device that was chosen for gathering the data, is the Fossil Gen 5[2]. It runs on a Snapdragon 3100 chipset[3], which is currently the latest chipset from Qualcomm for smartwatches, features 1 GB of RAM and 8 GB of storage. It comes equipped with accelerometer, gyroscope, magnetometer and heart rate sensor. For communication with other devices, it can use either Bluetooth or Wi-Fi. The hardware is managed by Wear OS[4] by Google, a modified version of Android for smartwatches and wearables. Although Wear OS targets devices with more limited hardware resources than smartphones, it has the same Application Programming Interface (API) as Android making the development process the same. The sensors that were used for creating the dataset were the 3-axial accelerometer and gyroscope. Each sensor was set to its maximum sampling rate allowed by the OS which is limited 50 Hz. For each gesture, the device captured a time window of 3 s of data (150 samples), which was enough for the subjects to perform gestures that involved a lot of hand movement.

Table 1. Dataset contents and participating subjects

Set	Characters	Subjects	No. of Chars
Train	A–Z	25	26
Validation	0–9	5	10
Test	@\$€#?!%*+=	5	10
Total		35	46

In order to create an homogeneous dataset, subjects were provided with instructions on how to draw each character. The instructions included the pattern they had to follow for each character along with the starting and ending point for the symbol, the lines or curves they had to draw and the order they had to follow, as shown in Fig. 1. The starting point was shown as a blank circle

---

[2] https://www.fossil.com/en-us/smartwatches/learn-more/gen-5/.
[3] https://www.qualcomm.com/products/snapdragon-wear-3100-platform.
[4] https://wearos.google.com/.

and the ending point as a solid filled circle. Additionally, dashed lines showed were the subject would have to lift the hand and not draw anything. Despite the pattern limitation, subjects were free to choose the hand that they could use (left of right), to choose whether they would be sitting or standing and to select the writing surface (paper, whiteboard or simply draw the character in the air).

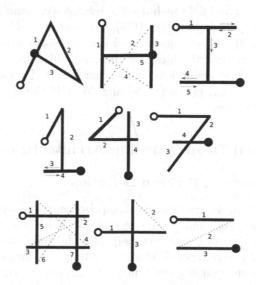

Fig. 1. A sample of the symbols used in the dataset

Two native Android applications were developed to build the dataset; one for smartphones and one for smartwatches. The smartwatch application was used to capture and save the raw data from the sensors, while the smartphone application was used for labeling the data. After wearing the smartwatch, the subject would select the character to execute from a list in the main screen of the smartphone application. Then, the device would send the symbol to the smartwatch and it would start capturing the data for the predefined duration. A vibration in the watch would signal the beginning and the ending of the capture. Afterwards, the data would be saved in Comma Separated Values (CSV) files in the smartwatch. When a subject would finish capturing the data, (s)he would tap a button on the mobile application to send the CSV files from the smartwatch to the smartphone and then another button to send the files to the server. Before actually sending the files, a random UUID (Universally Unique IDentifier) would be appended to the filename in order to easily distinguish each set. Files were deleted from both devices by tapping a button in the smartphone, before the devices was passed on the next subject. The reason for storing the output from each subject on separate file is application performance. By having small files, each write operation runs faster. Moreover, the files are sent faster between the devices and to the server. In order to avoid subjects executing the same gesture multiple times, the background of the character in the list would change color when a gesture was performed. In addition, if the subject would tap on a character that has already executed, a dialog would appear asking him/her if (s)he wants to execute again the same gesture.

File structure is uniform across subjects: it has 9 values in each row. The first field denotes the Epoch time in milliseconds, i.e. the time that the data arrived in the application, the second field includes the relative timestamp of data arrival, as reported by the Operating System (OS), the next six fields include the x, y, and z axis values of the accelerometer and the gyroscope sensors respectively, while the last field contains the label for the executed gesture. The label takes on values from 0 to 45, where 0 denotes the character "A", 25 the character "Z", 26 the character "0", 35 the character "9" and 36 to 45 the special characters in the order described above.

3   Benchmarked Deep Learning Architectures

3.1   One-Shot Learning Problem Definition

One-shot learning datasets are typically comprised of three sets: a) the training set, b) the validation set, and c) the testing set. Each one of them contains disjoint label spaces (i.e., different gestures) [14]. The main objective of few-shot learning setting is to extract transferable embeddings/features from the observed gestures included in the training set. One-shot learning is a subclass of few-shot learning setting, where the classification is done under the restriction that only a single example of each possible class is observed before making a prediction about a test sample [14]. Moreover, since SENSED contains ten unique classes in the validation and test sets, the one-shot problem is defined as 10-way.

To benchmark our dataset we investigated the three DL approaches for one-shot learning (described in the following subsections), which are based on two deep learning architectures that have been successfully applied to human activity/gesture recognition. The first one, called PerceptionNet, is a deep CNN model introduced in [12], which relies on late sensor fusion [22] using a 2D convolutional layer. The second one, called deep ConvLSTM, deploys a LSTM (Long-Short Term Memory) layer after the convolutional ones so as to fuse the sensor modalities [28].

3.2   Vanilla Embedding Extraction

The approach adopted here is the most commonly used in bibliography [21] when it comes to Transfer Learning (TL), and it is comprised of the following steps. The DL model is firstly trained on a source domain (i.e., English capital letters), just like in any vanilla classification task. After training, the weights of the trained model are "frozen" and applied to the target domain. The tensors produced by the last hidden convolutional layers, which represent all the knowledge from the input signal (called embedding), are stored. In our 10-way one-shot learning task in order to define the class of the anchor signal, we select that embedding e^c, which represents the class C that has the minimum norm distance from the anchor signal's embedding e^1.

The L_2 norm distance between the embeddings e^1, e^2 is given by:

$$d(e^1, e^2) = \left\| (e_i^1 - e_i^2) \right\|_2^2 \tag{1}$$

3.3   Pairwise Siamese Networks

A Siamese network similar to the one reported in [6], which is an end-to-end learning approach for extracting embeddings, has, also, been implemented. In this approach, the deep neural network is replicated twice (i.e., sharing the same filters for each input gesture sample). Just like the previous approach, the produced embeddings are compared using the Euclidean distance (i.e., L_2 norm) to directly predict whether the two input samples (i.e., anchor and candidate) belong to the same gesture class. However, this approach differs from the previous one because it does not aim at finding the nearest neighbor, but feeds the produced absolute difference to a fully connected layer followed by a sigmoid activation function. As a result, the output is mapped into a single logistic unit, where different gesture signals should produce a value equal to 0 and the same gestures equal to 1. To this end, a binary cross entropy function is used as a terminal step, to define the loss, similar to [14].

The binary cross entropy loss function is given by:

$$CE_b = -(y * log(p) + (1 - y) * log(1 - p)) \tag{2}$$

where y denotes the target label and p the probability produced by the sigmoid function.

3.4   Matching Network

Another network selected for evaluation here is the Matching Network (Match-Net) [27] which has been succesfully applied to previous human activity recognition tasks [30]. It shares the same logic with Pairwise Siamese classifiers, but here the anchor signal is compared with C candidate similar motion signals (i.e., ten in our case). MatchNet was developed on top of the two selected DL models (i.e., the CNN and the deep ConvLSTM). Figure 2 displays the network architecture for the case of CNN MatchNet.

The values of the selected window size are denoted by n_w, while the number of the sensor channels are depicted by n_c. Since the sensor signals in the selected architecture are stacked vertically, the number of the kernels is equal to 1. It should be noted that all the convolutional layers are followed by a ReLU activation function and a batch normalization layer, while all the pooling layers are followed by a dropout. After computing the embeddings, u for the anchor signal and v_i for the comparing signal, where $i = 1, ..., C$, we estimate the similarity score defined by:

$$similarity = \frac{u * v_i}{\|v_i\|} \tag{3}$$

Finally, the produced similarities scores are concatenated and normalized using a softmax function to compute the multi-class cross entropy loss:

$$CE_c = -\sum_{i=1}^{C} y_i \log(p_i) \qquad (4)$$

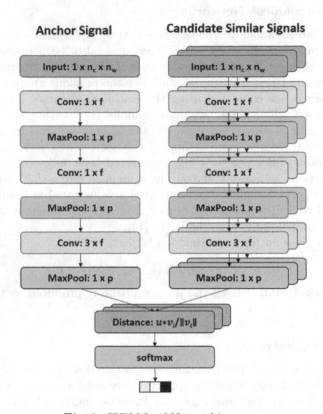

Fig. 2. CNN MatchNet architecture.

4   Experimental Set-Up

For our experiments we used a computer workstation equipped with a NVIDIA GTX 1080 Ti GPU featuring 11 gigabytes RAM, 3584 CUDA cores and a bandwidth of 484 GB/s. Python and specifically the Numpy library for matrix multiplications, data preprocessing and segmentation, was used as the programming language of choice, the scikit-learn[5] library was used for implementing the

---

[5] https://scikit-learn.org/stable/modules/generated/sklearn.manifold.TSNE.html.

t-SNE algorithm, and the Keras[6] high-level neural networks library with TensorFlow[7] library as backend was used for developing the model architectures. The CUDA Toolkit supported by the cuDNN[8], which is the NVIDIA GPU-accelerated library for deep neural networks, was used to accelerate the tensor multiplications. The software was installed on a 18.04 Ubuntu Linux operating system.

4.1   Data Sampling and Preprocessing

The data sampling process was done as follows. In the case of training set, the anchor gesture executed by a subject s_i was compared with 10 randomly chosen gestures executed by a subject s_j; we selected to make 2,000 10-way comparisons for each English character leading to 52,000 training samples. The same approach was followed in the cases of the validation and test sets; however, in these cases all possible 10-way combinations were taken into consideration, yielding 200 samples for each set. These are stored and published to be used for future algorithmic benchmarking.

Table 2. Examined hyperparameters

Name	Symbol	Range
Batch size	–	64, 128, 256
Learning rate	α	1e-03
Beta1	β_1	0.9
Beta2	β_2	0.999
Epsilon	ϵ	1e-08
Filter height	f_h	1–3
Filter width	f_c	7–15
Filter channels	f_c	16, 24, 32, 48, 64, 80
LSTM units	–	8, 16
Dropout probability	–	0.1–0.5
Maximum epoch	–	1000
Early stopping criterion	–	100

As a preprocessing step for all the sets, the collected gesture signals were normalized using the following equation:

$$z_i = \frac{(x_i - \mu_i)}{\sigma_i} \tag{5}$$

---

[6] https://keras.io/.
[7] https://www.tensorflow.org/.
[8] https://developer.nvidia.com/cudnn.

where x_i denotes the samples of sensor modality i, while μ_i, σ_i depict their corresponding mean and standard deviation values respectively, which were computed using only the training samples.

4.2   Hyperparameter Tuning

While training the selected models, the fine-tuning of several hyperparameters was attempted, based on the criterion of the lowest error in the validation set. The model's accuracy on the test set, was computed subsequently, using the same criterion. Table 2 illustrates all the examined hyperparameters. It should be noted that a set of the selected hyperparameters of a model (e.g., deep ConvLSTM) used in a certain one-shot learning architecture (e.g., MatchNet), could slightly differ from the optimal ones for the same model deployed to a different one-shot learning architecture (e.g., Siamese). Regarding the optimization of each model's weights, Adam algorithm [13] was selected, with the following hyperparameters: learning rate α equal to 0.001, β_1 equal to 0.9, β_2 equal to 0.999 and ϵ equal to 1e−08. Furthermore, the batch size was set 128 and the minimum number of epochs to 1,000. The training process was automatically terminated if the best validation accuracy had not improved after 100 epochs.

Table 3. 10-way accuracy performance of the one-shot learning techniques on SENSED

Network	Val acc	Test acc
CNN TL	52.5%	51.0%
ConvLSTM TL	56.5%	55.5%
CNN Siamese	63.00%	58.25%
ConvLSTM Siamese	62.25%	56.75%
CNN MatchNet	82.0%	76.5%
ConvLSTM MatchNet	71.5%	55.0%

5   Results and Discussion

Table 3 presents the accuracy reached by each network architecture. The MatchNet built on top of the PerceptionNet model obtained the best results by far, reaching 82.0% on the validation set and 76.5% for the test set. The three convolutional layers of this model had filter sizes $1 \times 32 \times 1 \times 11$, $32 \times 48 \times 1 \times 11$ and $48 \times 64 \times 3 \times 11$ resulting in 119,056 trainable parameters. Moreover, it is worth mentioning that while the ConvLSTM produced more generalizable embeddings than the CNN ones in the case of TL, this did not hold true for the Siamese and the MatchNet architectures.

Figure 3 illustrates the confusion matrices of the CNN MatchNet algorithm for the validation and the test sets. It should be noted that the algorithm misclassified many instances of class "6" to class "9". Apart from the fact that number "9"

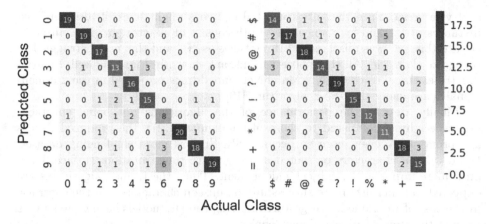

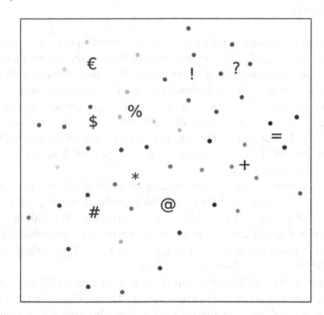

Fig. 3. Confusion matrices produced by CNN MatchNet for the validation (left) and the test (right) sets.

Fig. 4. t-SNE visualization of the test set's last hidden layer representations in CNN MatchNet.

is a reversed number "6", this occurred because the users were free to execute the gestures using hand, posture and writing surface of their choice. Consequently, the trained MatchNet seem to be a non-orientation-free algorithm and does not discriminate between the starting and the ending point of a gesture.

In the test set's confusion matrix some misclassification patterns can be observed. In particular, the algorithm confused a few instances of "−" with "+"

and vice versa, since they are consisted of two straight lines; it also confused instances of "*" and "#", since they both consist of six straight lines. In addition to this, "$" was misclassified three times as "€" and the model struggled to recognize class "%". All these observations, are shown in Fig. 4, as well. Figure 4 illustrates the extracted CNN MatchNet embeddings projected in the 2 dimensional space using the t-SNE algorithm [19].

Finally, despite the performance of the algorithms not being spectacular, especially if compared to those of Omniglot [14,27], the produced results are promising - even more so because SENSED is more challenging dataset. Hand-written characters presented as images are time, rotation, surface, hand and, more importantly, subject independent. Thus, the trained algorithms are expected to generalize more successfully on unseen characters. On the contrary, in the case of wearable-based gesture analysis, the DL models have to generalize against the aforementioned dependencies.

6   Conclusions

In this paper, we presented a publicly available wearable-based gesture recognition dataset, called SENSED, designed and built specifically to meet the needs of the one-shot learning setting. It is considered to be a fairly small dataset for deep learning algorithms to be trained on, since it contains only one instance of each gesture performed by each subject, while the gestures contained in the training, validation and test sets are disjoint with each other and are performed by different users. In our belief, the current dataset will assist researchers to test the generalizability of their algorithms on unseen gestures; it can also serve as a benchmark for one-shot learning.

Moreover, we have exploited the dataset to evaluate three one-shot learning techniques. The Matching Network architecture built on top of a deep CNN produced the best results, 82.0% and 76.5% accuracy on the validation and test respectively. Such recognition scores are considered to be promising for dynamic gesture-based user interactions with smart devices, as they might enable users to add moves of their own choice to smartwatches.

Exploitation of SENSED opens up a variety of new challenges and opportunities for one-shot learning. Future steps are currently being taken towards exploring more generalizable algorithms for domain-adaptation. Along a different line, data augmentation techniques based on Generative Adversarial Networks (GANS) could also be investigated.

Acknowledgements. This research is co-financed by Greece and the European Union (European Social Fund- ESF) through the Operational «Programme Human Resources Development, Education and Lifelong Learning 2014-2020» in the context of the project "On applying Deep Learning techniques to insufficient labeled sensor data for gesture recognition" (MIS 5050324).

References

1. Akbari, A., Jafari, R.: Transferring activity recognition models for new wearable sensors with deep generative domain adaptation. In: 2019 18th ACM/IEEE International Conference on Information Processing in Sensor Networks (IPSN), pp. 85–96 (2019)
2. Arnault, A., Hanssens, B., Riche, N.: Urban sound classification: striving towards a fair comparison. arXiv abs/2010.11805 (2020)
3. Brigato, L., Iocchi, L.: A close look at deep learning with small data. arXiv abs/2003.12843 (2020)
4. Chavarriaga, R., et al.: The opportunity challenge: a benchmark database for on-body sensor-based activity recognition. Pattern Recognit. Lett. **34**, 2033–2042 (2013)
5. Choi, Y., Hwang, I., Oh, S.: Wearable gesture control of agile micro quadrotors. In: 2017 IEEE International Conference on Multisensor Fusion and Integration for Intelligent Systems (MFI), pp. 266–271 (2017)
6. Chopra, S., Hadsell, R., LeCun, Y.: Learning a similarity metric discriminatively, with application to face verification. In: 2005 IEEE Computer Society Conference on Computer Vision and Pattern Recognition (CVPR 2005), vol. 1, pp. 539–546 (2005)
7. Costante, G., Porzi, L., Lanz, O., Valigi, P., Ricci, E.: Personalizing a smartwatch-based gesture interface with transfer learning. In: 2014 22nd European Signal Processing Conference (EUSIPCO), pp. 2530–2534 (2014)
8. Feng, S., Duarte, M.F.: Few-shot learning-based human activity recognition. arXiv abs/1903.10416 (2019)
9. Garber, L.: Gestural technology: moving interfaces in a new direction. Computer **46**, 22–25 (2013)
10. Jacot, A., Gabriel, F., Hongler, C.: Neural tangent kernel: convergence and generalization in neural networks. In: NeurIPS (2018)
11. Kasnesis, P., Chatzigeorgiou, C., Toumanidis, L., Patrikakis, C.Z.: Gesture-based incident reporting through smart watches. In: 2019 IEEE International Conference on Pervasive Computing and Communications Workshops (PerCom Workshops), pp. 249–254 (2019)
12. Kasnesis, P., Patrikakis, C.Z., Venieris, I.S.: PerceptionNet: a deep convolutional neural network for late sensor fusion. ArXiv abs/1811.00170 (2018)
13. Kingma, D.P., Ba, J.: Adam: a method for stochastic optimization. CoRR abs/1412.6980 (2015)
14. Koch, G.R.: Siamese neural networks for one-shot image recognition (2015)
15. Lake, B.M., Salakhutdinov, R., Gross, J., Tenenbaum, J.: One shot learning of simple visual concepts. Cognit. Sci. **33**, 2568–2573 (2011)
16. Laput, G., Xiao, R., Harrison, C.: Viband: high-fidelity bio-acoustic sensing using commodity smartwatch accelerometers. In: Proceedings of the 29th Annual Symposium on User Interface Software and Technology (2016)
17. Liu, J., Wang, Z., Zhong, L., Wickramasuriya, J., Vasudevan, V.: uWave: accelerometer-based personalized gesture recognition and its applications. In: PerCom (2009)
18. Luna, M.M., Carvalho, T.P., Soares, F., Nascimento, H.A.D., Costa, R.M.: Wrist player: a smartwatch gesture controller for smart TVs. In: 2017 IEEE 41st Annual Computer Software and Applications Conference (COMPSAC), vol. 02, pp. 336–341 (2017)

19. Maaten, L.V.D., Hinton, G.E.: Visualizing data using t-SNE. J. Mach. Learn. Res. **9**, 2579–2605 (2008)
20. Morales, F.J.O., Roggen, D.: Deep convolutional and LSTM recurrent neural networks for multimodal wearable activity recognition. Sensors (Basel, Switzerland) **16**, 115 (2016)
21. Morales, F.J.O., Roggen, D.: Deep convolutional feature transfer across mobile activity recognition domains, sensor modalities and locations. In: ISWC 2016 (2016)
22. Münzner, S., Schmidt, P., Reiss, A., Hanselmann, M., Stiefelhagen, R., Dürichen, R.: CNN-based sensor fusion techniques for multimodal human activity recognition. In: Proceedings of the 2017 ACM International Symposium on Wearable Computers (2017)
23. Nascimento, T.H., Soares, F.A.A.M.N., do Nascimento, H.A.D., Vieira, M.A., Carvalho, T.P., de Miranda, W.F.: Netflix control method using smartwatches and continuous gesture recognition. In: 2019 IEEE Canadian Conference of Electrical and Computer Engineering (CCECE), pp. 1–4 (2019)
24. Reiss, A., Stricker, D.: Introducing a new benchmarked dataset for activity monitoring. In: 2012 16th International Symposium on Wearable Computers, pp. 108–109 (2012)
25. Ronao, C.A., Cho, S.B.: Human activity recognition with smartphone sensors using deep learning neural networks. Expert Syst. Appl. **59**, 235–244 (2016)
26. Villani, V., Sabattini, L., Battilani, N., Fantuzzi, C.: Smartwatch-enhanced interaction with an advanced troubleshooting system for industrial machines (2016)
27. Vinyals, O., Blundell, C., Lillicrap, T.P., Kavukcuoglu, K., Wierstra, D.: Matching networks for one shot learning. In: NIPS (2016)
28. Wang, J., Zheng, V., Chen, Y., Huang, M.: Deep transfer learning for cross-domain activity recognition. In: ICCSE 2018 (2018)
29. Wang, J., Chen, Y., Hu, L., Peng, X., Yu, P.S.: Stratified transfer learning for cross-domain activity recognition. In: 2018 IEEE International Conference on Pervasive Computing and Communications (PerCom), pp. 1–10 (2018)
30. Wijekoon, A., Wiratunga, N., Sani, S.: Zero-shot learning with matching networks for open-ended human activity recognition. In: SICSA ReaLX (2018)
31. Zhu, P., Zhou, H., Cao, S., Yang, P., Xue, S.: Control with gestures: a hand gesture recognition system using off-the-shelf smartwatch. In: 2018 4th International Conference on Big Data Computing and Communications (BIGCOM), pp. 72–77 (2018)

NetFlow Datasets for Machine Learning-Based Network Intrusion Detection Systems

Mohanad Sarhan[1](✉), Siamak Layeghy[1], Nour Moustafa[2], and Marius Portmann[1]

[1] University of Queensland, Brisbane, QLD 4072, Australia
{m.sarhan,siamak.layeghy}@uq.net.au, marius@ieee.org
[2] University of New South Wales, Canberra, ACT 2612, Australia
nour.moustafa@unsw.edu.au

Abstract. Machine Learning (ML)-based Network Intrusion Detection Systems (NIDSs) have become a promising tool to protect networks against cyberattacks. A wide range of datasets are publicly available and have been used for the development and evaluation of a large number of ML-based NIDS in the research community. However, since these NIDS datasets have very different feature sets, it is currently very difficult to reliably compare ML models across different datasets, and hence if they generalise to different network environments and attack scenarios. The limited ability to evaluate ML-based NIDSs has led to a gap between the extensive academic research conducted and the actual practical deployments in the real-world networks. This paper addresses this limitation, by providing five NIDS datasets with a common, practically relevant feature set, based on NetFlow. These datasets are generated from the following four existing benchmark NIDS datasets: UNSW-NB15, BoT-IoT, ToN-IoT, and CSE-CIC-IDS2018. We have used the raw packet capture files of these datasets, and converted them to the NetFlow format, with a common feature set. The benefits of using NetFlow as a common format include its practical relevance, its wide deployment in production networks, and its scaling properties. The generated NetFlow datasets presented in this paper have been labelled for both binary- and multiclass traffic and attack classification experiments, and we have made them available for to the research community [1]. As a use-case and application scenario, the paper presents an evaluation of an Extra Trees ensemble classifier across these datasets.

Keywords: Network intrusion detection system · NetFlow · Machine learning · Network datasets · Network features

1 Introduction

Anomaly-based Network Intrusion Detection Systems (NIDSs) aim to learn and extract complex network behaviours to classify incoming traffic into various

Z. Deze et al. (Eds.): BDTA 2020/WiCON 2020, LNICST 371, pp. 117–135, 2021.
https://doi.org/10.1007/978-3-030-72802-1_9

attacks and benign classes [2]. Network attack vectors can be obtained from various features transmitted through network traffic, such as packet counts/sizes, protocols, services and flags. Each network attack's type has a different identifying pattern, known as a set of events that may compromise the security principles of networks if undetected [3]. The fact that these patterns are learnt from network traffic data shows the importance of data collection for Machine Learning (ML) training and evaluation stages. Real network data is challenging to obtain due to security and privacy issues. Also, production networks do not generate labelled flows, which is necessary for following a supervised ML learning approach.

As such, researchers have used network testbeds to create synthetic datasets that are publicly available for research purposes [4]. These NIDS datasets contain labelled network flows that are made up of certain features extracted from network traffic. These features are pre-determined by the datasets' authors based on their domain knowledge and tools used during their extraction. Network data features have a great impact on the performance of ML-based NIDSs [5]. Over the past few years, researchers have evaluated their proposed models on datasets using their original sets of features. However, as these features are very different, evaluating ML models often is not reliable, as each ML-based NIDS is trained and validated using different data features. Moreover, due to their complex techniques of extraction, these network feature sets might not be feasible for collection or storage in real-production networks.

In order to address this gap, we have created five NIDS datasets, which all have the same sets of features that facilitate reliable NIDS evaluation over multiple datasets. These datasets are created by converting four well-known modern NIDS datasets into NetFlow format. NetFlow is a widely deployed protocol of network flow collection [6]. Obtaining NetFlow features from existing NIDS datasets will enable researchers to evaluate ML models across various datasets using the same set of features. Moreover, it will also determine the performance of NetFlow features in detecting various attack types present in the datasets.

The rest of this paper is organised as below. Section 2 illustrates the limitations faced by existing datasets and how they can be overcome. Section 3 explains the importance and methodology of creating NetFlow datasets as well as the distribution of various benign/attack flows in the newly created datasets. Finally, the new datasets are evaluated in Sect. 4, by comparing their binary-class and multi-class classification performance to the original features of their corresponding datasets. The main contribution of this paper is to provide the research community with five NetFlow datasets, with the same feature sets, using four existing benchmark datasets, along with an initial set of results collected while evaluating the new datasets using binary-class and multi-class classification experiments.

2   Limitations of Existing Datasets

Due to the complexity in obtaining labelled real-world network flows, researchers have generated synthetic benchmark NIDS datasets. These datasets are made publicly available for use in the training and testing stages of the ML-based NIDSs. Currently, there are more than 15 NIDS datasets available in the field [7] containing labelled network flows. These datasets reflect network benign behaviour combined with synthetic attack scenarios. Each dataset contains a few attack categories conducted over a testbed network. The packets are captured, during the experiments, in the packet capture (pcap) format, and then pre-determined network features are extracted from these pcap files. A key stage of designing an ML-based NIDS is the selection of these features. The selected features must be feasible in count and extraction's complexity for efficient storage and collection. The sets should also provide adequate information for the efficient classification by the ML model.

Due to lack of a standard set of features for generating NIDS datasets, the authors of these datasets have applied their own domain knowledge to create network features, which they believe would aid in the classification process. As a result, each available dataset has been created with an almost exclusive set of network features. The variance of information represented in each dataset has caused limitations in the field that keeps aggravating with the new releases and production of NIDS datasets. The two main issues of having different feature sets in benchmark datasets are 1. dimensional overload due to collection and storage of various features, some of which are irrelevant and 2. inability to evaluate an ML model's generalisation across multiple NIDS datasets using a targeted or a proposed feature set. We believe the unreliable evaluation methods have caused a gap between the extensive academic research conducted and the actual deployments of ML-based NIDS models in the real-world.

Identifying the ideal set of network features to be used in NIDS datasets has been an ongoing research topic over the last decade. However, due to the subjection to the datasets used in the experiments, the identified feature sets have been custom to each dataset. These are also subjected to the feature selection techniques and ML models used to identify and evaluate them respectively. Moreover, due to the differences in datasets', the selected or identified features can not be evaluated using other datasets, simply due to their absence. The rest of this section discusses four of the most recent and common publicly available NIDS datasets. These datasets have been released within the last five years so they represent modern behavioural network attacks.

- **UNSW-NB15.** The Cyber Range Lab of the Australian Centre for Cyber Security (ACCS) released the widely used, UNSW-NB15, dataset in 2015. The IXIA PerfectStorm tool was utilised to generate a hybrid of testbed-based benign network activities as well as synthetic attack scenarios. Tcpdump tool was implemented to capture a total of 100 GB of pcap files. Argus and Bro-IDS now called Zeek, and twelve additional algorithms were used to extract the dataset's original 49 features [8]. The dataset contains 2,218,761 (87.35%) benign flows and 321,283 (12.65%) attack ones, that is, 2,540,044 flows in total.
- **BoT-IoT.** The Cyber Range Lab of the Australian Centre for Cyber Security (ACCS) designed a network environment in 2018 that consists of normal and

botnet traffic [9]. The Ostinato and Node-red tools were utilised to generate the non-IoT and IoT traffic respectively. A total of 69.3GB of pcap files were captured and Argus tool was used to extract the dataset's original 42 features. The dataset contains 477 (0.01%) benign flows and 3,668,045 (99.99%) attack ones, that is, 3,668,522 flows in total.

- **ToN-IoT.** A recent heterogeneous dataset released in 2020 [10] that includes telemetry data of Internet of Things (IoT) services, network traffic of IoT networks and operating system logs. In this paper, we utilise the portion containing network traffic flows. The dataset is made up of a large number of attack scenarios conducted in a representation of a medium-scale network at the Cyber Range Lab by ACCS. Bro-IDS, now called Zeek, was used to extract the dataset's original 44 features. The dataset is made up of 796,380 (3.56%) benign flows and 21,542,641 (96.44%) attack samples, that is, 22,339,021 flows in total.

- **CSE-CIC-IDS2018.** A dataset released by a collaborative project between the Communications Security Establishment (CSE) & Canadian Institute for Cybersecurity (CIC) in 2018 [11]. The victim network consisted of five different organisational departments and an additional server room. The benign packets were generated by network events using the abstract behaviour of human users. The attack scenarios were executed by one or more machines outside the target network. The CICFlowMeter-V3 tool was used to extract the original dataset's 75 features. The full dataset has 13,484,708 (83.07%) benign flows and 2,748,235 (16.93%) attack flows, that is, 16,232,943 flows in total.

Figure 1 illustrates all the shared and exclusive features of these datasets. As seen, the list of features shared by all four datasets includes only 3 features, and the pairwise shared features numbers vary from 1 to 5. Most of the features are exclusive to individual datasets. This has made it challenging for researchers to measure the performance of their proposed ML models using the same set of features across the four datasets. Apart from the small number of shared features, other differences make it even more difficult for using these datasets in the evaluation of ML-based NIDSs. The first issue is the vast differences in the ratio of the benign/attack flows. The UNSW-NB15 and CSE-CIC-IDS2018 datasets have very high benign to attack ratios (20 and 7.2 respectively) whereas for the ToN-IoT and BoT-IoT datasets this ratio is about 0.2 and 0.02 respectively.

The next issue is the number and type of features in each dataset. The UNSW-NB15 and ToN-IoT datasets have approximately the same number of original features. The CSE-CIC-IDS2018 dataset has almost double the number of their features and the BoT-IoT dataset has a slightly lower number. The original feature sets in UNSW-NB15, BoT-IoT and CSE-CIC-IDS2018 contain handcrafted features that are not present in network traffic but are statistically measured from other features, such as the average or sum of the number of bytes transferred over the last 100 s. All these differences, and the necessity of having multiple NIDS datasets with the common ground feature set, to generalise the evaluation of NIDSs, has led to the generation of the new datasets. This will

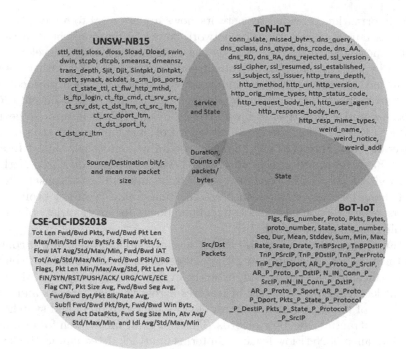

Fig. 1. List of the shared and exclusive features of four NIDS datasets

enable researchers to evaluate their proposed ML-based NIDS model's performance across various network designs and attack scenarios to make sure their measured model performance well generalises.

3 NetFlow Datasets

3.1 NetFlow

Collecting and recording network traffic is necessary to monitor and analyse network environments. There are two main trends for this process, capturing the complete network packets, and extracting a summary in the form of flows. While packet capturing provides full access to the network information, it is not scalable as it might necessitate large-capacity data storage to record a short period of traffic. The large volume of such data not only makes it difficult for the analysis, but it also faces privacy and security concerns. The alternative method is extracting network traffic summary as flows, which is very common in the networking industry due to its practical relevance and scaling properties. A network flow identifies a sequence of packets between two endpoints sharing a number of attributes. The packets flow can be unidirectional or bidirectional. These common attributes include; source/destination IP address and L4 (transport layer) ports, and the L4 protocol. These shared attributes are often referred to as the five-tuple.

The information provided by network flows are essential to analyse network traffic for security events [12]. The network flows can be represented in various formats where the NetFlow is the de-facto industry standard developed and proposed by Darren and Barry Bruins from Cisco in 1996 [13]. Other network hardware manufacturers have also implemented and adopted their protocols such as *NetStream* by Huawei, *Jflow* by Juniper, *Cflow* by Alcatel-Lucent, *Rflow* by Ericsson and *s-flow* that is supported by 3Com/HP, Dell, and Netgear. In response to the need for a universal standard of flow information, the Internet Engineering Task Force (IETF) has developed a new protocol, named Internet Protocol Flow Information Export (IPFIX) which is based on Cisco NetFlow. Similar to NetFlow, IPFIX considers a flow to be any number of packets sharing certain characteristics observed in a specific time-frame. NetFlow evolved over the years, where version 9 is the most common due to its larger variety of features and bidirectional flow support [14].

NetFlow makes it possible to convert any available dataset into a common ground feature set. Accomplishing that, researchers would be able to compare datasets efficiently and most importantly evaluate their proposed ML-based NIDS models using the same set of features across various datasets and attack types. Most of the production network devices such as routers and switches are capable of extracting NetFlow records. This is a great motivation for evaluating the performance of NetFlow features in terms of attack detection, as the level of complexity and resources required to collect and store them is lower. Moreover, the generated datasets sharing the same set of features can be merged together to generate a universal NIDS dataset containing data flows from various network environments consisting of various attack scenarios. Finally, the same set of features can be extracted from any future generated NIDS dataset and be merged into the current ones, increasing the value of the datasets.

3.2   Conversion

Figure 2 shows the procedure of creating the NetFlow datasets by extracting flows (in NetFlow format) from the pcap files of the original datasets, and labelling extracted flow records based on the grand truths provided by dataset authors. We utilised the publicly available pcap files of each dataset to generate

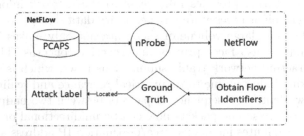

Fig. 2. NetFlow datasets' extraction and labelling procedure

Table 1. List of NetFlow fields included in the datasets proposed in this paper

Feature	Description
IPV4_SRC_ADDR	IPv4 source address
IPV4_DST_ADDR	IPv4 destination address
L4_SRC_PORT	IPv4 source port number
L4_DST_PORT	IPv4 destination port number
PROTOCOL	IP protocol identifier byte
TCP_FLAGS	Cumulative of all TCP flags
L7_PROTO	Layer 7 protocol (numeric)
IN_BYTES	Incoming number of bytes
OUT_BYTES	Outgoing number of bytes
IN_PKTS	Incoming number of packets
OUT_PKTS	Outgoing number of packets
FLOW_DURATION_MILLISECONDS	Flow duration in milliseconds

the NetFlow datasets. The nProbe tool by Ntop [15] was utilised to convert the pcaps into NetFlow version 9 format and selecting 12 features to be extracted. Table 1 lists the extracted NetFlow features along with their brief description. Using nProbe we create a text file listing the pcaps path of the original datasets. We specify NetFlow version 9 due to its popularity.

The dump format is chosen as text flows, in which each feature is separated by a comma (,) to be utilised as CSV files. The maximum number of flows in a file is 100 m dumped in a maximum of 100 m seconds, and nProbe is set not to modify the original pcaps timestamps. In the last step, we create two label features by matching the five flow identifiers; source/destination IPs and ports and protocol to the ground truth attack events published with the original datasets. If a flow is located in the attack events it would be labelled as an attack, class 1, in the binary label and its respective attack's type would be recorded in the attack label, otherwise, the record is labelled as a benign flow, class 0.

3.3 Datasets

Table 2 lists the NetFlow datasets, and compares their properties to the original datasets, in terms of Feature Extraction (FE) tool, number of features, files size and the benign to attack samples ratio. As illustrated, there is one NetFlow dataset corresponding to each original NIDS dataset, and the fifth NetFlow dataset is the comprehensive dataset that combines all the four.

- **NF-UNSW-NB15.** The NetFlow-based format of the UNSW-NB15 dataset, named NF-UNSW-NB15, has been developed and labelled with its respective attack categories. The total number of data flows are 1,623,118 out of which 72,406 (4.46%) are attack samples and 1,550,712 (95.54%) are benign. The

Table 2. Specifications of the datasets proposed in this paper, compared to the original datasets that have been used to generate them

Dataset	Release year	Feature extraction tool	Number of features	CSV size (GB)	Benign to attack samples ratio
UNSW-NB15	2015	Argus, Bro-IDS and MS SQL	49	0.55	8.7 to 1.3
NF-UNSW-NB15	**2020**	**nProbe**	**12**	**0.11**	**9.6 to 0.4**
BoT-IoT	2018	Argus	42	0.95	0.0 to 10
NF-BoT-IoT	**2020**	**nProbe**	**12**	**0.05**	**0.2 to 9.8**
ToN-IoT	2020	Bro-IDS	44	3.02	0.4 to 9.6
NF-ToN-IoT	**2020**	**nProbe**	**12**	**0.09**	**2.0 to 8.0**
CSE-CIC-IDS2018	2018	CICFlowMeter-V3	75	6.41	8.3 to 1.7
NF-CSE-CIC-IDS2018	**2020**	**nProbe**	**12**	**0.58**	**8.8 to 1.2**
NF-UQ-NIDS	**2020**	**nProbe**	**12**	**1.0**	**7.7 to 2.3**

attack samples are further classified into nine subcategories, Table 3 represents the NF-UNSW-NB15 dataset's distribution of all flows.

- **NF-BoT-IoT.** An IoT NetFlow-based dataset generated using the BoT-IoT dataset, named NF-BoT-IoT. The features were extracted from the publicly available pcap files and the flows were labelled with their respective attack categories. The total number of data flows are 600,100 out of which 586,241 (97.69%) are attack samples and 13,859 (2.31%) are benign. There are four attack categories in the dataset, Table 4 represents the NF-BoT-IoT distribution of all flows.

- **NF-ToN-IoT.** We utilised the publicly available pcaps of the ToN-IoT dataset to generate its NetFlow records, leading to a NetFlow-based IoT network dataset called NF-ToN-IoT. The total number of data flows are 1,379,274 out of which 1,108,995 (80.4%) are attack samples and 270,279 (19.6%) are benign ones, Table 5 lists and defines the distribution of the NF-ToN-IoT dataset.

- **NF-CSE-CIC-IDS2018.** We utilised the original pcap files of the CSE-CIC-IDS2018 dataset to generate a NetFlow-based dataset called NF-CSE-CIC-IDS2018. The total number of flows are 8,392,401 out of which 1,019,203 (12.14%) are attack samples and 7,373,198 (87.86%) are benign ones, Table 6 represents the dataset's distribution.

- **NF-UQ-NIDS.** A comprehensive dataset, merging all the aforementioned datasets. The newly published dataset represents the benefits of the shared dataset feature sets, where the merging of multiple smaller datasets is possible. This will eventually lead to a bigger and more universal NIDS dataset containing flows from multiple network setups and different attack settings. It includes an additional label feature, identifying the original dataset of each flow. This can be used to compare the same attack scenarios conducted over two or more different testbed networks. The attack categories have been modified to combine all parent categories. Attacks named DoS attacks-Hulk, DoS attacks-SlowHTTPTest, DoS attacks-GoldenEye and DoS attacks-Slowloris

Table 3. NF-UNSW-NB15 distribution

Class	Count	Description
Benign	1550712	Normal unmalicious flows
Fuzzers	19463	An attack in which the attacker sends large amounts of random data which cause a system to crash and also aim to discover security vulnerabilities in a system
Analysis	1995	A group that presents a variety of threats that target web applications through ports, emails and scripts
Backdoor	1782	A technique that aims to bypass security mechanisms by replying to specific constructed client applications
DoS	5051	Denial of Service is an attempt to overload a computer system's resources with the aim of preventing access to or availability of its data
Exploits	24736	Are sequences of commands controlling the behaviour of a host through a known vulnerability
Generic	5570	A method that targets cryptography and causes a collision with each block-cipher
Reconnaissance	12291	A technique for gathering information about a network host and is also known as a probe
Shellcode	1365	A malware that penetrates a code to control a victim's host
Worms	153	Attacks that replicate themselves and spread to other computers

Table 4. NF-BoT-IoT distribution

Class	Count	Description
Benign	13859	Normal unmalicious flows
Reconnaissance	470655	A technique for gathering information about a network host and is also known as a probe
DDoS	56844	Distributed Denial of Service is an attempt similar to DoS but has multiple different distributed sources
DoS	56833	An attempt to overload a computer system's resources with the aim of preventing access to or availability of its data
Theft	1909	A group of attacks that aims to obtain sensitive data such as data theft and keylogging

have been renamed to the parent DoS category. Attacks named DDOS attack-LOIC-UDP, DDOS attack-HOIC and DDoS attacks-LOIC-HTTP have been renamed to DDoS. Attacks named FTP-BruteForce, SSH-Bruteforce, Brute Force -Web and Brute Force -XSS have been combined as a brute-force category. Finally, SQL Injection attacks have been included in the injection attacks category. The NF-UQ-NIDS dataset has a total of 11,994,893 records, out of which 9,208,048 (76.77%) are benign flows and 2,786,845 (23.23%) are attacks. Table 7 lists the distribution of the final attack categories.

Table 5. NF-ToN-IoT distribution

Class	Count	Description
Benign	270279	Normal unmalicious flows
Backdoor	17247	A technique that aims to attack remote-access computers by replying to specific constructed client applications
DoS	17717	An attempt to overload a computer system's resources with the aim of preventing access to or availability of its data
DDoS	326345	An attempt similar to DoS but has multiple different distributed sources
Injection	468539	A variety of attacks that supply untrusted inputs that aim to alter the course of execution, with SQL and Code injections two of the main ones
MITM	1295	Man In The Middle is a method that places an attacker between a victim and host with which the victim is trying to communicate, with the aim of intercepting traffic and communications
Password	156299	covers a variety of attacks aimed at retrieving passwords by either brute force or sniffing
Ransomware	142	An attack that encrypts the files stored on a host and asks for compensation in exchange for the decryption technique/key
Scanning	21467	A group that consists of a variety of techniques that aim to discover information about networks and hosts, and is also known as probing
XSS	99944	Cross-site Scripting is a type of injection in which an attacker uses web applications to send malicious scripts to end-users

Table 6. NF-CSE-CIC-IDS2018 distribution

Class	Count	Description
Benign	7373198	Normal unmalicious flows
BruteForce	287597	A technique that aims to obtain usernames and password credentials by accessing a list of predefined possibilities
Bot	15683	An attack that enables an attacker to remotely control several hijacked computers to perform malicious activities
DoS	269361	An attempt to overload a computer system's resources with the aim of preventing access to or availability of its data
DDoS	380096	An attempt similar to DoS but has multiple different distributed sources
Infiltration	62072	An inside attack that sends a malicious file via an email to exploit an application and is followed by a backdoor that scans the network for other vulnerabilities
Web Attacks	4394	A group that includes SQL injections, command injections and unrestricted file uploads

4   Evaluation

For the evaluation of the newly published NetFlow datasets, we use an ML classifier and compared the classifier performances with the corresponding measures on the original datasets. We drop the flow identifiers such as IDs, source/destination IP and ports, timestamps and start/end time to avoid bias towards attacking or victim nodes. For UNSW-NB15, we additionally drop Time To Live (TTL) based features i.e., `sttl`, `dttl` and `ct_state_ttl`, due to their extreme correlation with the labels. Furthermore, we utilise the min-max normalisation technique to scale all datasets' values between 0 to 1. Finally, we apply an *Extra Trees ensemble* classifier, made up of 50 randomised decision trees estimators. The chosen classifier belongs to the 'trees' family and has proven to achieve reliable performances on NIDS datasets. Due to the extreme imbalance in all datasets' binary-class and multi-class labels, we set a custom class weight parameter, using Eq. 1.

$$Class\ Weight = \frac{Total\ Samples\ Count}{Number\ Of\ Classes \times Class\ Samples\ Count} \tag{1}$$

To reliably evaluate the datasets, we conduct five cross-validation splits and collect the average metrics such as accuracy, *Area Under the Curve (AUC)*,

F1 Score, Detection Rate (DR), False Alarm Rate (FAR) and time required to predict a single test sample in microseconds (μs).

Table 7. NF-UQ-NIDS distrubution

Class	Count	Class	Count
Benign	9208048	Scanning	21467
DDoS	763285	Fuzzers	19463
Reconnaissance	482946	Backdoor	19029
Injection	468575	Bot	15683
DoS	348962	Generic	5570
Brute Force	291955	Analysis	1995
Password	156299	Shellcode	1365
XSS	99944	MITM	1295
Infilteration	62072	Worms	153
Exploits	24736	Ransomware	142

4.1 Binary-Class Classification

In this experiment, we evaluate the attack detection performance of the Net-Flow datasets compared to the original datasets. Table 8 lists the accuracy, AUC, F1 score, DR, FAR and prediction time results for both, the original and the NetFlow versions. The NF-UNSW-NB15 dataset achieved slightly lower performance than the UNSW-NB15 dataset, with almost the same DR but higher FAR, however, it used less time to predict the samples. The overall accuracy achieved by the NF-UNSW-NB15 dataset is 98.62% compared to 99.25% when using the UNSW-NB15 dataset. The NF-BoT-IoT dataset has achieved slightly lower classification performance, i.e. 93.70% DR and 0.97 F1 Score, compared to its parent BoT-IoT dataset which achieved a 100% DR and 1.00 F1 Score. The almost perfect results achieved by BoT-IoT has been deemed unreliable in a recent study [16], due to its extreme class imbalance of attack and benign samples which is unrealistic in a real-world network.

The NF-ToN-IoT dataset's performance was superior to its original ToN-IoT dataset, achieving a 99.67% DR and 0.37% FAR, it also consumed less prediction time. The accuracy achieved is 99.66% proving its significance compared to the ToN-IoT dataset, 97.86%. The NF-CSE-CIC-IDS2018 dataset performance was less efficient than the CSE-CIC-IDS2018 dataset achieving a similar DR of 94.71% but a higher FAR of 4.59%, however significantly less time was consumed in prediction. The overall accuracy achieved is 95.33%, significantly lowering the 98.31% accuracy of the CSE-CIC-IDS2018 dataset. The merged NF-UQ-NIDS dataset achieved an accuracy of 97.25%, a DR of 95.66% and a FAR of 2.27%, achieving a reliable classification performance of 20 different attack categories. Figure 3 shows the AUC achieved using the *Extra Trees* classifier on the four newly published NetFlow-based datasets. This comparison is conducted by using the same set of features across all datasets.

This fair comparison demonstrates the benefit of the newly published datasets, which was not possible to achieve due to each dataset's unique set of features. Overall, the NetFlow datasets containing only eight features used in the classification experiments achieved a very similar attack detection performance compared to the original 36 features of the BoT-IoT, 38 features of both the UNSW-NB15 and ToN-IoT datasets and the 77 features of the CSE-CIC-IDS2018 dataset. We noticed a consistent prediction time decrease in using all the NetFlow datasets. Therefore, in terms of feasibility and practicality in real-world networks, using NetFlow features might lead to an overall superior performance if additional metrics are measured such as storage and computation power required to extract and store the utilised features.

Table 8. Binary-class classification results

Dataset	Accuracy	AUC	F1 score	DR	FAR	Prediction time (μs)
UNSW-NB15	99.25%	0.9545	0.92	91.25%	0.35%	10.05
NF-UNSW-NB15	**98.62%**	**0.9485**	**0.85**	**90.70%**	**1.01%**	**7.79**
BoT-IoT	100.00%	0.9948	1.00	100.00%	1.05%	7.62
NF-BoT-IoT	**93.82%**	**0.9628**	**0.97**	**93.70%**	**1.13%**	**5.37**
ToN-IoT	97.86%	0.9788	0.99	97.86%	2.10%	8.93
NF-ToN-IoT	**99.66%**	**0.9965**	**1.00**	**99.67%**	**0.37%**	**6.05**
CSE-CIC-IDS2018	98.31%	0.9684	0.94	94.75%	1.07%	23.01
NF-CSE-CIC-IDS2018	**95.33%**	**0.9506**	**0.83**	**94.71%**	**4.59%**	**17.04**
NF-UQ-NIDS	**97.25%**	**0.9669**	**0.94**	**95.66%**	**2.27%**	**14.35**

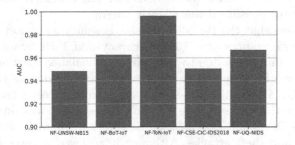

Fig. 3. Binary-class classification's AUC

Table 9. NF-UNSW-NB15 multi-class classification results

Class name	UNSW-NB15		NF-UNSW-NB15	
	DR	F1 score	DR	F1 score
Benign	99.72%	1.00	99.02%	0.99
Analysis	4.39%	0.03	28.28%	0.15
Backdoor	13.96%	0.08	39.17%	0.17
DoS	13.63%	0.18	31.84%	0.41
Exploits	83.25%	0.80	81.04%	0.82
Fuzzers	50.50%	0.57	62.63%	0.55
Generic	86.08%	0.91	57.13%	0.66
Reconnaissance	75.90%	0.80	76.89%	0.82
Shellcode	53.61%	0.59	87.91%	0.75
Worms	5.26%	0.09	52.91%	0.55
Weighted average	**98.19%**	**0.98**	**97.62%**	**0.98**
Prediction time (μs)	**9.94**		**9.35**	

4.2 Multi-class Classification

In this experiment, we measure the DR and F1 score of each attack's type present in each dataset. Tables 9, 10, 11, 12 and 13 list the DR and F1 score of each attack type for the NF-UNSW-NB15, NF-BoT-IoT, NF-ToN-IoT, NF-CSE-CIC-IDS2018 and NF-UQ-NIDS datasets respectively. The average accuracy and prediction time are calculated and the results are compared to their respective original datasets. In Table 9, we can conclude that by using the NF-UNSW-NB15 dataset, we can increase the DR of analysis, backdoor, DoS, fuzzers, shellcode and worms attacks, however, it was inefficient against generic attacks. The overall accuracy achieved which is 97.62% is slightly lower than the UNSW-NB15 dataset, 98.19%, due to the number of miss-correctly classified samples, however, the prediction time consumed was slightly lower.

Table 10 shows that the BoT-IoT dataset is achieving almost perfect multi-classification performances of a 100% accuracy and 1 F1 Score. Again, these results might be unreliable due to the extreme imbalance mentioned in [16]. In addition, there might be certain 'hidden label' features, such as the TTL-based features in the UNSW-NB15 dataset, that are extremely correlated to the attack types present in the dataset. The NF-BoT-IoT dataset was unreliable in the detection of the DDoS and DoS attacks. However, it achieved a 90% DR against reconnaissance and theft attacks. Although it achieved a lower DR of 73.58% and F1 Score of 0.77, the NetFlow dataset maintained the lower prediction time compared to the BoT-IoT dataset.

In Table 11, the NF-ToN-IoT dataset increased the DR of DoS attacks but lowered the DDoS, injection, MITM, password, scanning and XSS attacks compared to the ToN-IoT dataset. Further analysis is required to identify which fea-

Table 10. NF-BoT-IoT multi-class classification results

Class name	BoT-IoT		NF-BoT-IoT	
	DR	F1 score	DR	F1 score
Benign	99.58%	0.99	98.65%	0.43
DDoS	100.00%	1.00	30.37%	0.28
DoS	100.00%	1.00	36.33%	0.31
Reconnaissance	100.00%	1.00	89.95%	0.90
Theft	91.16%	95.37	88.06%	0.18
Weighted average	**100.00%**	**1.00**	**73.58%**	**0.77**
Prediction time (µs)	**12.63**		**9.19**	

tures of the original dataset were critical in the detection of the missed attacks and to be added to the NetFlow dataset. Overall, in multi-class classification, the NF-ToN-IoT dataset was not as effective in terms of overall accuracy and prediction time compared to the ToN-IoT dataset. It achieved a low prediction accuracy of 56.34% and a high prediction time of 21.21 µs. However, a binary-class classification deemed it was very efficient, therefore, it seems like the ML classifier is detecting the overall pattern of attacks present in the dataset, but not the pattern of individual attacks. We suspect that specific features present in the original dataset contain payload information that was enabling the ML classifier to detect certain attack types. Further analysis is required to investigate which features from the ToN-IoT dataset are necessary to identify each attack's type.

In Table 12, the performance of the NF-CSE-CIC-IDS2018 dataset can prove that attacks such as FTP-bruteforce and infiltration were better detected using the NetFlow features compared to the CSE-CIC-IDS2018 features. However, Brute Force -Web, Brute Force -XSS, DDOS attack-HOIC and SQL injection attack samples were mostly undetected by using the NetFlow features. The DoS attacks-SlowHTTPTest attack samples were fully undetected by the ML classifier. Similar to the NF-ToN-IoT dataset, the ML classifier was unable to efficiently detect the pattern of certain attack types. Overall, the accuracy and prediction time achieved while using the NF-CSE-CIC-IDS2018 dataset being 71.92% and 17.29 µs respectively were lower compared to the CSE-CIC-IDS2018 dataset.

Table 13 displays the full attack identification results of the merged dataset named NF-UQ-NIDS. The chosen ML classifier was efficient in the detection of certain attack's types such as backdoor, bot, bruteforce, exploits, shellcode, DDoS and ransomware. However, attacks such as analysis, DoS, fuzzers, generic, infiltration, worms, injection, MITM, password, scanning and XSS were not reliably detected. Further analysis is required to identify the features that are critical in identifying these attacks and to add them to the NetFlow features. The overall accuracy of 70.81% and prediction time 14.74 (µs) were achieved.

Table 11. NF-ToN-IoT multi-class classification results

Class name	ToN-IoT		NF-ToN-IoT	
	DR	F1 score	DR	F1 score
Benign	89.97%	0.94	98.97%	0.99
Backdoor	98.05%	0.31	99.22%	0.98
DDoS	96.90%	0.98	63.22%	0.72
DoS	53.89%	0.57	95.91%	0.48
Injection	96.67%	0.96	41.47%	0.51
MITM	66.25%	0.16	52.81%	0.38
Password	86.99%	0.92	27.36%	0.24
Ransomware	89.87%	0.11	87.33%	0.83
Scanning	75.05%	0.85	31.30%	0.08
XSS	98.83%	0.99	24.49%	0.19
Weighted average	**84.61%**	**0.87**	**56.34%**	**0.60**
Prediction time (µs)	**12.02**		**21.21**	

Table 12. NF-CSE-CIC-IDS2018 multi-class classification results

Class Name	CSE-CIC-IDS2018		NF-CSE-CIC-IDS2018	
	DR	F1 score	DR	F1 score
Benign	89.50%	0.94	69.83%	0.82
Bot	99.92%	0.99	100.00%	1.00
Brute Force -Web	71.36%	0.01	50.21%	0.52
Brute Force -XSS	72.17%	0.72	49.16%	0.39
DDOS attack-HOIC	100.00%	1.00	45.66%	0.39
DDOS attack-LOIC-UDP	83.59%	0.82	80.98%	0.82
DDoS attacks-LOIC-HTTP	99.93%	1.00	99.93%	0.71
DoS attacks-GoldenEye	99.97%	1.00	99.32%	0.98
DoS attacks-Hulk	100.00%	1.00	99.65%	0.99
DoS attacks-SlowHTTPTest	69.80%	0.60	0.00%	0.00
DoS attacks-Slowloris	99.44%	0.62	99.95%	1.00
FTP-BruteForce	68.76%	0.75	100.00%	0.79
Infilteration	36.15%	0.08	62.66%	0.04
SQL Injection	49.34%	0.30	25.00%	0.22
SSH-Bruteforce	99.99%	1.00	99.93%	1.00
Weighted average	**90.28%**	**0.94**	**71.92%**	**0.80**
Prediction time (µs)	**24.17**		**17.29**	

Table 13. NF-UQ-NIDS multi-class classification results

Class name	NF-UQ-NIDS	
	Detection rate	F1 score
Analysis	69.63%	0.21
Backdoor	90.95%	0.92
Benign	71.70%	0.83
Bot	100.00%	1.00
Brute Force	99.94%	0.85
DoS	55.54%	0.62
Exploits	80.65%	0.81
Fuzzers	63.24%	0.54
Generic	58.90%	0.61
Infilteration	60.57%	0.03
Reconnaissance	88.96%	0.88
Shellcode	83.89%	0.15
Theft	87.22%	0.15
Worms	52.97%	0.46
DDoS	77.08%	0.69
Injection	40.58%	0.50
MITM	57.99%	0.10
Password	30.79%	0.27
Ransomware	90.85%	0.85
Scanning	39.67%	0.08
XSS	30.80%	0.21
Weighted average	**70.81%**	**0.79**
Prediction time (µs)	**14.74**	

5   Conclusion

This paper provides the research community with five new NIDS datasets based on NetFlow features as shown in Table 2. These datasets can be used in ML-based NIDS training and evaluation stages. The datasets are showing positive results by achieving similar binary-class detection performance compared to the complete set of their corresponding original datasets. Though, in the case of multi-class detection experiments, the NF-BoT-IoT, NF-ToN-IoT and NF-CSE-CIC-IDS2018 datasets were not similarly efficient. Further feature analysis is required to identify the strength of each NetFlow feature, and how these datasets can be improved by adding key features from the original datasets to aid in the detection of missed attack types.

These published NetFlow datasets offer a promising performance, and serve three advantages; 1. the level of complexity and resources required to collect and store NetFlow features are lower, 2. proposed ML models can be evaluated using the same set of features across various attack types, and 3. datasets can be merged to generate a more comprehensive data source including collected over various network environments. Overall, the practicality and initial performance of NetFlow features' collection and attack detection, requires increased attention and interest by researchers in applying them into the real-world models for ML-based NIDS. Future works include enhancing the current datasets with additional NetFlow features which can potentially improve both the binary and multi-class classification performances. Finally, key features from the original datasets required to detect certain attack types must be identified to be included in NetFlow features.

References

1. "Netflow datasets." (2020). http://staff.itee.uq.edu.au/marius/NIDS_datasets/
2. Garcia-Teodoro, P., Diaz-Verdejo, J., Maciá-Fernández, G., Vázquez, E.: Anomaly-based network intrusion detection: techniques, systems and challenges. Comput. Secur. **28**(1–2), 18–28 (2009)
3. Sahu, S.K., Sarangi, S., Jena, S.K.: A detail analysis on intrusion detection datasets. In: 2014 IEEE International Advance Computing Conference (IACC), pp. 1348–1353 (2014)
4. Shiravi, A., Shiravi, H., Tavallaee, M., Ghorbani, A.A.: Toward developing a systematic approach to generate benchmark datasets for intrusion detection. Comput. Secur. **31**(3), 357–374 (2012)
5. Binbusayyis, A., Vaiyapuri, T.: Identifying and benchmarking key features for cyber intrusion detection: an ensemble approach. IEEE Access **7**, 106495–106513 (2019)
6. Claise, B., Sadasivan, G., Valluri, V., Djernaes, M.: Cisco systems netflow services export version 9 (2004)
7. Ring, M., Wunderlich, S., Scheuring, D., Landes, D., Hotho, A.: A survey of network-based intrusion detection data sets. Comput. Secur. **86**, 147–167 (2019)
8. Moustafa, N., Slay, J.: UNSW-NB15: a comprehensive data set for network intrusion detection systems (UNSW-NB15 network data set). In: 2015 Military Communications and Information Systems Conference (MilCIS) (2015)
9. Koroniotis, N., Moustafa, N., Sitnikova, E.,Turnbull, B.: Towards the development of realistic botnet dataset in the Internet of Things for network forensic analytics: BoT-IoT dataset, CoRR, vol. abs/1811.00701 (2018)
10. Moustafa, N.: ToN-IoT datasets (2019)
11. Sharafaldin, I., Habibi Lashkari, A., Ghorbani, A.A.: Toward generating a new intrusion detection dataset and intrusion traffic characterization. In: Proceedings of the 4th International Conference on Information Systems Security and Privacy (2018)
12. Li, B., Springer, J., Bebis, G., Hadi Gunes, M.: A survey of network flow applications. J. Netw. Computer Appl. **36**(2), 567–581 (2013)
13. Kerr, D.R., Bruins, B.L.: Network Flow Switching and Flow Data Export (2001)

14. Cisco Systems: Cisco IOS NetFlow Version 9 Flow-Record Format - White Paper. https://www.cisco.com/cn/US/technologies/tk648/tk362/technologies_white_paper09186a00800a3db9.pdf (2011)
15. Ntop: nProbe, An Extensible NetFlow v5/v9/IPFIX Probe for IPv4/v6. https://www.ntop.org/guides/nprobe/cli_options.html (2017)
16. Al-Othman, Z., Alkasassbeh, M., Baddar, S. A.-H.: A state-of-the-art review on IoT botnet attack detection (2020)

WiCON 2020

Performance Evaluation of Energy Detection, Matched Filtering and KNN Under Different Noise Models

Xiaoyan Wang[1], Jingjing Yang[1], Tengye Yu[2], Rui Li[2], and Ming Huang[1(✉)]

[1] School of Information Science and Engineering of Yunnan University,
Kunming 650091, China
huangming@ynu.edu.cn

[2] Radio Management Office of Honghe Prefecture, Mengzi 661199, Yunnan, China

Abstract. Due to the broadcast nature of radio transmission, both authorized and unauthorized users can access the network, which leads to the increasingly prominent security problems of wireless network. At the same time, it is more difficult to detect and identify users in wireless network environment due to the influence of noise. In this paper, the performance of energy detection (ED), matched filtering (MF) and K-nearest neighbor algorithm (KNN) are analyzed under different noise and uncertain noise separately. The Gaussian noise, α-stable distribution noise and Laplace distribution noise models are simulated respectively under the different uncertainty of noise when the false alarm probability is 0.01. The results show that the performance of the detectors is significantly affected by different noise models. In any case, the detection probability of KNN algorithm is the highest; the performance of MF is much better than ED under different noise models; KNN is not sensitive to noise uncertainty; MF has better performance on noise uncertainty which makes ED performance decline fleetly.

Keywords: Spectrum security · Radio monitoring · Noise uncertainty

1 Introduction

The amount of Internet of Things (IoT) devices based on wireless cellular network architecture has been increasing explosively with the advent of the 5G era, and the security of IoT has attracted much attention. Iot devices often suffer from various attacks, such as Denial of Service Attack (DoS), the User to Root Attack (U2R), Remote to Local Attack (R2L), and Probing Attack which may disrupt device workflow, impair product quality, and even lead to serious privacy issues and economic losses [1, 2]. In addition, the rapidly increasing IoT devices will not only bring convenience to daily life, but also bring greater consumption of mobile bandwidth, putting forward a higher requirement for radio spectrum safety and making radio monitoring particularly important. Identify the unauthorized radio users effectively is the basis of radio spectrum management [3].

Generally, the common methods for signal detection are cyclostationary feature detection [4], matched filter detection [5, 6], energy detection [7–9] and its improved

© ICST Institute for Computer Sciences, Social Informatics and Telecommunications Engineering 2021
Published by Springer Nature Switzerland AG 2021. All Rights Reserved
Z. Deze et al. (Eds.): BDTA 2020/WiCON 2020, LNICST 371, pp. 139–149, 2021.
https://doi.org/10.1007/978-3-030-72802-1_10

algorithms [10–12]. ED and MF detection are the two most commonly used detection methods in radio monitoring [13], which have a good performance under Gaussian noise. However, there are many electromagnetic interferences in complex environment, resulting in many monitoring data accompanied by non-Gaussian noise. For example, the non-Gaussian noise that has a long tailed is described by α-stable distribution model [14, 15]; the impulse noise that generated by the electromechanical switches in the indoor environment, the lightning in the air and the wires in the outdoor environment [16], etc. A signal detection method based on matched filter under α-stable distribution noise is proposed in [17], which improves the detection performance of traditional matched filter in non-Gaussian noise environment; the method in [18] uses hyperbolic tangent function to suppress impulse noise, which obtains an improved robustness of detection under non-Gaussian noise. More unfortunately, the time-varying intensity of these non-Gaussian noises makes the noise change in a certain range, which seriously interferes with the signal detection process. And when the signal-to-noise ratio (SNR) of the signal detected is smaller than the threshold, the detector is no longer robust [19]. Different from the traditional methods, KNN algorithm based on ML learns from training samples, compares the new-coming signal sample with the training set, then labels the new-coming signal sample to reflect the specific attribute information, such as amplitude, phase, energy, frequency.

In this paper, the models of ED, MF and KNN under different noises are established and simulated to analyze the influence of different noises and noise with uncertain variance on the performance of the detectors (model). The remainder of this paper is organized as follows. Section 2 gives the signal model and detectors, Sect. 3 presents the simulation and analysis and Sect. 4 summarizes the whole paper.

2 Signal Model and Detectors

In this section, signal model and three detectors: ED, MF and the detector based on KNN algorithm are introduced respectively.

2.1 Signal Model

Signal existence detection mainly focuses on whether the signal exists in the channel. A binary hypothesis can be used to represent the detection problem of the signal:

$$H_0 : x[n] = w[n]$$
$$H_1 : x[n] = s[n] + w[n] \tag{1}$$

Here $n = 1, 2, 3, \ldots, N$ is the sampling time; H_0 refers to the absence of signal; H_1 refers to the occurrence of signal; $w[n]$ is the noise sequence; $s[n]$ is the radio signal sequence; $x[n]$ refers to the signal received by the radio monitoring station.

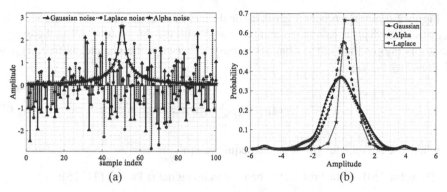

Fig. 1. Different noises wave with length of 100 (a) and their PDF (b). For the Gaussian noise, it has the parameters of $\mu = 0, \sigma^2 = 1$; the α-stable noise has the $\alpha = 0.5, \beta = 0, \gamma = 0.223, \mu = 0$, which has an obvious peak; Laplace noise with $\mu = 0, \sigma^2 = 1$, which has a heavy tail.

For convenience, we assume that $\{s[n]\}, \{w[n]\}$ are both independent and identically distributed, and they are independent of each other [20, 21]. In this paper, w[n] is studied by taking Gaussian noise [22], α-stable distribution noise [23] and Laplace noise [22] respectively. As shown in Fig. 1, the time-domain waveforms (a) and probability distribution curves (b) of the three noise models are given.

2.2 Detectors

ED Detector. ED is the best detection scheme when the radio signal information is unknown, which is widely used in the field of radio monitoring [13]:

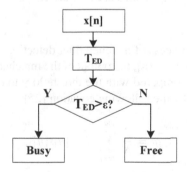

Fig. 2. Energy detection.

Figure 2 shows the processing of classical energy detection. After receiving x[n], the energy statistic T_{ED} is calculated and compared with the threshold ε. When the energy statistic is bigger than ε, the channel is busy; otherwise, the channel is free. T_{ED} is calculated by the Eq. (2):

$$T_{ED} = \frac{1}{N} \sum_{i=1}^{N} |x[i]|^2,$$

(2)

where the N is the length of signal sequence x[n].

MF Detector. MF is the best way when the radio signal is known [24, 25]:

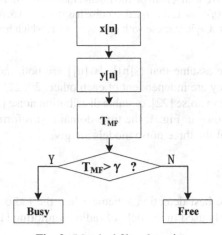

Fig. 3. Matched filter detection.

Figure 3 illustrates the process of matched filter detection. Assuming that the signal received by the matched filter is x[n]; the output of the matched filter is denoted as y[n], and the energy statistics is compared with the threshold γ to determine the state of the channel. T_{MF} is calculated by the following equation [25]:

$$T_{MF} = \frac{1}{N} \sum_{i=1}^{N} |C_m y[n] s[n]|,$$

(3)

where the Cm is the channel state information (CSI); s[n] is the radio signal sequence.

KNN Detector. KNN algorithm based on machine learning is a supervised learning algorithm [26], which needs to build training set and label.

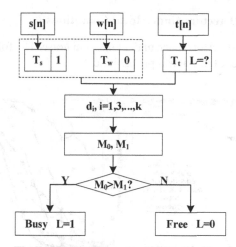

Fig. 4. Detection based on KNN algorithm.

Figure 4 depicts the process of method based KNN algorithm. The energy statistics are calculated form radio signal s[n] and labeled as 1; for noise w[n], the energy statistics are labeled as 0. In this way, we build a training set that includes data and tags showed as dotted box in Fig. 4, 75% of them are used as training data, 25% are used as testing data to test the performance of KNN. In addition, t[n] is the sample signal to be tested. Energy statistics are given by Eq. (4):

$$T_s = \frac{1}{N} \sum_{i=1}^{N} |s[i]|^2, \, T_w = \frac{1}{N} \sum_{i=1}^{N} |w[i]|^2, \, T_t = \frac{1}{N} \sum_{i=1}^{N} |t[i]|^2 \tag{4}$$

Euclidean distance is widely used as the measure distance of KNN algorithm. The Euclidean distance between any two samples X, Y is given by Eq. (5):

$$disy(X, Y) = \sqrt{\sum_{i=1}^{n} (x_i - y_i)^2} \tag{5}$$

Distance between the energy statistics of t[n] and each sample in the training set is calculated, then K samples that is closest to the T_t is selected to calculate the number M_0 and M_1 of T_w and T_S. Finally, t[n] will be labeled with 0 when $M_0 > M_1$, otherwise with 1.

3 Simulation and Analysis

In order to analyze the performance of different detectors, we assume that the channel state information (CSI) is fixed, $C_m = 1$. The signal sequence is BPSK modulated signal, and the noise sequence is established according to the SNR.

3.1 Performance of Detectors Under Ideal Conditions

ED and MF have the best performance under Gaussian noise. The following experiments are performed at different false alarm probabilities:

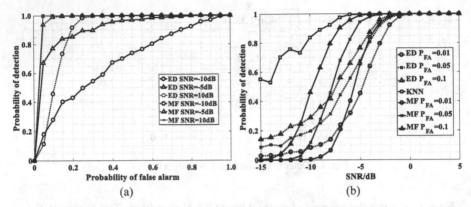

Fig. 5. Performance of detectors under Gaussian noise. (a) depicts the ROC curve of ED and MF; (b) describes the performance of detectors under different SNR. The detection probability of KNN is the highest; with the increase of false alarm probability, the detection probability of ED and MF is also increasing; under the same false alarm probability, the detection probability of MF is much higher than ED.

Figure 5 (a) indicates that probability of false alarm is helpful to improve the probability of detection, the detection probability of ED or MF is increased with the increasing of false alarm probability. On the other hand, under a certain false alarm probability, the higher the SNR is, the higher the detection probability will be.

Figure 5 (b) shows that under the simulated signal-noise environment, when P_{FA} is equal to 0.01, the detection probability of MF reaches 1 near SNR $= -2.7$ db, and ED is 1 near SNR $= -1.5$ dB; the detection probability of MF reaches 1 near SNR $= -5$ dB, ED is 1 near SNR $= -1$ dB when $P_{FA} = 0.1$. In addition, the detection principle of KNN algorithm is very different from ED and MF, the probability of detection of KNN depends on the quality of the sample to be tested and the actual detection. KNN detector has excellent performance when the SNR $= -15$ dB, and the detection probability reaches 0.56, while the detection probability of ED and MF detector is smaller than 0.2; in any cases of P_{FA}, detection probability of KNN is the fastest detector to reach 1, which shows the great potential of KNN in radio monitoring.

3.2 Performance of Detectors Under Non-Gaussian Noise

Compared with the ideal Gaussian channel shown in Fig. 5, the performance of detectors changes greatly under non-Gaussian noise like α-stable distribution noise and Laplace distribution noise. The parameter configuration of the simulation experiment is shown in Table 1.

Table 1. Parameter configuration

Items	Parameter/statement	Value	Items	Parameter/statement	Value
s[n]	BPSK	–	Gaussian Noise	μ (mean value)	0
K	Parameter of KNN algorithm	3		σ^2(Variance)	1
P_{FA}	Target false alarm probability	0.01	α-stable Noise	α (Characteristic index)	1
Laplace noise	μ (mean value)	0		β (Symmetrical coefficient)	0
	σ^2((Variance)	1		γ (Dispersion coefficient)	0.223
	λ (scale parameter)	0.7		μ(Positional arguments)	0
ρ	Noise uncertainty	[0, 3]	SNR	Signal to noise ratio	[−15, 15]

In Table 1, the radio signal sequence s[n] is the BPSK modulated signal with length N = 100, which has a power 1; the noise power is calculated according to the SNR, and the noise sequence w[n] is obtained by multiplying the Gaussian noise with mean of 0 and variance of 1; K is the only parameter of KNN algorithm, and is the number of nearest neighbors; P_{FA} is the target false alarm probability set in the following simulation experiment; there are three main parameters of Laplace noise: μ is the position parameter of Laplace noise, λ is related to the variance of noise ($\sigma^2 = 2\lambda^2$); Generally, the larger λ is, the longer the tail is when the position parameter μ is fixed; The α-stable noise has a serious towing and the parameter $\alpha \in (0,2]$ determines the towing; The smaller α is, the more serious towing is. The symmetric parameter β determines the inclination of the distribution. The larger the dispersion coefficient γ, the more dispersed the sample is relative to the mean value.

Taking the Gaussian noise detection probability curve as the baseline, the performance of both ED and MF decrease under the Laplace noise; under the α-stable noise, the detection performance of MF improves rapidly, while the detection probability of ED decreases sharply. In addition, the detection probability of MF is higher than ED, which shows that MF has higher flexibility than ED in dealing with different noises. KNN has the highest detection probability under different noises. When the noises are non-Gaussian noises, the detection probability is maintained at 1 (Fig. 6).

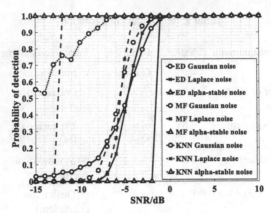

Fig. 6. Performance of detectors under different noise

Observingly, the detection probability curves of ED and MF under α-stable noise have a jump from 0 to 1 without any transition. Trying to adjust the parameters of a-distribution many times, but nothing is changed. Consider that it's related to noise characteristics, three kinds of noise waveforms are given in Fig. 1(a), which shows that α-stable noise only has a single pulse with a small amplitude in a limited range, while in other ranges its amplitude is generally close to 0.

3.3 Performance of Detectors with Uncertain Noise Variance

In practice, the noise is uneven and time-varying, which causes the variance to fluctuate in a certain range [20]. Analysis of the influence of noise uncertainty on the performance of three detectors under different noise.

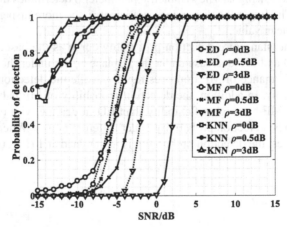

Fig. 7. Detection probability of three detectors under noise uncertainty in ideal Gaussian channel. The dotted line in the figure represents the detection probability curve of ED and the solid line represents the detection probability curve of MF.

Figure 7 points out that KNN has a good performance against noise uncertainty, and the increase of noise uncertainty does not reduce the detection probability of KNN. Even in an ideal Gaussian channel, the detection performance of ED and MF will be degraded due to the small uncertainty of Gaussian noise variance. With the uncertainty $= 0$ dB as the baseline, when the uncertainty of Gaussian noise was 0.1 dB, the ED detection probability curve moved down significantly and reached 1 at SNR $= 0$ dB, while the trend of MF detection probability curve was not as obvious as that of ED, and the detection probability reached 1 at SNR $= -1.5$ dB When the uncertainty of Gaussian noise is 3 dB, the ED detection probability curve drops significantly, the detection probability reaches 1 at SNR $= 4$ dB, and the MF detection probability reaches 1 at SNR $= 0$.

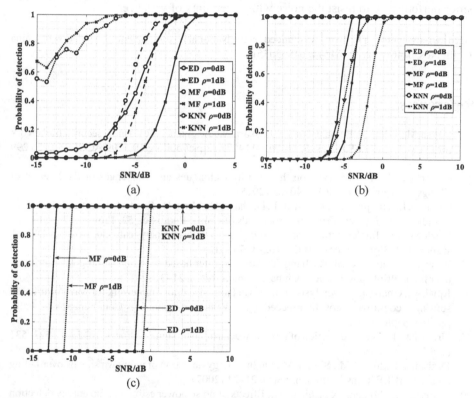

Fig. 8. Detection performance of three kinds of noise with uncertainty of ρ. (a) shows the detection probability of ED, MF and KNN when under Gaussian noise with uncertainty; (b) shows the detection probability of detector under Laplace noise with uncertainty; (c) shows the detection probability of detector under uncertain α-stable noise.

The simulation results in Fig. 8 show that whether Gaussian noise or non-Gaussian noise, once there is a small uncertainty in the noise variance, it will cause a great change in detection performance. As a result, the detection performance of ED and MF decreases; MF has a stronger ability to resist the uncertainty of noise than ED; KNN has a detection probability of 1 under non-Gaussian noise.

4   Conclusions

In this paper, the detection performance of ED, MF and KNN under different noise models are analyzed and simulated. The simulation results show that: 1) KNN is not sensitive to noise uncertainty, and the detection probability stays at 1 when dealing with non-Gaussian noise; 2) the detection probability of MF and ED under Gaussian noise model is higher than that under non Gaussian noise model; 3) under Gaussian or non-Gaussian noise model, MF has a higher detection probability than ED, MF holds a better performance to resist all kinds of noise; 4) considering the uncertainty of noise, the detection performance of MF and ED declines no matter what noise model; 5) under the same noise uncertainty, MF has a better detection probability than ED, MF holds a better performance to resist the noise with uncertainty of variance.

Acknowledgement. This work was funded by the National Natural Science Foundation of China (Grant Nos. 61461052, 11564044, 61863035).

References

1. Bagaa, M., Taleb, T., Bernal Bernabe, J., Skarmeta, A.: A machine learning security framework for IoT systems. IEEE Access **8**, 114066–114077. https://doi.org/10.1109/ACCESS.2020.299 6214
2. Chuankun, W.: An overview on the security techniques and challenges of the Internet of Things. J. Cryptol. Res. **2**(01), 40–53 (2015)
3. Qiannan, L., Jingjing, Y., Zhaoyuan, J., Dezhang, C., Ming, H.: State-of-the-art and challenges of radio spectrum monitoring in borderlands of China. Radio Sci. **52**, 1261–1267 (2017)
4. Kozlowski, S.: Implementation and verification of cyclostationary feature detector for DVB-T signals. IET Signal Process. **10**(2), 162–167 (2016)
5. Zhang, X., Gao, F., Chai, R., Jiang, T.: Matched filter based spectrum sensing when primary user has multiple power levels. China Commun. **12**(2), 21–31 (2015)
6. Iqbal, M., Ghafoor, A.: Analysis of multiband joint detection framework for waveform-based sensing in cognitive radios. In: Proceedings of Vehicular Technology Conference (VTC Fall), pp. 1–5, September 2012
7. Urkowitz, H.: Energy detection of unknown deterministic signals. Proc. IEEE **55**(4), 523–531 (1967)
8. Digham, F., Alouini, M., Simon, M.: On the energy detection of unknown signals over fading channels. IEEE Trans. Commun. **55**(1), 21–24 (2007)
9. Mariani, A., Giorgetti, A., Chiani, M.: Effects of noise power estimation on energy detection for cognitive radio applications. IEEE Trans. Commun. **59**(12), 3410–3420 (2011)
10. Singh, A., Bhatnagar, M., Mallik, R.: Performance of an improved energy detector in multihop cognitive radio networks. IEEE Trans. Veh. Technol. **65**(2), 732–743 (2016)
11. Song, J., Feng, Z., Zhang, P., Liu, Z.: Spectrum sensing in cognitive radios based on enhanced energy detector. IET Commun. **6**(8), 805–809 (2012)
12. Chen, Y.: Improved energy detector for random signals in Gaussian noise. IEEE Trans. Wirel. Commun. **9**(2), 558–563 (2010)
13. Seven, M.K.: Fundamentals of Statistical Signal Processing: Estimation and Detection Theory. Electronic Industry Press, Beijing (2014)
14. Krämer, W.: Signal processing with alpha-stable distributions and applications. Comput. Stat. Data Anal. **22**(3), 334 (1996). https://doi.org/10.1016/0167-9473(96)81457-5

15. Kassam, S.: Signal Detection in Non-Gaussian Noise. Springer, New York (1988). https://doi.org/10.1007/978-1-4612-3834-8
16. Middleton, D.: Statistical-physical models of man-made radio noise, part I. First-order probability models of the instantaneous amplitude. In: Proceedings of ACM Joint Meeting Foundations of Software Engineering, pp. 175–233 (1974)
17. Xing, Q., Shouyong, W.: Signal detection based on matched filtering under α stable distributed noise. J. Air Force Radar Acad. China **04**, 270–272 (2007)
18. Hua, Q., Xiguang, X., Jihong, Z., Feiyu, Y., Weihua, W.: Robust Spectrum Sensing Based on Hyperbolic Tangent in Gaussian and Non-Gaussian Noise Environments, pp. 283–288 (2018)
19. Tandra, R., Sahai, A.: SNR walls for signal detection. IEEE J. Sel. Top. Signal Process. **2**(1), 4–16 (2008)
20. Zhu, X., Zhu, Y., Bao, Y., Zhu, W.: A pth order moment based spectrum sensing for cognitive radio in the presence of independent or weakly correlated Laplace noise. Signal Process. **137**(C), 109–123 (2017)
21. Karimzadeh, M., Rabiei, A., Olfat, A.: Soft-limited polarity-coincidence-array spectrum sensing in the presence of non-Gaussian noise. IEEE Trans. Veh. Technol. **66**(2), 1418–1427 (2017)
22. Nadarajah, S., Kotz, S.: On the linear combination, product and ratio of normal and Laplace random variables. J. Franklin Inst. **348**(4), 810–822 (2011)
23. Ilow, J.: Signal processing in alpha-stable noise environments: noise modelling, detection and estimation. Ph.D. dissertation, Dept. Elect. Eng., Univ. Toronto, Toronto, Canada (1995)
24. Kapoor, S., Rao, S., Singh, G.: Opportunistic spectrum sensing by employing matched filter in cognitive radio network. In: Proceedings of IEEE CSNT, Katra, Jammu, pp. 580–583, June 2011
25. Liangping, M., Yingxue, L., Demir, A.: Matched filtering assisted energy detection for sensing weak primary user signals. In: 2012 IEEE International Conference on Acoustics, Speech and Signal Processing (ICASSP), Kyoto, pp. 3149–3152 (2012). https://doi.org/10.1109/ICASSP.2012.6288583.
26. Cover, T., Hart, P.: Nearest neighbor pattern classification. IEEE Trans. Inf. Theory **13**(1), 21–27 (1967). https://doi.org/10.1109/TIT.1967.1053964

Hybrid Deep-Readout Echo State Network and Support Vector Machine with Feature Selection for Human Activity Recognition

Shadi Abudalfa[1](✉) and Kevin Bouchard[2]

[1] IT Department, University College of Applied Sciences, Gaza, Palestine
sabudalfa@ucas.edu.ps
[2] LIARAlab, Université du Québec à Chicoutimi, Saguenay, Canada
kevin_bouchard@uqac.ca

Abstract. Developing sophisticated automated systems for assisting numerous humans such as patients and elder people is a promising future direction. Such smart systems are based on recognizing Activities of Daily Living (ADLs) for providing a suitable decision. Activity recognition systems are currently employed in developing many smart technologies (e.g., smart mobile phone) and their uses have been increased dramatically with availability of Internet of Things (IoT) technology. Numerous machine learning techniques are presented in literature for improving performance of activity recognition. Whereas, some techniques have not been sufficiently exploited with this research direction. In this paper, we shed the light on this issue by presenting a technique based on employing Echo State Network (ESN) for human activity recognition. The presented technique is based on combining ESN with Support Vector Machine (SVM) for improving performance of activity recognition. We also applied feature selection method to the collected data to decrease time complexity and increase the performance. Many experiments are conducted in this work to evaluate performance of the presented technique with human activity recognition. Experiment results have shown that the presented technique provides remarkable performance.

Keywords: Hybrid technique · Echo state networks · Support Vector Machine · Feature selection · Human activity recognition · Smart system

1 Introduction

Human activity recognition is an important task in developing many smart technologies (e.g., smart homes). Human activity recognition can be used by numerous systems and applications that serve many fields such as healthcare [1], security [2] and physical rehabilitation [3]. Mainly, this task is achieved by employing machine learning techniques [4]. Thereby, using recent machine learning techniques reveal a significant improvement in human activity recognition. This motivated us to explore performance of employing more recent machine techniques with human activity recognition.

Z. Deze et al. (Eds.): BDTA 2020/WiCON 2020, LNICST 371, pp. 150–167, 2021.
https://doi.org/10.1007/978-3-030-72802-1_11

Based on our knowledge, there is an extension of neural networks entitled reservoir computing framework [5] has not been adequately exploited with human activity recognition. Therefore, we present a technique based on such machine learning technique and show its efficiency with this research direction. The presented technique entitled Hybrid Echo State Network and Support Vector Machine (HESNSVM).

The presented technique includes specifically a part of reservoir computing framework which is referred to as Echo State Network (ESN) [6]. ESN [7] mimics a conceptual and practical distinction between a dynamical component entitled reservoir and a feed-forward readout tool. ESN is based on training a deep neural network (recurrent neural network) which causes a high computational time. Thus, we use feature selection [8] for decreasing time complexity. Moreover, the feature selection step improves the overall performance of human activity recognition with the collected dataset used for this work.

Additionally, the presented technique combines ESN with Support Vector Machine (SVM) [9]. As a result of this, the presented technique improves performance of human activity recognition in comparison with ESN. Numerous experiments are conducted in this research to show performance of the presented technique with human activity recognition. Performance of the presented technique has been compared as well with performance of applying ESN, SVM and an extension of ESN called BDESN [10]. Additionally, we compare performance of the presented technique with performance of applying a related work presented by Alalshekmubarak et al. [11].

In this work, the authors focus on developing a supervised learning technique for human activity recognition as an extension to another work conducted for evaluating performance of applying unsupervised and semi-supervised learning techniques [12]. It is worth noting here that this research direction is based on developing activity recognition system that collects data from different inertial central units [13]. Such sensors are located in a smart home and send collected data to an activity recognition system for making suitable decisions that assist patients and elder people. The activity recognition system may be remotely connected to a larger system through Internet of Things (IoT) technology.

The contributions of the present work used to solve the problem of human activity recognition are highlighted below:

- We have designed a hybrid technique named as HESNSVM by combining ESN and SVM models, which has been used for applying human activity recognition to a data collected from different inertial central units.
- In this presented technique, we have used logits resulted from ESN model and probabilities resulted from SVM model. This combination makes our solution unique.
- A comparative study of presented HESNSVM and other models is performed. The reported results aid to confirm the idea of choosing particularly ESN and SVM.
- We have evaluated the presented HESNSVM on a collected dataset and reported results through various perspectives.

The rest of paper is organized as follows: Sect. 2 presents a review for some related studies. Section 3 explains the presented technique. Section 4 describes the experiment environment. Section 5 discusses the experiment results and provides due analysis. Finally, Sect. 6 concludes the paper and reveals some suggestions for future work.

2 Literature Review

A lot of approaches have been presented in the literature for developing human activity recognition systems. Some approaches convert the problem into image processing by collecting data from video camera sensors [14]. While, other approaches [15], similar to our research work, are based on identifying human actions by collecting data from different sensors.

Most of research works are based on employing supervised learning techniques that use only labeled data for human activity recognition [16]. However, some supervised learning techniques have not been adequately exploited in this research direction. Based on our knowledge, limited research works used echo state networks for human activity recognition. Thereby, our work enriches this research direction by showing performance of employing echo state networks with additional methodology in collecting data and recognizing human activities. In the sequel of this section, we present some related works and show the difference in comparison with our research work.

Some research works employed deep learning techniques such as Long Short-Term Memory models (LSTM) and Temporal Convolutional Network (TCN) with human activity recognition [17]. While, other works [18] adopted a deep Convolutional Neural Network (CNN) for improving performance of human activity recognition. Additionally, Wan et al. [19] designed a smartphone inertial accelerometer-based architecture for human activity recognition. They utilized CNN, LSTM, BLSTM, MLP and SVM models.

Miciet al. [20] presented experiment work with echo state networks for classifying human activities extracted from video data. While, our research work is different in using data collected from inertial central units. In the same context, Basterrechand Ojha [21] presented an approach for modeling the human activities by using a temporal learning with ESN. They analyzed a dataset collected with an embedded Gyroscope sensor. Whereas, we presented different learning technique and analyzed different dataset.

Moreover, Gallicchio and Micheli [22] provided an experimental analysis of ESN for ambient assisted living. They analyzed data consists in the 4-dimensional stream of Received Signal Strength (RSS) and sampled at the frequency of 8 Hz. Thereby, it is obvious that they use different evaluation strategy with different dataset.

Based on previous discussion, we conclude that our research work presents additional knowledge for showing performance of applying ESN with human activity recognition. Moreover, there are some unknown factors that were not studied nor evaluated by previous related works. Thereby, our paper fills some gaps and enriches this research direction.

3 Solution Approach

The presented system is firstly based on collecting data from sensors and extracting features from the collected data. Then, a feature selection method is applied for using the most dominant attributes included in the dataset. Next, a data scaling method is applied to normalize attribute values. After that, the normalized data points (attribute values) are used as input to the presented technique HESNSVM. Finally, the output of HESNSVM model shows the predicted activity expressed in the corresponding data point. All phases of the presented system are shown in Fig. 1.

As shown in the figure, the presented technique HESNSVM combines ESN and SVM models. This technique is inspired by an approach presented by Alalshekmubarak et al. [11]. However, we presented in this work another method for combining ESN and SVM as described below.

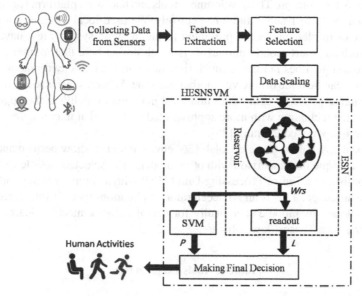

Fig. 1. The presented system structure.

The HESNSVM model should be firstly trained by inputting normalized data points (training set) selected from the dataset. Then, each data point is mapped to higher dimensions by using the reservoir network of ESN. As a result of this, reservoir states Wrs_train are computed by using the input data points. Next, the reservoir states Wrs_train along with the corresponding target labels (actual human activities) are used to train SVM model and the readout layer of ESN model. After that, the presented system becomes ready to predict human activates.

To evaluate performance of the trained HESNSVM model, another set of normalized data points (testing set) should be selected from the dataset. Then, the corresponding reservoir states Wrs_test are computed. Next, the reservoir states Wrs_test are classified by using both SVM and readout models. As a result of this, the trained SVM model provides a vector P which denotes a set of class membership probabilities that are corresponding to each input data point. While, the output of trained readout model is a set of logits L [23]. After that, the presented technique makes the final decision by combining the output of both models by multiplying P by L. Applying the multiplication operation increases the confidence of predicting input data points. Finally, the vector O resulted from the multiplication operation ($O = P \times L$) is used as input to *argmax* function to find the predicted label (predicted human activity). The *argmax* function returns the index (corresponding class label) of the maximum value in vector O.

4 Experiment Setup

We conducted many experiments to evaluate performance of the presented technique with human activity recognition. The development tools and hardware platform specifications are described in Table 1 and Table 2 respectively. We used local machine for showing performance of implementing the presented technique with systems that have limited recourses such as smart mobile phones. It is worth noting here that implementing the presented technique does not cause much time delay in the real environment since the training phase can be done offline via another machine. Whereas, we also show effect of applying training phase by using the same local machine to highlight the applicability of the presented technique with more sophisticated systems that may use unsupervised [24] and semi-supervised learning [25].

Additionally, we used Google Colab [26] environment to show performance of the presented technique in comparison with other models. The selected Google Colab environment consists of a Tensor Processing Unit (TPU) with a compiler to support version 3 of Python language. TPU is an AI accelerator Application-Specific Integrated Circuit (ASIC) developed by Google specifically for neural network machine learning and it uses Google's own TensorFlow software.

Table 1. Tools and programs

Tool	Version	Purpose
Python	3.7.1	Building and learning models for developing experiments
Anaconda	4.2.0	Open data science platform powered by Python for providing development environment that facilitates developing our experiments
Spyder	2.3.8	Graphical platform for editing, testing and debugging Python codes
TensorFlow	1.14.0	Open source platform used for implementing echo state networks

Table 2. Platform specifications

Host	Component	Specification
Local	CPU	Intel(R) Celeron (R) N3060 1.6 GHZ
	Memory	4.00 GB
	OS	Windows 10 (64-bit)
Cloud	CPU	Tensor Processing Unit (TPU)
	Memory	12.72 GB

4.1 Dataset

Our experiment work is conducted by using a dataset entitled ActivitiesExercisesRecognition[1] that includes 1150 samples (data points) collected by Kévin Chapron et al. [27] affiliated to the LIARA laboratory at University of Québec in Chicoutimi. The dataset includes ten classes of activities collected from ten participants as shown in Table 3. The table reports same description provided by Chapron et al. In addition, we used same features extracted and reported by Chapron et al. The feature set includes 105 features as shown in Table 4.

For evaluating performance ESN model, we used 70/30 split method for dividing the dataset into training and testing sets. Thereby, the training set (70%) includes 805 samples (data points). While, the testing set includes the rest 345 samples. We also used 10-fold cross validation [28] to show performance of the presented technique in comparison with other models.

Table 3. Activities included in the used dataset

#	Activity	Description
1	ExoFente	Typical Front Lunge
2	ExoMarche	Front Step Down
3	ExoSitUp	Sit-to-Stand
4	ExoSquat	Typical Squat on chair
5	shortRunning	Continuously running for 30 s
6	shortSeat	Staying sit in a chair for 30 s
7	shortSitting	Transition Stand-to-Sit
8	shortStanding	Transition Sit-to-Stand
9	shortSwitch	Fast rotation of the wrist
10	shortWalking	Continuously walking for 30 s

4.2 Evaluation Measures

Empirical results obtained from experiments provide a good way to evaluate performance of the presented technique with human activity recognition. Thereby, we use classification accuracy and F1-score [29] for evaluating the presented model. The accuracy is the ratio of all samples that are classified correctly. While, the F1-score (also known as F-score or F-measure) is the harmonic mean of precision and recall, and its best value is 1 while the worst score is 0.

Recall (which also known as sensitivity or true positive rate) is the ratio of samples which are classified correctly as positive to all positive samples. While, precision is the

---

[1] https://github.com/LIARALab/Datasets/tree/master/ActivitiesExercisesRecognition.

ratio of samples which are correctly classified as positive to all samples classified as positive. The F1-score is basically applied to binary classification and there are different types of averaging [30] used for applying multiclass classification such as macro, micro, and weighted. In this work, we use weighted average for studying how the system performs across overall sets of data. This method calculates metrics for each label and finds their mean weighted by number of true samples for each label.

Table 4. Feature Set Included in the Used Dataset

Domain	Feature	Count
Temporal	Mean value for each axis	9
	Mean value of mean values	3
	Standard Deviation for each axis	9
	Mean value of standard deviation	3
	Skewness Value for each axis	9
	Mean value of Skewness value	3
	Kurtosis Value for each axis	9
	Mean value of Kurtosis value	3
	Zero Crossing Rate for each axis	9
	Mean value of Zero Crossing Rate	3
	Correlation between every axis	18
Frequential	DC Component for each axis	9
	Energy for each axis	9
	Entropy for each axis	9
	Total	105

4.3 Data Scaling

Applying data scaling is a very important phase that improve significantly performance of the presented technique with the used dataset. In this work we apply data scaling by using a method entitled StandardScaler implemented in Scikit-learn [31] library. StandardScaler purely centers the data by using the following Z-Score formula, where μ is the mean and σ is the standard deviation.

$$Z = (x - \mu)/\sigma \tag{1}$$

4.4 Feature Selection

We evaluated performance of selecting a set of best features that discern robustly all data points existed in the used dataset. For applying feature selection, we firstly removed features that have redundant attribute values. As a result of this, number of remaining features becomes 35 features. Then, we applied feature selection by using a method entitled SelectKBest implemented in Scikit-learn [31] library. SelectKBest selects the top k features that have maximum score that is relevance to every feature with the target variable. In this work, we selected the best 18 features to evaluate performance of the presented technique.

5   Results and Analysis

We conducted numerous experiments to evaluate performance of applying the presented technique to the used dataset. This section shows experiment results provided when applying the presented technique through various perspectives.

5.1   Feature Selection and Normalization

Applying feature selection makes a significant effect on the shape of activity classes in the multi-dimensional space. Figure 2 visualizes the distributions of features embedded in the used dataset by using t-SNE [32]. Colors of the figure show the ten activity classes included in the dataset.

Figure 2(a) depicts the real data points included in the dataset. Figure 2 (b) visualizes effect of removing features that have redundant attribute values. We note that activity classes have become more clearly. Figure 2 (c) illustrates effect of selecting the best 18 features included in the dataset. It is clear that the ten activity classes have become more separable. Figure 2 (d) shows effect of applying data scaling. Based on this analysis, we conclude that applying feature selection and normalizing data points make an obvious change in shape of activity classes.

5.2   Performance of ESN

In this subsection, we show performance of applying ESN model by using the local host with 70/30 split method for dividing the dataset into training and testing sets. It is necessary to evaluate performance of the ESN model since it is the core of the presented technique. To train ESN model, we should set some hyperparameters. Table 5

Table 5.   List of hyperparameters used for training ESN

Hyperparameter	Description
N_r	Size of the reservoir
β	Percentage of nonzero connections in reservoir
ρ	Largest eigen value of the reservoir
ω	Scaling of the input weights
£	Noise in the reservoir state update
λ	Regularization coefficient for ridge regression

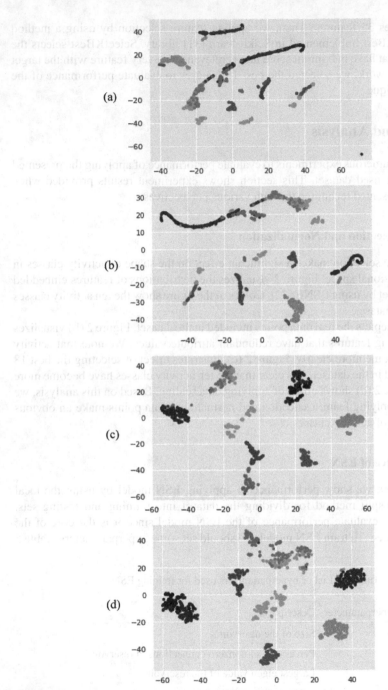

Fig. 2. Visualizing effect of applying feature selection and normalization in terms of t-SNE. (a) The real data points. (b) Removing features that have redundant attribute values. (c) Selecting the best set of features. (d) Applying data scaling.

shows a list of hyperparameters used for setting ESN model. Additionally, we initialized *embedding_method* for ESN as "identity".

For showing performance of applying ESN model to the used dataset, we conducted a sequence of experiments to find the best results. Firstly, we changed value of N_r hyperparameter and fixed value of rest hyperparameters. In this experiment, we set β = 0.33, ρ = 1.12, ω = 0.47, £ = 0.7, and λ = 2.12. It is worth to clarify that running same experiment through training ESN model provides different results when using fixed values of hyperparameters. For taking into consideration this randomness, we repeated each run 3 times and reported the average value with each corresponding value of N_r.

Figure 3 shows classification accuracy (in percent) of changing value of N_r and fixing value of rest hyperparameters through applying ESN with feature selection. We notice clearly that classification accuracy is improved when increasing size of the reservoir network.

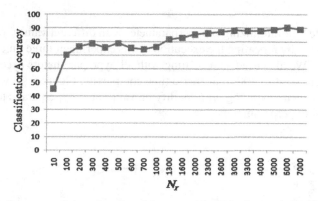

Fig. 3. Performance of changing size of the reservoir (N_r) when training ESN model.

We also evaluated time complexity to show whether the presented technique is applicable to smart systems that have limited recourses such as using smart mobile phones. Figure 4 shows effect of increasing size of the reservoir on computational time consumed when training ESN model. We notice clearly that computational time is sharply grown when increasing size of the reservoir network. Based on these experiment results, we conclude that complexity of ESN model is increased when rising size of the reservoir. We also notice that fixing size of the reservoir to 2000 neurons decreases significantly time complexity with acceptable classification accuracy.

To check effect of setting the rest of hyperparameters, we initialized each hyperparameter with different values and reported classification accuracy. Based on our experiment results, modifying value of β hyperparameter does not provide significant change in performance. While, changing value of ρ hyperparameter affects sharply on the performance. It is interested to clarify that both β and ρ hyperparameters do not significantly affect on computational time.

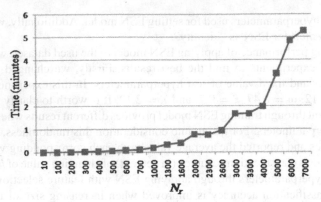

Fig. 4. Time complexity provided with changing size of the reservoir (N_r) when training ESN model.

To show effect of initializing ρ hyperparameter with different values, we used same evaluation strategy by repeating the execution of this experiment three times and reporting the average. We also used same setting with all hyperparameters except Nr hyperparameter which is set to 700 to decrease time complexity. Figure 5 shows the change in classification accuracy along with modifying value of ρ hyperparameter and fixing value of the rest hyperparameters.

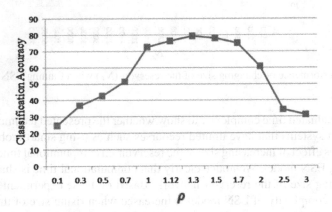

Fig. 5. Effect of changing value of ρ hyperparameter when training ESN model.

Since value 1.3 provides the best accuracy with ρ hyperparameter, we used this value with the rest of experiments. Then, we check effect of changing value of ω hyperparameter. Initializing ω hyperparameter with different values affects significantly on the performance as shown in Fig. 6. After that, we fixed value of ω hyperparameter to 1.7 (achieved best accuracy) and changed value of £ hyperparameter. Figure 7 shows an effect of changing value of £ hyperparameter on classification accuracy.

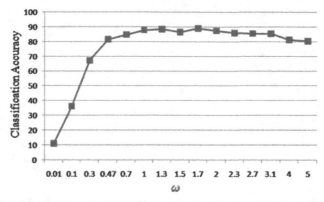

Fig. 6. Effect of changing value of ω hyperparameter when training ESN model.

Finally, we fixed value of £ hyperparameter to 0.00001 and modified value of λ hyperparameter. Figure 8 shows accuracy of initializing λ hyperparameter with different values. It is also worth mentioning that changing value of ω, £ and λ hyperparameters does not significantly affect time complexity. Thereby, N_r is the only hyperparameter that affects significantly time complexity.

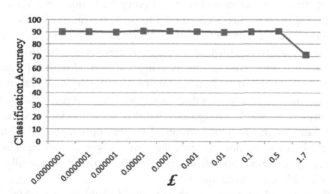

Fig. 7. Effect of changing value of £ hyperparameter when training ESN model.

Based on our experiment results, the best achieved average results are 92.08% and 91.90% for classification accuracy and F1-score respectively. However, better results may be provided if we conduct more experiments with using more settings for the hyperparameters. These results are reported when tuning hyperparameters to β = 0.33, ρ = 1.3, ω = 1.7, £ = 0.00001, λ = 15.12, and N_r = 700. The computational time consumed for running this experiment is about 0.09 min (5.4 s). Thereby, we conclude that the presented technique is efficient and can be employed with smart systems that use limited resources (e.g., small memory and slow processor) such as using smart mobile phone.

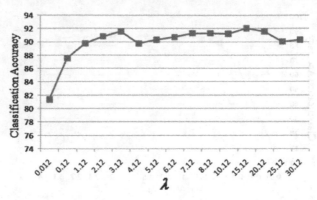

Fig. 8. Effect of changing value of λ hyperparameter when training ESN model.

5.3 Comparison Framework

In this subsection, we show performance of the presented techniques in comparison with other models. We compare performance of the presented technique HESNSVM with performance of ESN, SVM, BDESN [10] and a related work entitled ESNSVM [11]. We used the cloud host to enable us making numerous evaluations in a short time.

We used *SVC* function included in sklearn library for building SVM model. Default settings are selected for building SVM model to decrease number of possibilities and present a well comparative perspective when comparing with other models. Based on our experiment work, using default settings provides competitive performance. Thereby, the SVM classifier provides fixed results by using 'rbf' kernel with C parameter equals to 1.0, degree parameter equals to 3 and gamma parameter equals to 'auto'. The 'auto' value means that the model uses a value equals to $1/n\_$features. Where, n denotes a number of features. It is worth noting here that this SVM model uses one-versus-rest (OvR) decision function as multiclass strategy [33] for applying the SVM model to our classification problem which contains more than two classes (ten activity classes). Using multiclass strategy is essential operation since the SVM model is basically designed to solving binary classification problem.

Additionally, we used an open source code that is publicly available[2] for building both ESN and BDESN models. Moreover, we developed a code based on our expectation for implementing ESNSVM model that fits the technique presented by Alalshekmubarak et al. [11].

To make the comparison fair enough, we applied 10-fold cross validation. In addition, a random search approach [34] is used to identify the optimal values for some hyperparameters of ESN and BDESN models. SHERPA library[3] is used for tuning hyperparameters of ESN and BDESN models. Due to the larger number of hyperparameters in ESN model, a total of 500 random configurations are evaluated. Of course, using larger number of random configurations may reveal global optimal values of the hyperparameters. We could not investigate this matter further because it is a time-consuming

---

[2] https://github.com/FilippoMB/Bidirectional-Deep-readout-Echo-State-Network.

[3] https://parameter-sherpa.readthedocs.io/en/latest/.

process. After finding the optimal values for the hyperparameters of ESN, we used them for training ESN, ESNSVM and the presented technique HESNSVM.

Similarly, we identified optimal values for the hyperparameters of BDESN model. In this stage, we mainly employed random search approach for tuning additional hyperparameters: P_{drop}, γ and $\lambda 2$. P_{drop} used specifically for estimating dropout (keep) probability in the multilayer perceptron (MLP) of BDESN model. While, γ denotes learning rate in Adam optimizer and $\lambda 2$ is a L2 regularization weight in loss function. Thereby, we used the optimal values of hyperparameters selected with ESN model for tuning the other hyperparameters of BDESN model. Based on our experiment work, this scenario provides better results in comparison with searching immediately for all optimal values of the hyperparameters in BDESN model. In this experiment, a total of 67 random values are evaluated for tuning P_{drop} hyperparameter.

Table 6 shows all optimal values of the hyperparameters identified to training ESN, BDESN, ESNSVM and the presented technique HESNSVM. We also report the intervals where each hyperparameter is sampled from during the optimization procedure.

It is worth noting here that the MPL of BDESN model includes three hidden layers and each of them contains 18 neurons. We also used 1000 epochs and 25 samples in the mini-batches with gradient descent training. In addition to that, Principal Component Analysis (PCA) [35] is used as dimensionality reduction method while the space size of reduced dimensionality equals to 18 features.

Table 6. Optimal values of the hyperparameters identified for training ESN, BDESN, ESNSVM and HESNSVM models

Hyperparameter	Opt. Val	Intervals
N_r	1500	[750, 1000, 1250, 1500, 1750, 2000]
β	0.2758	[0.1, 0.6]
ρ	1.3130	[0.5, 1.8]
ω	0.4319	[0.01, 1.0]
$\pounds$	0.0217	[0, 0.1]
λ	8.6215	[0.03, 32]
P_{drop}	0.8707	[0.6, 1.0]
γ	0.0008	[0.0001, 0.001]
$\lambda 2$	0.0345	[0.00001, 0.1]

Table 7 shows results of comparing SVM, ESN, BDESN, ESNSVM and HESNSVM models in terms of classification accuracy (Acc), F1-score (F1). While, Table 8 shows the results in term of computation time (T) in minutes. To make our comparison more accurate and fair enough, we used 10-fold cross validation. We run each model 11 times with each fold by using different random initializations. Then, average values of performance measures (Acc, F1 and T) are reported for each fold.

As shown in the table, the presented technique HESNSVM outperforms all compared models in terms of average classification accuracy and F1-score. It is noteworthy that behavior of each model is different with some folds. We note as well that BDESN model provides low accuracy with high time complexity. Our explanation for this result tends to the nature of used dataset which has small number of selected features. Thereby, using MLP in BDESN model increases time complexity without adding a significant improvement in accuracy.

Table 7. Comparing performance of different techniques for human activity recognition

Fold	SVM		ESN		BDESN		ESNSVM		HESNSVM*	
	Acc	F1	Acc	F1	Acc	F1	Acc	F1	Acc	F1
1	85.2	82.1	83.4	80.0	83.1	79.9	86.6	83.5	85.8	82.8
2	95.7	95.6	93.7	93.6	94.8	94.7	91.9	91.6	95.2	95.1
3	96.5	96.5	97.4	97.4	95.4	95.3	93.2	92.8	97.3	97.3
4	95.7	95.6	93.4	92.9	93.6	93.0	96.1	96.0	95.4	95.4
5	87.0	84.9	86.6	85.0	86.7	85.1	85.8	83.6	86.2	84.8
6	87.8	85.9	91.7	91.1	88.3	86.5	86.2	83.8	90.5	89.8
7	87.0	84.8	91.5	91.2	91.6	90.8	90.7	89.8	88.9	87.5
8	85.2	82.3	85.1	81.5	87.5	85.5	87.4	84.5	87.3	84.8
9	97.4	97.3	97.6	97.6	94.9	94.7	96.4	96.0	98.6	98.6
10	91.3	90.8	91.5	91.1	88.1	87.3	91.9	91.3	91.9	91.6
Avg	90.9	89.6	91.2	90.14	90.4	89.3	90.6	89.3	**91.7**	**90.8**

*The presented technique

Additionally, we noticed obviously that time complexity of using SVM model is very low. Thus, combining SVM and ESN models does not affect sharply on time complexity of the presented technique HESNSVM. It is clear also that performance of HESNSVM model is better than performance of the related work ESNSVM.

5.4   Threats to Validity

We run each experiment many times with different random initializations. All our experiment results show that the presented technique outperforms always other compared models: SVM, ESN, BDESN and ESNSVM. The margin of performance difference between the compared models may be varied based on some threats that should be considered when conducting the experiment work. Two threats to the validity are discussed in the sequel.

It is not conclusive that applying the presented technique to other datasets with different distributions would result in the same classification accuracy. We could not

Table 8. Comparing time complexity of different techniques for human activity recognition

Fold	SVM	ESN	BDESN	ESNSVM	HESNSVM*
	T× 10–3	T	T	T	T
1	0.310	0.077	6.915	0.139	0.126
2	0.320	0.077	6.834	0.137	0.127
3	0.360	0.077	6.825	0.136	0.127
4	0.330	0.077	6.710	0.136	0.127
5	0.310	0.077	6.844	0.136	0.127
6	0.310	0.077	6.926	0.139	0.128
7	0.310	0.077	6.874	0.136	0.127
8	0.320	0.076	4.933	0.137	0.128
9	0.310	0.077	4.902	0.136	0.126
10	0.310	0.077	4.941	0.137	0.128
Average	0.319	0.077	6.270	0.137	0.127

*The presented technique

investigate this matter further because there were no other relevant public datasets available. Moreover, our experiments revealed that results are sensitive to initial values that are used when setting the hyperparameters in models.

6 Conclusion and Future Work

This research work evaluates performance of applying echo state networks with feature selection to human activity recognition. Thus, this work helps scholars to assess their solutions proposed in this research direction. We also present a technique for improving performance of human activity recognition. The experiment results show that performance of the presented technique outperforms performance of SVM, ESN, BDESN and ESNSVM models in terms of classification accuracy and F1-score. Based on our experiment work, we conclude that applying data scaling and feature selection along with echo state networks provide competitive results. Thereby, using the presented technique for human activity recognition is a promising research direction.

This research can be extended in different ways. It is interesting to show performance of applying the presented technique to more datasets. Additionally, evaluating the presented technique by using more reservoir computing models will be a promise research direction. The future work maybe also extended by investigating performance of applying more feature selection methods.

Moreover, it is interested to evaluate more random configurations when initializing the hyperparameters used with ESN, BDESN, ESNSVM and HESNSVM models. Using optimization methods for finding optimal values of hyperparameters is also a good direction that may improve performance of applying the presented technique to human activity recognition.

References

1. Liu, X., Liu, L., Simske, S.J., Liu. J.: Human daily activity recognition for healthcare using wearable and visual sensing data. In Proceedings of the IEEE International Conference on Healthcare Informatics (ICHI), Chicago, IL, pp. 24–31 (2016)
2. Taha, A., Zayed, H., Khalifa, M.E., El-Horbarty, E.M: Human activity recognition for surveillance applications. In: Proceedings of the 7th International Conference on Information Technology (2015)
3. Leightley, D., Darby, J., Li, B., McPhee, J.S., Yap, M.: Human activity recognition for physical rehabilitation. In: Proceedings of the 2013 IEEE International Conference on Systems, Man, and Cybernetics (2013)
4. Abudalfa, S., Al-Mouhamed, M., Ahmed, M.: Comparative study on behavior-based dynamic branch prediction using machine learning. Int. J. Comput. Digit. Syst. 7(3), 155–160 (2018)
5. Lukoševičius, M., Jaeger, H.: Reservoir computing approaches to recurrent neural network training. Comput. Sci. Rev. 3(3), 127–149 (2009)
6. Lukoševičius, M.: A practical guide to applying echo state networks. In: Montavon, G., Orr, G.B., Müller, K.-R. (eds.) Neural Networks: Tricks of the Trade. LNCS, vol. 7700, pp. 659–686. Springer, Heidelberg (2012). https://doi.org/10.1007/978-3-642-35289-8_36
7. Gallicchio, C., Micheli, A.: Architectural and markovian factors of echo state networks. Neural Netw. 24(5), 440–456 (2011)
8. Guyon, I., Elisseeff, A.: An introduction to variable and feature selection. J. Mach. Learn. Res. 3, 1157–1182 (2003)
9. Burg, G., Groenen, P.: GenSVM: a generalized multiclass support vector machine. J. Mach. Learn. Res. 17(224), 1–42 (2016)
10. Bianchi, F., Scardapane, S., Løkse, S., Jenssen, R.: Bidirectional deep-readout echo state networks. In: Proceedings of the European Symposium on Artificial Neural Networks, Computational Intelligence and Machine Learning. Bruges, Belgium (2018)
11. Alalshekmubarak, A., Smith, L.: A novel approach combining recurrent neural network and support vector machines for time series classification. In: Proceedings of the 9th International Conference on Innovations in Information Technology (IIT) (2013)
12. Abudalfa, S., Qusa, H.: Evaluation of semi-supervised clustering and feature selection for human activity recognition. Int. J. Comput. Digit. Syst. 8(6), 651–658 (2019)
13. Novak, D., Goršič, M., Podobnik, J., Munih, M.: Toward real-time automated detection of turns during gait using wearable inertial measurement units. Sensors 14, 18800–18822 (2014)
14. Yuan, H.: A semi-supervised human action recognition algorithm based on skeleton feature. J. Inf. Hiding Multimed. Signal Process. 6(1), 175–181 (2015)
15. Cvetković, B., Kaluža, B., Luštrek, M., Gams, M.: Multi-classifier adaptive training: specialising an activity recognition classifier using semi-supervised learning. In: Paternò, F., de Ruyter, B., Markopoulos, P., Santoro, C., van Loenen, E., Luyten, K. (eds.) AmI 2012. LNCS, vol. 7683, pp. 193–207. Springer, Heidelberg (2012). https://doi.org/10.1007/978-3-642-34898-3_13
16. Yang, J., Nguyen, M., San, P., Li, X., Krishnaswamy, S.: Deep convolutional neural networks on multichannel time series for human activity recognition. In: Proceedings of the 24th International Joint Conference on Artificial Intelligence (IJCAI), Buenos Aires, Argentina, pp. 3995–4001 (2015)

17. Browne, D., Giering, M., Prestwich, S.: Deep learning human activity recognition. In: Proceedings of the 27th AIAI Irish Conference on Artificial Intelligence and Cognitive Science (AICS 2019), CEUR Workshop Proceedings, NUI Galway, Ireland, 5–6 December, vol. 2563, pp. 76–87 (2019)
18. Sana, P., Kakara, P., Li, X., Krishnaswamy, S., Yang, J., Nguyen, M.: Deep learning for human activity recognition, big data analytics for sensor-network collected intelligence, intelligent data-centric systems, pp. 186–204 (2017)
19. Wan, S., Qi, L., Xu, X., Tong, C., Gu, Z.: Deep learning models for real-time human activity recognition with smartphones. Mobile Netw. Appl. **25**(2), 743–755 (2019). https://doi.org/10.1007/s11036-019-01445-x
20. Mici, L., Hinaut, X., Wermter, S.: Activity recognition with echo state networks using 3D body joints and objects category. In: Proceedings of the European Symposium on Artificial Neural Networks, Computational Intelligence and Machine Learning (ESANN), Bruges, Belgium, pp. 465–470 (2016)
21. Basterrech, S. , Ojha, V.: Temporal learning using echo state network for human activity recognition. In: Proceedings of the Third European Network Intelligence Conference, pp. 217–223 (2016)
22. Gallicchio, C., Micheli, A.: Experimental analysis of deep echo state networks for ambient assisted living. In: Proceedings of the 3rd Workshop on Artificial Intelligence for Ambient Assisted Living (AI*AAL 2017), Colocated with the 16th International Conference of the Italian Association for Artificial Intelligence (2017)
23. Cramer, J.S.: The Origins and Development of the Logit Model. Cambridge UP, Cambridge (2003)
24. Abudalfa, S., Mikki, M.: A dynamic linkage clustering using KD-Tree. Int. Arab J. Inf. Technol. (IAJIT), **10**(3), 283–289 (2013)
25. Abudalfa, S., Ahmed, M.: Semi-supervised target-dependent sentiment classification for micro-blogs. J. Comput. Sci. Technol. **19**(1), e06 (2019)
26. Bisong, E.: Google colaboratory. In: Proceedings of Building Machine Learning and Deep Learning Models on Google Cloud Platform. Apress, Berkeley (2019)
27. Chapron, K., Plantevin, V., Thullier, F., Bouchard, K., Duchesne, E., Gaboury, S.: A more efficient transportable and scalable system for real-time activities and exercises recognition. Sensors MDPI **18**, 268 (2018)
28. Cawley, G., Talbot, N.: On over-fitting in model selection and subsequent selection bias in performance evaluation. J. Mach. Learn. Res. **11**, 2079–2107 (2010)
29. Metz, C.: Basic principles of ROC analysis. Semin. Nucl. Med. **8**(4), 283–298 (1978)
30. Parambath, S., Usunier, N., Grandvalet, Y.: Optimizing F-measures by cost-sensitive classification. In: Proceedings of Neural Information Processing Systems (NIPS), pp. 2123–2131 (2014)
31. Pedregosa, F., et al.: Scikit-learn: machine learning in Python. J. Mach. Learn. Res. **12**, 2825–2830 (2011)
32. Maaten, L., Hinton, G.: Visualizing data using t-SNE. J. Mach. Learn. Res. **9**, 2579–2605 (2008)
33. Aly, M.: Survey on Multiclass Classification Methods, California Institute of Technology (2005)
34. Bergstra, J., Bengio, Y.: Random search for hyper-parameter optimization. J. Mach. Learn. Res. **13**, 281–305 (2012)
35. Miranda, A., Borgne, Y.-A., Bontempi, G.: New routes from minimal approximation error to principal components. Neural Process. Lett. **27**(3), 197–207 (2008). https://doi.org/10.1007/s11063-007-9069-2

Research on User Privacy Security of China's Top Ten Online Game Platforms

Lan-Yu Cui, Mi-Qian Su, Yu-Chen Wang, Zu -Mei Mo, Xiao-Yue Liang, Jian He, and Xiu-Wen Ye(✉)

Yulin Normal University, Yulin, China

Abstract. The privacy agreement presented to online game users is the basic guarantee of the running of an online game. An online game platform can have access to users' private information by setting various mandatory clauses. This paper takes the ten most popular online game platforms in China in recent years as examples, using documentary analysis and quantitative analysis to analyze their privacy clauses. The research results show that there are loopholes in protection of users' private information by online platforms that have gained access and rights to use them. Based on this, it is conducive to the protection of users' private information through improving information security protection system of online game platforms, adding the option for access denial of privacy information in the process of user registration, and mandatorily prolonging the time assigned for users to read the privacy agreements.

Keywords: Online game · Rights of privacy · Format clauses

1 Preface

The security of online games has become a frequently seen issue in network tort liability disputes and network service contract disputes. The premise for users to register for access to online game platform services is to accept the User Agreement and Privacy Policy provided by the platform. The content of these agreements is usually the format clauses prepared by online game companies in advance, which involves disclosure of personal identity information such as the users' name, ID, E-mail address, and head photo and so on. To wish to have access to the services, user can only passively click the "Agree" button to accept the terms. If online game companies do not protect the users' privacy, and the identity information is leaked, it will undoubtedly lead to the damage of the users' privacy. As a result, how to standardize the format clauses of online games is really important. Research on the user privacy agreements of China's top ten online game platforms can help deepen the understanding of the privacy security problems of Chinese online game platforms and improve the protection of users' private information on online game platforms and propose solutions accordingly.

© ICST Institute for Computer Sciences, Social Informatics and Telecommunications Engineering 2021
Published by Springer Nature Switzerland AG 2021. All Rights Reserved
Z. Deze et al. (Eds.): BDTA 2020/WiCON 2020, LNICST 371, pp. 168–175, 2021.
https://doi.org/10.1007/978-3-030-72802-1_12

2   Status Quo of Privacy Security on China's Top Ten Online Game Platforms

The privacy agreements of China's top 10 online game platforms are collected from their official websites and coded (see Table 1).

Table 1. Privacy agreements of China's top ten online game platforms

No.	China's top 10 game platforms	Code
1	GOG Privacy Agreement	A1
	GOG.COM User Agreement	B1
2	Origin Privacy Agreement	A2
	Origin Agreement	B2
3	Steam Privacy Agreement	A3
	Steam Subscriber Agreement	B3
4	Uplay Privacy Policies	A4
	splnproc1703	B4
5	WeGame Statement on Protection of Children's Privacy	A5
	WeGame Privacy Guidelines	A5-1
	WeGame Software License and User Agreement	B5
6	Blizzard Battlenet Privacy Policy	A6
	Blizzard Protection of Minors	B6
	Blizzard Battlenet End User License Agreement	B6-1
7	Cubejoy Privacy Protection Policy	A7
	Cubejoy User Agreement	B7
8	Nintendo Privacy Agreement	A8
	Nintendo User agreement	B8
9	Sguo Privacy Agreement	A9
	Sguo Service Agreement	B9
10	Netease Privacy Agreement	A10
	Netease User Agreement	B10

Based on the privacy agreements of China's top ten online game platforms, this paper analyzes the format clauses involving usage of users' identity information. It can be seen that in China's top ten online game platforms, users' e-mail address and username are used respectively. A1, A2, A3, A5, A5-1, A6, A8, A9 and A10 all include provisions on child protection, while A4 and A7 do not have relevant provisions. A3, A5 and A8 do not require users to be older than 16. For example, A3 has clearly shown in its agreements that the minimum age for registering a steam user account is 13, a restriction tougher than before. B6 requires minor users to conduct real name authentication. A1, A2 and A3 do not mention the collection and use of users' mobile phone numbers while the agreements of the other seven game platforms have clearly pointed this out. A6, A7, A9 and A10 include clauses involving the use of ID information of users. A3 indicates that when setting up a user account, a number ("steam ID") will be automatically assigned to the account, without requiring providing or using a real name. The number will be used to refer to the user account, but it is stressed that the users' private identity information will not be directly exposed. Similar content does not exist in corresponding agreements provided by other game platforms. A9 doesn't mention the use of users' name, while Steam clearly points out that the users' name will not be used for the user account with the other eight game platforms saying that they will use the users' name for their accounts. Eight of the ten platforms use the users' date of birth. A6 requires to obtain information about the users' age, date of birth, gender and other non-private information, while the agreements of A7, A9 and A10 do not mentioned this part. A1, A2, A3, A5-1, A8 and A10 all include contents about the users' account avatar, while A4, A6, a7 and A9 do not have similar provisions on this issue. Statement released by A5 indicates that children should not upload real portraits as avatars when accessing the platform's services, while other agreements do not have such provisions. Except A9, all of the other online game platforms require users to share their geographic locations. For example, in A3, Steam requires information about users' geographic location to deliver content through the use of distributed server system. As for data sharing, however, A1, A2, A3, A5, A6 and A10 all agree to purchase content through third-party platforms that share direct connected account information through the use of relevant direct connected account information. On top of that, four of China's top ten online game platforms are not developed by Chinese companies, and the agreements of A1, B1, A2, B2, A8, B8, A9, and B9 are not formulated exclusively for Chinese users but for users worldwide. Online game platforms will encrypt the users' account and password information after collecting it, in case users forgets their password and cannot log in. It can retrieve the password through e-mail verification of identity information. (see Fig. 1).

Among all private information collected, the mobile phone number and E-mail address have to be provided by users to access the platforms' services, which users will need in registering an account and setting a password and username. Apart from that, in order to meet the demands for user identity verification and service security, platforms will also require users' ID card number, name and facial information, which is relatively more important identity information for users. If this kind of information is accessed by the platforms but not well protected, its leakage will lead to the infringement of users' privacy. In order to provide more personalized services to users, some platforms will collect the date of birth, avatar and other contents of the users. None of these platforms mention the restrictions on the use of real minors' portraits except Statement in A5, and such information is not prerequisite to use services. Additionally, these platforms share a feature, that is, users' information may be changed by Cookies. Moreover, Cookies are not bound by privacy agreement, so users' information cannot be guaranteed after being used by a third party. The abuse of identity information of users,

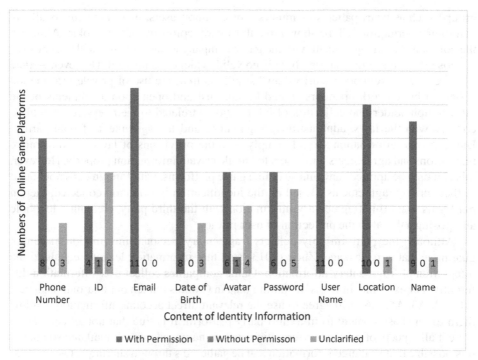

Fig. 1. Identity information required by agreements from China's top 10 online game platforms

especially of minors, may lead to the infringement of their privacy rights. If their information is leaked, it may be purposefully collected by lawbreakers, subjecting minors who have not maturely developed physically and psychologically to mental damage.

3 Research and Analysis

Through research and analysis on China's ten most popular online game platforms, it is shown that game platforms need to collect personal or non-personal information of users such as mobile phone number, avatar, geographical location, device information, etc. to provide their services, such as improving experience of reality in the game, limiting illegal behaviors and helping minor avoid addiction to games. Although personal information has not been collected excessively, the risk of personal information being abused due to the leakage still exists. Among the ten online game platforms, A3 and B3 clearly point out that the users' name would not be used to set up the users' account, while the other eight game platforms have a different policy. However, A1, A2 and A3 do not include collection of the private information and use of mobile phone number, which is, however, covered by the agreements of the other seven game platforms. Moreover, A6 needs to collect users' age, date of birth, gender and so on, but the agreements of A7, A9, A10 and other game platforms does not have similar provisions. Agreements of A2, B2 and A4 belong to foreign game platforms, whose common feature is that they require less from common users but include more provisions particularly for special groups such as heart patients or minors. For common users, these agreements all say that their information will be shown to a third-party company called Cookie. Although the company has an agreement with the game company ensuring that it will not abuse or disclose the users' information, there is no valid evidence to prove it. However, Article 11 of China's "Network Security Law" stipulates that, the use of private information collected by network operators should be fair, just and open upon agreements of the information holder and collection of information unrelated to their services should be comply with the laws, administrative regulations and the agreement of both parties. Using private information should comply with the provisions of laws, administrative regulations and agreements with users to handle private information properly. However, this can only be applied for Chinese online game platforms, with foreign ones not bound in their privacy agreements. Based on the identification information collected, the ten platforms share this fragmentary information with the third party, creating a loophole and posing a threat to the protection of user privacy.

Although the platform only collects fragmentary personal information, it cannot guarantee that zero leakage. Zhou (2013) said that information leakage equals to the integration of fragmentary information. Game companies collect user information differently. For example, in terms of sharing data in China's top ten popular online games, A1, A2, A3, A5, A6, A10 agree to use the relevant direct account information to allow them to purchase content from a third-party platform. It is true that not all companies collect all aspects of personal information such as name, address, E-mail and so on, but it is possible that scattered information can be gathered s through sharing between third-party platforms or game company platforms, which is highly likely to lead to leakage of user information. In the case of Li Hanbin and Li Yuehua, the Appellants at Maoming Intermediate People's Court in Guangdong Province, Xie Jingdong, the defendants in the original trial, illegally sold citizens' private information through the Internet. This constituted the crime of infringing citizens' private information. The case shows that after the identity information is leaked, lawbreakers may take the opportunity to sell their information illegally, leading to abuse and exposure of personal information.

According to Jiang and Zhang (2012), there are security risks in the personal privacy of online games. There is a lack of restraint in preventing online game operators from selling or leaking users' personal information. Compared with anonymous users, real name users have relatively larger losses. After the real name system of online games, this disadvantage has become more obvious, not only in China, but also in foreign countries. Amanda and Mike (2020) pointed out that "organizations have been increasingly using information technology (IT) to enhance business operations and decision-making processes and thus information security is one of the most pressing issues facing organizations worldwide, influencing organizational sustainable information systems and business continuity. However, many managers and employees do not pay sufficient attention to information security issues in their organizations. As a result, the computer systems of most organizations are far less secure than they should be, and damages due to information security breaches are on the rise". Although this is a description of information leakage among enterprises' employees, it is similar to personal information leakage of Chinese online game platforms. It can be seen that the leakage of identity information of Internet users is a problem that cannot be ignored. In the age of big data, fragmented identity information may also be integrated, leading to its illegal sale and abuse, and its leakage by the third-party platforms also aggravates its risk of abuse.

4 Suggestions on Users' Privacy Protection of Online Game Platforms

4.1 Suggestions for the Regulatory Bodies of Online Game Platforms

China's Internet platforms are supervised by Ministry of Industry and Information Technology of P.R.C, State Administration for Market Regulation, Internet Society of China and other departments. In order to achieve the best supervision effect and prevent the information leakage of internet users, the regulatory bodies themselves should first follow the principles of law enforcement, and not abuse their power to punish, or cover up the online platforms because of their illegal collection and sale of users' identity information for the purpose of profit. Secondly, they should limit and manage the content of user identity information collected by online platforms at different levels. Through the investigation and statistics of the information required by the developers of each platform and the feedback provided by users voluntarily, the regulatory bodies can formulate the format clauses for collecting personal identity information in the agreement of game platforms and specify the content of information that can be collected. Meanwhile, the platforms can be required to improve their technology of information security protection, and manage the crucial and the less crucial identity information at different levels to avoid the risk of excessive collection and information leakage. Finally, they should also consider the domestic users on foreign game platforms, strictly formulate the access mechanism of foreign platforms and restrict the cross-border transfer of personal information to better protect the identity information of domestic users.

4.2 Suggestions for Game Platforms

Platforms should strengthen the refinement of format clauses, set the minimum time limit for reading these clauses, highlight their options, and reduce the unnecessary clauses unilaterally beneficial to the platform side. The collection of users' ID, telephone number, E-mail address, head photo, date of birth, name and other information must be approved by the user first, protected and legally used. If the platform cooperates with a third party, it is necessary to inform the users in advance and emphasize the interest involved through words. Except that it shall not disclose the users' information, it has the obligation to guarantee that the third party acts in the same way. Zhang (2019) mentioned that the personal information right is positive on right holders, and they can request the actors to change or delete their personal information when it has been collected and used without permission. Therefore, a denial option should be added in the process of users' permission for platform services. At the same time, for users who have refused to fill in the unnecessary personal information on the platforms, services should be provided as well. Wang (2020) found out that some online game platforms have separate terms in their network service agreement with the privacy policy included. It is clearly stipulated that the users' consent to the network service agreement is regarded as the acceptance of their privacy policy, too. This practice should be changed. The platforms should separate the privacy agreement from the service agreement, and get the users' personal information only after obtaining their consent to the privacy policy. Moreover, the minimum age of game users and time limit of playing games should be promoted among platforms. For registration, users need to use their real names, ID, and face recognition which will also be carried out regularly in the later stage. The real name registration also ensures the security of game transactions, and the minimum age, face recognition and time limit reduce the excessive exposure of minors to games, protecting their rights of education as well as physical and mental health. At the same time, the game platforms can establish a database for regular information management of ordinary users, and protect the key information of special groups. In pursuit of economic benefits, they should also reflect their social values to ensure the privacy and security of users' information.

4.3 Suggestions for Users

The types of users online are adults and minors, respectively. Chen (2018) believed that mature adults need to change their concept of negative power (i.e. hoping that their privacy will not be leaked by others, and being accustomed to putting themselves in the passive and defensive positions), so as to improve their abilities of personal information protection. On the one hand, when the users log in to a game, they should pay attention to whether the information to be filled in is reasonable or necessary, such as race, religion, marital status, political inclination and other sensitive information unrelated to the use of the game. If the platform still requires such information, the users can send opinions to platform or feedbacks to the regulatory bodies due to the excessive collection of personal information. On the other hand, the users should not click the links that pop up in the process of game running or the links sent by other players on the Internet, so as to prevent law breakers from embedding Trojan Horse into computers to steal users' identity information. As minors, they should follow the age rules stipulated in the agreements of game platforms. Those under the age should register and use the platforms under the guidance of their parents. In addition, parents should educate the minors on online security, and tell them not to trust other players in the game easily, so as to avoid the leakage of personal and family identity information due to their ignorance.

5   Conclusion

The identity information of online game users is an important part of their right of privacy. It is the responsibility of the online game platforms to protect their users' identity information from being leaked. It is also of great significance to the protection of users' privacy and the healthy development of online games. Therefore, the regulatory bodies of online game platforms are required to exercise their rights in accordance with the law, improve their regulatory system, as well as standardize and restrict the format clauses of the platforms; the online game platforms shall collect and use the identity information with the consent of the users, refines the format clauses and strictly performs their security obligations; online game users should strengthen their awareness of security protection of personal information, and take reasonable measures when their privacy is violated. As for minors, they can use the platforms in a proper way. When the three parties join hands and work together, the privacy of online game users can be protected and the sound development of online games can be promoted.

References

Chu, A.M.Y., So, M.K.P.: So organizational information security management for sustainable information systems: an unethical employee information security behavior perspective. Sustainability **12**(8), 3163 (2020)

Chen, T.F.: Research on legal issues of privacy protection under the new media environment. Fudan Univ. **76** (2018)

Jiang, Y.Z., Zhang, P.: Analysis on the legal issues of the real name system of online games. Wuhan Univ. J. (Philos. Soc. Sci.), **65**(01), 55–58 (2012)

Wang Y.G.: On the effectiveness of network privacy policy–focus on the protection of personal information. Comp. Law Res. (01), 124–138 (2020)

Zhang, L.: Research on trace information protection of personal network activities–comments on the first case of privacy dispute over cookie in China. Hebei Law Sci. **37**(05), 135–150 (2019)

Zhou, S.Q.: On misuse and safeguard of personal information in the network crowd movement. Soc. Sci. Beijing **123**, 13–18 (2013)

Spectrum Sensing and Prediction for 5G Radio

Małgorzata Wasilewska[(✉)] [ID], Hanna Bogucka [ID], and Adrian Kliks [ID]

Institute of Radiocommunications, Poznan University of Technology, Poznan, Poland
{malgorzata.wasilewska,hanna.bogucka,adrian.kliks}@put.poznan.pl

Abstract. In future wireless networks, it is crucial to find a way to precisely evaluate the degree of spectrum occupation and the exact parameters of free spectrum band at a given moment. This approach enables a secondary user (SU) to dynamically access the spectrum without interfering primary user's (PU) transmission. The known methods of signal detection or spectrum sensing (SS) enable making decision on spectrum occupancy by SU. The machine learning (ML), especially deep learning (DL) algorithms have already proved their ability to improve classic SS methods. However, SS can be insufficient to use the free spectrum efficiently. As an answer to this issue, the prediction of future spectrum state has been introduced. In this paper, three DL algorithms, namely NN, RNN and CNN have been proposed to accurately predict the 5G spectrum occupation in the time and frequency domain with the accuracy of a single resource block (RB). The results have been obtained for two different datasets: the 5G downlink signal with representation of daily traffic fluctuations and the sensor-network uplink signal characteristic for IoT. The obtained results prove DL algorithms usefulness for spectrum occupancy prediction and show significant improvement in detection and prediction for both low signal-to-noise ratio (SNR) and for high SNR compared with reference detection/prediction method discussed in the paper.

Keywords: Spectrum sensing · Spectrum prediction · Machine learning · 5G · LTE · Convolutional neural network · Recurrent neural network · Neural network · Deep learning

1 Introduction

According to the Ericsson Mobility Report [3], there will be 8,9 billion mobile subscriptions in 2025, out of which 2.8 billion 5G subscriptions are forecast. This number adds to 24,6 billion of machines and devices comprising future Internet of Things (IoT). Moreover, data traffic increased by 20–100% as a consequence

This work was supported by the DAINA project no. 2017/27/L/ST7/03166 "Cognitive Engine for Radio environmenT Awareness In Networks of the future" (CERTAIN) funded by the National Science Centre, Poland.

of COVID-19 lockdowns. Particularly in times of crisis, digital communication capabilities need to be supported. Future IoT communication also poses challenges, never encountered before. Regarding 5G wireless communication, it aims at achieving 1000 times the system capacity; 10 times the data rate, and spectral efficiency, and 25 times the average mobile cell throughput compared with 4G [2]. One of the enablers of meeting these requirements is system's spectrum awareness and flexible spectrum reuse, the concept contained in the notion of cognitive radio. Cognitive features of 5G are indicated already in [2], and become subject of many publications, e.g. [7], even now, after the 3GPP standardization group announced the completion of 3GPP Release 15 – the first full set of 5G standards in 2018, and its update in 2019 [1] and Release 16 in 2020. The mentioned cognition and wireless intelligence is also envisioned as one of the prerequisites for future 6G communication systems [13].

The main issue regarding spectrum occupancy awareness is how to assure its accuracy, i.e. precision (in terms of high probability of detection and low probability of false alarm) and granularity of detected spectrum opportunities, as well as to efficiently take these opportunities for the transmission purposes. An important direction of research to address these challenges is to apply machine learning (ML) methods to detect and predict the spectrum gaps (temporarily unused frequency bands). This is because spectrum occupation has some time-patterns reflecting daily traffic variations. Moreover, patterns in frequency can be observed due to propagation-dependent resource (channels) allocation among the cells, while spatial correlation reflects shadowing effect in the radio communication channel. ML methods can, thus, be efficient in recognizing these patterns in time, frequency and space.

This paper considers the application of neural networks to improve spectrum sensing and spectrum prediction based on energy values calculation. The energy calculation is used in energy detection (ED) sensing method. i.e. [4,10,15], which is simple and is considered as semi-blind, it does not require any knowledge on signal's properties, however, the noise-level cognition is essential [14]. In this paper the noise estimation is not mandatory, as an information on Signal-to-Noise Ratio (SNR) can be obtained in other ways, for example as a value associated with a given location and formerly calculated. Also the noise level is not important in the decision making process, as a calculated energy is not compared with any threshold to decide on spectrum occupancy - this task belongs to the machine learning algorithm. The considered ML algorithms involve a neural network (NN) with dense-layers, a recurrent neural network (RNN) structure with Long Short-Term Memory (LSTM) layers, and a convolutional neural network (CNN). CNNs are broadly used for image recognition, whilst in our paper, the novelty is to consider them for spectrum sensing and prediction using two-dimensional images formed of energy values and additional features in time and frequency dimensions. As far as it is known to authors, the CNN algorithm for spectrum occupancy prediction are usually used as a sensing or prediction tool for two dimensional data in cooperative sensing [11,12,21], where data collected from each of sensing SUs is merged into a set of input information for CNN algorithm. In [16] also NN, RNN and CNN are applied to predict the type, form and number of transmitting users in a frequency band, but data used for detection and prediction is a one-dimensional time-series data. The long-term prediction that has been based on spatial-spectral-temporal data has been addressed in [19], where a hybrid convolutional long short-term memory has been proposed for future spectrum state prediction. Another interesting hybrid DL approach has been presented in [18] which also exploits CNN and LSTM combination. Here, as an input data a set of IQ samples is considered for each moment in time.

The rest of the paper is organized as follows. In Sect. 2, we first define the system model and the spectrum sensing and prediction problem. In Sect. 3, we describe NN-based algorithmic solutions of the stated problem. In Sect. 4, we present computer-simulation results, whilst in Sect. 5, we derive the conclusions.

2   System Model and Problem Definition

Below, we consider a certain area in which an unlicensed user (called secondary user – SU) aims at detecting and predicting 5G transmission activity of the licensed 5G/4G users (called primary users – PUs) in time and frequency. (Note that 4G LTE-A transmission can be considered as a special case of 5G.) Since 5G numerology allows for high flexibility in resource blocks (RBs) assignment, the goal is to opportunistically make use (by SU) of the spectrum gaps (created by PUs).

In order to define the spectrum occupation state, two hypotheses can be considered. Hypothesis $\mathcal{H}_0$ applies to the situation, when the received signal consists of just the Additive White Gaussian Noise (AWGN). Furthermore, hypothesis $\mathcal{H}_1$ is that the received signal consists of the PU's transmitted signal distorted by the radio fading channel and AWGN. Both hypotheses can be described as:

$$
\begin{aligned}
\mathcal{H}_0 &: y(t) = n(t), \\
\mathcal{H}_1 &: y(t) = h(t) * s(t) + n(t),
\end{aligned}
\tag{1}
$$

where $y(t)$ is the received signal, $n(t)$ depicts AWGN, $s(t)$ is a transmitted signal, and $h(t)$ is an impulse response of a radio fading channel.

A given sensing algorithm chooses the most probable of the two hypotheses. In order to do so, the algorithm defines test function $T(y)$, which is applied on collected received signal samples y. A decision on spectrum occupancy is made by comparing the value of the test function to threshold value λ defined by algorithm. If the test function value is higher or equal to the threshold, the spectrum is considered to be occupied, otherwise, the spectrum is considered free. The spectrum sensing algorithm's performance is determined by the probability of detection P_d (the probability of correctly detecting a present signal) and the probability of false alarm P_{fa} (the probability that signal presence is detected, even though it is not true), i.e.:

$$P_{\text{d}} = \Pr\{T(y) > \lambda|\mathcal{H}_1\},$$
$$P_{\text{fa}} = \Pr\{T(y) > \lambda|\mathcal{H}_0\}. \tag{2}$$

Transmission detection is the decision regarding the present state of spectrum occupation, i.e., at time moment t, while SU may be interested in prediction of the future states. For the prediction, the main issue is to make a decision on a future spectrum state, i.e. at the next, or several next time moments in the time interval [t, t+τ], where $\tau > 0$. This decision, however, is based on the current signal data, i.e., collected at time moment t.

Although there are multiple well known spectrum detection methods, ML algorithms have proved their usefulness in spectrum sensing area. Future spectrum state prediction is another area in which machine learning performs well thanks to its adaptability and ability to find patterns in input data.

In the problem described in the paper, SU is collecting data samples of a received, distorted by channel signals. We assume a system consisting of one base station (BS) transmitting to multiple users. The considered SU is receiving the BS's signal and is trying to decide by employing machine learning (ML) techniques whether it is possible to transmit now or in near future. SU is collecting signal samples and calculates energy for every RB in every first OFDM symbol in a given time slot. Having this information, SU tries to make a decision whether a considered slot is occupied. By calculating energy in a single OFDM symbol SU has time to make a decision and transmit in the remaining part of the time slot. It would be beneficial however, to simultaneously gain knowledge of occupancy of the same RBs in the future time slots in order to prepare for longer transmission. Proposed ML algorithms try to evaluate occupancy for current and six next time slots. The ML input data is calculated based on energy values per RB. The ML algorithms are trained separately for different signal to noise ratio (SNR) values.

3   Deep Learning for Spectrum Sensing and Prediction - Algorithmic Solution

Deep Learning (DL) algorithms are known for their ability of finding complicated dependencies in input data [8]. In the prediction problem, it is crucial to recognize any patterns that may occur in the receiving signal and DL algorithms should be a good choice. Three DL algorithms have been implemented for spectrum sensing and prediction. First, NN algorithm has been implemented as an example of a simplest algorithm. The second algorithm is a RNN algorithm. The RNNs are usually used in language and audio signal processing, as a tool of predicting sequences [6]. Their particular usefulness in this field is due to the fact that basic elements of RNNs layers called cells feedback their own output as an additional input information which makes possible for RNNs to notice intricate patterns occurring in input data in time. The last algorithm implemented is a CNN. CNNs are broadly used for image recognition, processing and classification [17].

Fig. 1. First dataset - cyclical intensity of RBs occupancy

All of the proposed algorithms are supervised classification algorithms. Each one of them is trying to establish an occupancy status of a current of future RBs, so it indicates a binary classification problem. The proposed NN-based method is the simplest and requires least calculations, but is able to perform only a single RB classification. This means that based on the current input data, the NN classifies one current or one of the future RBs' as free or occupied. On the other hand, the RNN as a more complicated method, is able to perform a detection and prediction for several next RBs, but only for single frequency range. The CNN is able to perform most complex calculations and classify multiple RBs both in time and in frequency.

Each proposed algorithm receives slightly different input data based on RB energy values. A single input dataset for NN algorithm consists of four values that characterize a single RB: frequency index (values from range 0–49), time slot index (values from range 0–79), energy value for the considered RB, and sum of energies of neighboring RBs. Each element of an input sequence of RNN consists of 3 values: time slot index, energy value, and sum of neighboring RBs' energy values. To take full advantage of CNN advantages, the input data in proposed algorithm is constructed as an 2D image, whose first dimension is frequency, second dimension is time, and pixels contain RB energy values. Input images also have three layers, similarly as color images have three RGB components. The first layer consists of aforementioned RBs' energy values, the second layer contains frequency index values, and the third one, the time slot indexes.

4   Simulation Experiment

4.1   Assumptions and Settings

Two different cases of signals received by SU are considered. First signal is a symbolic representation of daily fluctuations in traffic intensity typical to wireless communication systems. Figure 1 presents signal for 400 slots as RBs in frequency and time. The yellow areas indicates occupied RBs, and blue means free RBs. The intensity dependency in time is clearly visible, as an intensity rises and drops every 80 slots. The signal is correlated in time, also, probability of occupied

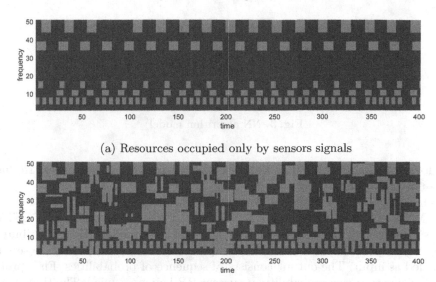

(a) Resources occupied only by sensors signals

(b) Resources occupied by sensors signals and random signals

Fig. 2. Second dataset - sensor network signals

RB in frequency is not uniform, which is dictated by the fact that the channel may prevent effective transmission on certain frequencies to some users. In this example it is assumed, that signal is most probable to appear on the middle frequencies, and least probable on the marginal frequencies.

The second considered case concerns a system, where there are multiple sensor-like devices that need to transmit information in the form of short signals and with high periodicity. The signal occurs in every cycle with high probability, although from time to time devices hold back the transmission. The simulated sensors' transmitted signal is presented on Fig. 2a. Additionally to the sensors' signals, a random signal which is characterized by a certain correlation over time is transmitted with uniform probability throughout the band. The random signal with sensors signal is presented on Fig. 2b.

As mentioned before, three DL algorithms have been implemented. Figure 3 shows a structure of the NN model. It consists of three dense layers, proceeded by a Softmax layer [5], which convert received data into probability values. First two dense layers consist of 10 neurons. The last dense consists of two neurons.

Neural network is used here for classification problem, so as a loss function, Sparse Categorical Cross Entropy [8] has been used. The output data consists of two probabilities – probability of a considered RB belonging to 'occupied' category and probability of belonging to 'free' category. Those two probability values sum up to one. In order to achieve a classification result for current RB's signal detection or for further RB occupancy prediction, separate NNs must be trained. In the experiments shown in the paper, detection, and prediction from first to sixth next time slot is performed, which required to create seven NNs

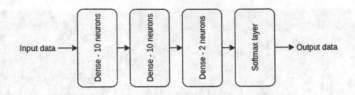

Fig. 3. NN algorithm model

one four each application. The Stochastic Gradient Descent optimizer [20] has been used in training process.

The proposed RNN model consists of three Long Short-Term Memory (LSTM) layers [9]. A dropout of 0.5, 0.3 and 0.2 is applied after each of LSTM layers respectively to prevent overfitting. The last layer is a time distributed dense layer consisting of 4 neurons. A sequence consisting of 100 feature sets is provided as input. The output consists of sequence of probabilities. First probability value concerns probability of current RB being occupied. The three next probabilities are for predicting occupancy of next RBs for the same frequency, but future time slots. Since the RNN accepts as an input a one-dimensional data, there is a need of training separate RNNs for each frequency separately. The Adam optimizer [20] has been used, with learning rate 0.001. As a loss function, binary cross entropy has been implemented. Figure 4 portrays the RNN model.

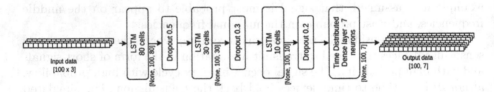

Fig. 4. RNN algorithm model

The last implemented algorithm is a CNN. Figure 5 shows proposed algorithm's model. This method accepts as an input a spectrogram-like image of energy values and other features per each RB. The input data is padded with zero values on the top, bottom and on the right side. Output results achieved by this network, are two-dimensional layers of the size of 50 pixels by 7 pixels. It means that a results is a detection and prediction results for each of 50 frequencies for current and next 7 time slots. One pixel represents one RB.

The created CNN model consists of four convolutional layers. The first one has 8 kernels (filters) are the size of 9 by 80 pixels. This layer returns image of the same size as input. The second layer uses 16 kernels of size 5 by 50, and the third one uses 32 kernels of size 3 by 25. The growing number of kernels in each layer is to ensure better recognition of any more abstract features of input data. The output layer has only two kernels, each for every RB's occupancy category - free or occupied. The filters are the size of 1 by 27, to ensure a proper output image size. Each of the layers uses rectifier function (ReLU) as an activation function, except of the last layer, which uses softmax function. As an optimizer, Adam algorithm is implemented with learning rate equal 0.0001. Since the output consists of two categorical probabilities, the Sparse Categorical Crossentropy is used as a loss function.

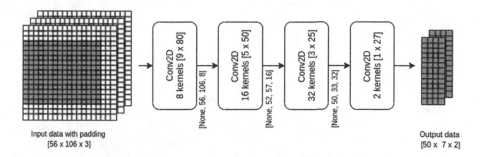

Fig. 5. CNN algorithm model

4.2 Simulation Results

In order to test algorithms' performance on detection and future spectrum state prediction, experiments have been conducted for different SNR values. Additionally a primitive algorithm (PA) for prediction has been proposed in order to evaluate whether DL algorithms introduce any improvement into prediction. This primitive method uses detection results of a currently considered ML and assumes that all RBs for a given frequency in every future time slot that is considered will have the same occupancy state as those that just have been detected. A simple prediction method as that can give quite good results if the spectrum is occupied most of the time, or it is occupied in continuous in time groups of RB. The latter case is true in both of considered datasets.

For all of the considered ML algorithms and their corresponding PA results, plots of P_d and P_{fa} for a range of SNR values have been obtained. To facilitate the interpretation of the results, the bar charts have been drawn of the probabilities P_d and P_{fa} for each of prediction steps. These charts are created for highest SNR value, where the difference between ML and PA is the biggest. Additionally, an overall measure of improvement - a total difference between both probabilities has been determined, according to the formula:

$$D_{total} = P_{d_{ML}} - P_{d_{PA}} + P_{fa_{PA}} - P_{fa_{ML}}, \tag{3}$$

where D_{total} is a total evaluation measure, $P_{d_{ML}}$, $P_{fa_{ML}}$, $P_{d_{PA}}$, $P_{fa_{PA}}$ are probabilities of detection and false alarm for a considered ML and for a corresponding PA respectively.

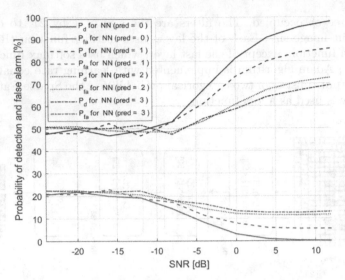

(a) NN probability of detection and false alarm results

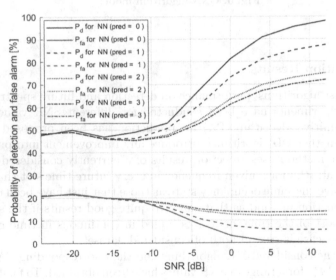

(b) PA probability of detection and false alarm results based on NN)

Fig. 6. NN and PA results depending on SNR for first dataset

First Dataset. Results for first dataset have been achieved by applying all of the proposed DL algorithms. Figure 6 shows plots of probabilities of detection and false alarm for detection and prediction for next three slots. Figure 6a shows probabilities for NN algorithm, while Fig. 6b contains results for primitive prediction based on NN detection results. It can be observed that for low SNR values, NN algorithm is able to achieve probability of detection equal around

50%, while keeping lower values of probability of false alarm around 20%. Typical detection algorithms like ED method usually achieve the same values of P_d and P_{fa} for low SNR, so results achieved by NN are beneficial, although P_{fa} could be considered as high depending on the detection/prediction requirements for transmission. The results for prediction and detection for both NN and PA are the same for low SNR. This is a common rule among all of the following results. For low SNR, the noise prevents any time-depending sequences being found, hence there are no differences in the detection and prediction results. At the same time, there are some dependencies of resource allocation in time, which is a reason for a significant difference between P_d and P_{fa}. All of the results of NN and PA for high SNR, are very similar, although PA shows a slight advantage.

The differences in results for SNR $= 12$ dB are much easier to compare on Fig. 9. Here, all of the blue bars correspond to P_d and P_{fa} NN results on top and bottom plot respectively. The grey bars overlapping blue bars represent PA results based on NN detection. It can be observed that P_d for all predictions for NN is lower than PA results, but at the same time P_{fa} results are lower. The overall prediction evaluation is presented on Fig. 10. Figures 9 and 10 are described in more detail below.

For second set of results, the RNN results are presented on Fig. 7. Here, the differences between RNN and PA results are more visible, especially for P_d, which is significantly higher for RNN for prediction of next second and third slots. The gap between P_d and P_{fa} results for low SNR is even more substantial than for the NN. Here, the P_{fa} stays on value of 20%, while P_d reaches values of even 70%. For high SNR values and for bigger number of prediction steps, RNN results are also compared in more detail on Fig. 9.

CNN results are presented on Fig. 8. It can be expected, that CNN would work as good or even better than RNN algorithm. The achieved results prove it's true. The results of P_d for high SNR are almost as good as those of RNN, and P_{fa} are even lower. Although the P_d values for low SNR are not as high as RNN P_d, the P_{fa} are lower, which ensures that the difference of these results is preserved, and still equal to around 50%.

As mentioned above, all of the detection and prediction results for high SNR are compared collectively in order to evaluate which of the algorithms works best on the first dataset. On Fig. 9 one can observe differences between P_d (top chart) and P_{fa} (bottom) for each of DL algorithms and their corresponding PA. Each of the DL bars has a corresponding overlapping grey PA bar. It can be observed that PA results of prediction are very dependent on ML algorithm detection that they are based on. For instance PA based on NN are significantly worse than PA based on RNN and CNN, although all three ML algorithms reach very similar results for detection (prediction $= 0$). The P_{fa} for NN based PA grow much faster with each prediction step. In fact for sixth predicted slot, the P_{fa} and P_d values of PA are only 15% apart.

The NN P_d results are usually a few percent worse than PA results, but since $P_{fa_{PA}}$ values grow fast with each prediction step, $P_{fa_{NN}}$ reach lower values, although are still higher than P_{fa} of other DL algorithms. It is also quite clear

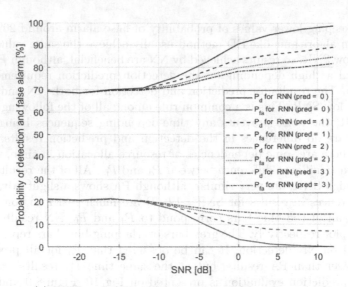

(a) RNN probability of detection and false alarm results

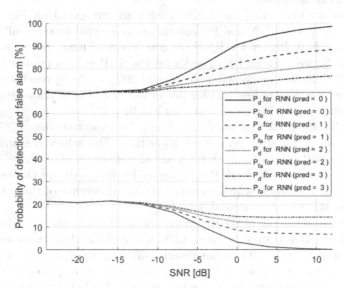

(b) PA probability of detection and false alarm results based on RNN

Fig. 7. RNN and PA results depending on SNR for first dataset

that the best P_d results are achieved by RNN, but the best P_{fa} belong to CNN algorithm. Either way, both methods work comparably for first dataset.

The top graph of Fig. 10 shows how each of DL algorithms performs comparing to it's PA. These results were obtained through use of Eq. 3. This bar graph represents whether it is better to use simple PA method based on a chosen ML algorithm and how much better or worse performance can be achieved. Figures 9

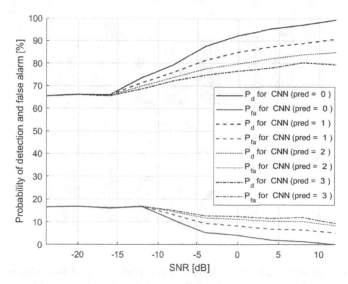

(a) CNN probability of detection and false alarm results

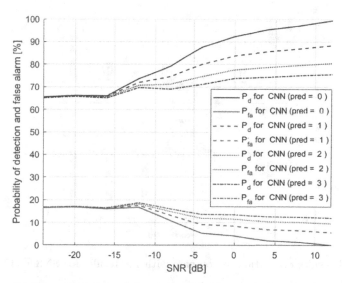

(b) PA probability of detection and false alarm results (CNN)

Fig. 8. CNN and PA results depending on SNR for first dataset

and 10 provide the complete set of information needed for the assessment of a given method. The negative results indicate that a PA is better than a ML for a given prediction step. The bottom part of Fig. 10 presents also comparison between ML results and PA results, although only one set of PA results is chosen to be compared with every ML result. It is dictated by the fact that some PA

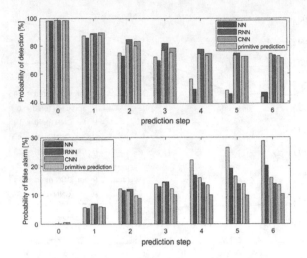

Fig. 9. Comparison of probability of detection and probability of false alarm values for SNR = 12 dB (first dataset)

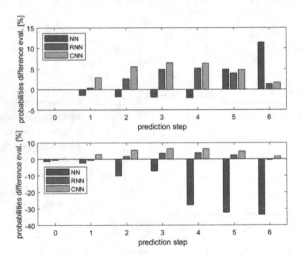

Fig. 10. Final results evaluation in compare with PA results for SNR = 12 dB (first dataset)

results for a given DL can be much worse than ML and give false impression on a top graph that a given ML performs better than the others. The example of this phenomenon is evaluation result for NN algorithm for prediction 6, where the $P_{fa_{PA}}$ are so high that NN appears to achieve significant improvement, when it fact it still performs much worse than RNN and CNN. To address this issue, on the bottom graph, all of the DL results have been compared, to the PA results of CNN, which are the best. It is clearly visible now that NN is the worst algorithm for this dataset.

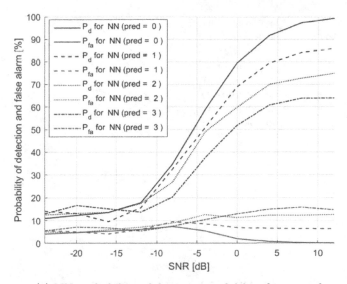

(a) NN probability of detection and false alarm results

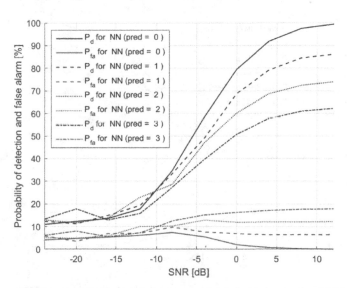

(b) PA probability of detection and false alarm results (NN)

Fig. 11. NN and PA results depending on SNR for second dataset

Second Dataset. As a second dataset a signals from sensor network has been considered. Unlike the results of first dataset, this time the gap between P_d and P_{fa} for low SNR for all of the considered DL algorithms. Figure 11 presents results for NN and NN-based PA. The P_d for low SNR is equal only around 12%, while P_d equals 5%.

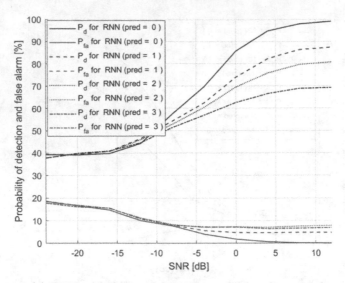

(a) RNN probability of detection and false alarm results

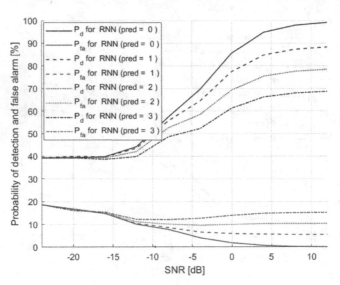

(b) PA probability of detection and false alarm results (RNN)

Fig. 12. RNN and PA results depending on SNR for second dataset

Figure 12 presents results for RNN algorithm. Same as for the first dataset, in case of the second dataset RNN also performs generally better in terms of both P_d and P_{fa} than NN. The RNN is better suited for recognizing the patterns in signal despite the noise and random signals. For low SNR values it is not possible anymore to associate a specific time with higher or lower communication traffic intensity, but it is still possible to predict sensor's activity, hence the gap between

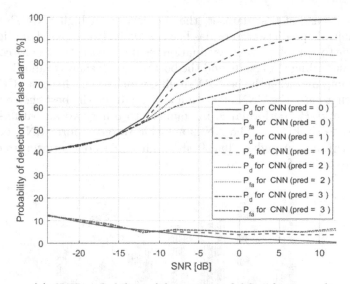

(a) CNN probability of detection and false alarm results

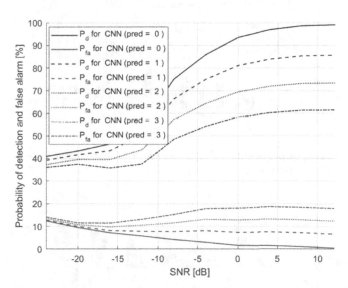

(b) PA probability of detection and false alarm results (CNN)

Fig. 13. CNN and PA results depending on SNR for second dataset

P_d and P_{fa}. It is worth noting that for high SNR, values P_{fa} of RNN are lower than corresponding values of P_{fa} for RNN-based PA.

Figure 13 shows results for CNN. In this case, the differences between the two CNN and CNN-based PA results can be seen more clearly than before. The advantage of the CNN algorithm over PA in terms of high SNR P_d is growing with each prediction step. Also it is very clear that P_{fa} can be achieved much lower thanks to the use of CNN than PA.

Just like in case of first dataset, the comparison of high SNR P_d and P_{fa} results for multiple prediction steps has been collectively compared on Fig. 14. As previously, the top graph presents evaluation results of each ML results compared to their corresponding PA results and the bottom graph shows evaluation of each ML results compared with the best PA results, which are in this case RNN-based PA. Also in that case, the CNN algorithm appears to be the best choice in terms of overall P_d and P_{fa} performance in compare to other two algorithms, which is clearly visible on Fig. 15. The NN is not able to outperform RNN-based PA for any prediction step higher than 0 although it does outperform its own PA results for prediction from 1 to 3.

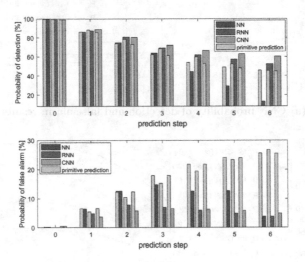

Fig. 14. Comparison of probability of detection and probability of false alarm values for SNR = 12 dB (second dataset)

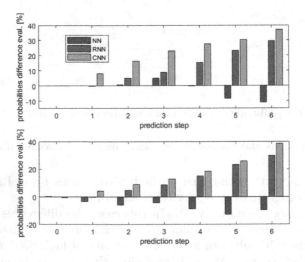

Fig. 15. Final results evaluation for SNR = 12 dB (second dataset)

5   Conclusions

In this paper, we considered three deep learning algorithms for 4G/5G spectrum detection and prediction. Two datasets have been investigated. The chosen datasets represent different cases of communication systems, namely the periodic changes in communication traffic intensity and sensor networks with repeating signals. Neural Network, Recurrent Neural Network and Convolutional Neural Network have been used for detection and future spectrum state prediction. All of them present different set of advantages and disadvantages, although the CNN turned out to be the best fitting method in both of the considered cases. All three of the algorithms have been compared to the very simple detection/ prediction method based on each of the machine learning methods, called as primitive algorithm in the paper. In the paper, there has been derived an overall evaluation of proposed algorithms in order to facilitate the selection of the most appropriate algorithm for specific needs.

References

1. 3GPP technical specification group services and system aspects. https://www. 3gpp.org/release-15
2. 5G vision: the next generation of communication networks and services (2015). https://5g-ppp.eu/wp-content/uploads/2015/02/5G-Vision-Brochure-v1.pdf
3. The Ericsson mobility report, June 2020. https://www.ericsson.com/49da93/ assets/local/mobility-report/documents/2020/june2020-ericsson-mobility-report. pdf
4. Alom, M.Z., Godder, T.K., Morshed, M.N., Maali, A.: Enhanced spectrum sensing based on energy detection in cognitive radio network using adaptive threshold. In: 2017 International Conference on Networking, Systems and Security (NSysS), pp. 138–143 (2017)
5. Bishop, C.M.: Pattern Recognition and Machine Learning. Springer, Heidelberg (2006)
6. De Mulder, W., Bethard, S., Moens, M.F.: A survey on the application of recurrent neural networks to statistical language modeling. Comput. Speech Lang. **30**(1), 61–98 (2015)
7. Ahmad, W.S.H.M.W., et al.: 5G technology: towards dynamic spectrum sharing using cognitive radio networks. IEEE Access **8**, 14460–14488 (2020)
8. Goodfellow, I., Bengio, Y., Courville, A.: Deep Learning. MIT Press, Cambridge (2016)
9. Hochreiter, S., Schmidhuber, J.: Long short-term memory. Neural Comput. **9**(8), 1735–1780 (1997)
10. Joshi, M., Borde, S.D.: Comprehensive analysis of various energy detection parameters in spectrum sensing for cognitive radio systems. In: 2014 International Conference on Advances in Communication and Computing Technologies (ICACACT 2014), pp. 1–4 (2014)
11. Lee, W., Kim, M., Cho, D.: Deep cooperative sensing: cooperative spectrum sensing based on convolutional neural networks. IEEE Trans. Veh. Technol. **68**(3), 3005–3009 (2019)

12. Liu, H., Zhu, X., Fujii, T.: Ensemble deep learning based cooperative spectrum sensing with semi-soft stacking fusion center. In: 2019 IEEE Wireless Communications and Networking Conference (WCNC), pp. 1–6 (2019)

13. Latva-aho, M., et al.: Key drivers and research challenges for 6G ubiquitous wireless intelligence. 6G Research Visions 1 (2019)

14. Mariani, A., Giorgetti, A., Chiani, M.: Effects of noise power estimation on energy detection for cognitive radio applications. IEEE Trans. Commun. **59**(12), 3410–3420 (2011)

15. Ribas, A.O.P., Dias, U.S.: On the double threshold energy detection-based spectrum sensing over κ-μ fading channel. In: 2015 IEEE Radio and Wireless Symposium (RWS), pp. 82–85 (2015)

16. Omotere, O., Fuller, J., Qian, L., Han, Z.: Spectrum occupancy prediction in coexisting wireless systems using deep learning. In: 2018 IEEE 88th Vehicular Technology Conference (VTC-Fall), pp. 1–7 (2018)

17. Qin, Z., Yu, F., Liu, C., Chen, X.: How convolutional neural network see the world-a survey of convolutional neural network visualization methods. arXiv preprint arXiv:1804.11191 (2018)

18. Roy, D., Mukherjee, T., Chatterjee, M., Pasiliao, E.: Primary user activity prediction in DSA networks using recurrent structures. In: 2019 IEEE International Symposium on Dynamic Spectrum Access Networks (DySPAN), pp. 1–10 (2019)

19. Shawel, B.S., Woldegebreal, D.H., Pollin, S.: Convolutional LSTM-based long-term spectrum prediction for dynamic spectrum access. In: 2019 27th European Signal Processing Conference (EUSIPCO), pp. 1–5 (2019)

20. Sra, S., Nowozin, S., Wright, S.J.: Optimization for Machine Learning. MIT Press, Cambridge (2012)

21. Yu, L., et al.: Spectrum availability prediction for cognitive radio communications: a DCG approach. IEEE Trans. Cogn. Commun. Netw. **6**(2), 476–485 (2020)

Towards Preventing Neighborhood Attacks: Proposal of a New Anonymization's Approach for Social Networks Data

Requi Djomo[1]($\boxtimes$) and Thomas Djotio Ndie[2]

[1] National Polytechnic School of Douala (ENSPD), University of Douala, Douala, Cameroon
[2] National Polytechnic School
of Yaounde (ENSPY), University of Yaounde, Yaounde, Cameroon

Abstract. Anonymization is a crucial process to ensure that published social network data does not reveal sensitive user information. Several anonymization approaches for databases have been adopted to anonymize social network data and prevent the various possible attacks on these networks. In this paper, we will identify an important type of attack on privacy in social networks: "neighborhood attacks". But it is observed that the existing anonymization methods can cause significant errors in certain tasks of analysis of structural properties such as the distance between certain pairs of nodes, the average distance measure "APL", the diameter, the radius, etc. This paper aims at proposing a new approach of anonymization for preventing attacks from neighbors while preserving as much as possible the social distance on which other structural properties are based, notably APL. The approach is based on the principle of adding links to have isomorphic neighborhoods, protect published data from neighborhood attacks and preserve utility on the anonymized social graph. Our various experimental results on real and synthetic data show that the algorithm that combines the addition of false nodes with the addition of links, allows to obtain better results compared to the one based only on the addition of links. They also indicate that our algorithm preserves average distances from the existing algorithm because we add edges between the closest nodes.

Keywords: Anonymization · Social network · Neighborhood attacks · Confidentiality · Graph isomorphism · APL

1 Introduction

Currently, more and more social network data is made available to the public in one way or another, protecting personal information while publishing social network data is becoming a very important concern. With some local knowledge about the individuals in a social network, an adversary can easily invade the privacy of some victims. Is it possible that posting social media data, even with anonymous individuals, still threatens privacy? Many social networks collect confidential information about their users, information

Z. Deze et al. (Eds.): BDTA 2020/WiCON 2020, LNICST 371, pp. 195–208, 2021.
https://doi.org/10.1007/978-3-030-72802-1_14

that could potentially be misused. The development of online social networks and the publication of social network data has created a risk of personal information leaking from individuals (example: salary, illness, connection to a specific group, etc.) (See Fig. 1. This requires the preservation of privacy before such data is published. In this paper, we focus on an important type of attack on privacy in social networks: "neighborhood attacks". If an adversary has some knowledge about a target victim's neighbors and the relationships between those neighbors, the victim can be re-identified even if the victim's identity is preserved using conventional anonymization techniques.

Most of the previous privacy studies can only deal with relational data, and cannot be applied directly to social media data. However, Bin Zhou and Jian Pei [1] have proposed a method of anonymizing a social network to prevent re-identification of nodes through structural "neighborhood" information, which is an initiative in this direction and which provides a practical solution to the problem. Subsequently, other research works were also proposed to solve the same problem as in [2–4].

The in-depth study of the neighborhood attack gave us a good understanding of the anonymization approach proposed by Zhou and Pei against these attacks. This approach, which works based on the principle of adding links to have isomorphic neighborhoods, considerably preserves privacy against neighborhood attacks but can significantly modify the structural properties of the original graph and therefore its potential utility. Our issue falls within this context, namely the protection of privacy while preserving a very important structural property, namely "APL (Average Shortest Path Length)". Preserving such a property in anonymization could be extremely essential thereafter for the analysis of graphs of anonymized networks.

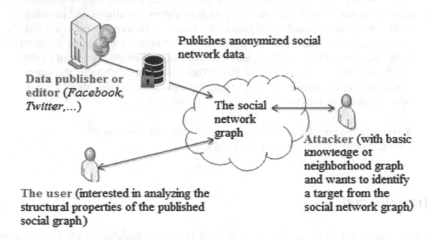

Fig. 1. Publication of social network data

The rest of this work is organized as follows: we start in Sect. 2 with an illustration of the neighborhood attack to show how an attacker can identify a person in the published graph using their neighborhood knowledge. Subsequently, we discuss the limits of the existing solution to prevent this attack. We present our contribution to improve this solution in Sect. 3. Our approach to social network anonymization that preserves as much as possible the ownership of the mean distance or APL is presented in Sect. 5. Finally, Sect. 7 is devoted to the conclusion, and then some tracks for future work are discussed.

2 Illustration of Neighborhood Attacks

As a concrete example, let us take a synthesized social network of "friends" shown in Fig. 2 (a). Each vertex in the network represents a person. The sensitive attribute associated with each node in the network represents a disease, and the non-sensitive attribute represents each person's occupation. An edge connects two people who are friends. Let us suppose that the network is to be published. To preserve privacy, is it sufficient to delete all identities as shown in Fig. 2 (b) (i.e. perform naive anonymization [11], where identifiers are replaced with random numbers)?

Unfortunately, if an adversary has some knowledge of an individual's neighbors, privacy may be disclosed. If an opponent wants to find information about "Walid" and knows that he has two friends who know each other and, two other friends who do not know each other, i.e. it knows the neighborhood graph of "Walid" as shown in Fig. 2 (c), then the vertex "2" representing "Walid" can be uniquely identified in the network since no other vertex has the same graph of neighborhood. The adversary can thus know that "Walid" suffers from epilepsy. This represents an intrusion into the privacy of "Walid". Likewise, "Lyes" can be identified in Fig. 2 (b) if the adversary knows the neighborhood graph of "Lyes".

Identifying Individuals in Published Social Networks Violates Privacy.

In this example, by identifying "Walid" and "Lyes", an adversary may even know from the published network (Fig. 2 (b)) that "Walid" and "Lyes" share a friend in common.

Now, let us assume the opponent wants to find information about "Lina" and knows that she has two friends who do not know each other in the network. Using this knowledge, he tries to find it in the network. There are 4 vertices in the network which have the same neighborhood: 5, 7, 3 and 4 as shown in Fig. 2 (b). "Lina" can be any of these. Thus, "Lina" cannot be identified in the social network with a probability greater than 1/4. If each node in the social network cannot be identified with a probability greater than 1/k, the network is said to follow the principle of "k-anonymity" [5].

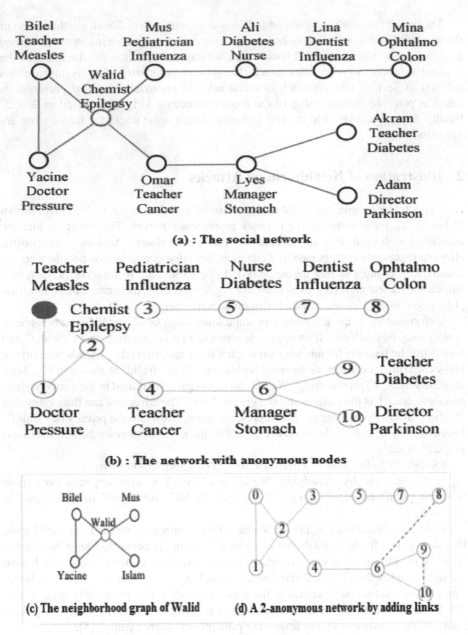

(a) : The social network

(b) : The network with anonymous nodes

(c) The neighborhood graph of Walid   (d) A 2-anonymous network by adding links

Fig. 2. Neighborhood attacks in a social network [12]

3 Contribution

To protect privacy satisfactorily, one solution is to ensure that any individual cannot be identified correctly in the anonymized social network with a probability greater than

1/k, where k is a user-specified parameter carrying the same characteristics of the k-anonymity model of L. Sweeney [5].

In the example of Fig. 2, an anonymous "2-neighborhood" graph of Fig. 2 (a) generated by adding links can be published. By adding two false links, one connecting "Lyes" and "Mina" and the other connecting "Akram" and "Adam", the neighborhood graph of each vertex in Fig. 2 (d) is no longer unique. An adversary with the knowledge of the neighborhood of a node, always gets at least two candidate nodes, so he cannot identify an individual in this anonymous graph with a probability greater than 1/2.

Zhou and Pei [1] took the initiative to address the problem of preserving privacy in the publication of social networks against neighborhood attacks, and proposed an anonymization method based on the addition of links, and subsequently, other research works [2–4] have appeared which are based on the solution of Zhou and Pei [1].

For example by connecting "Lyes" and "Mina" the distance between nodes 6 and 8 is changed from 6 to 1 in Fig. 2 (d). We note that this addition of link significantly modified the value of the distance and therefore any analysis (data mining) on this data could obtain erroneous or invalid conclusions. The advantage of the method of adding links already proposed keeps the nodes in the original graph unchanged, however, it can greatly affect the structure of the graph. This method can sometimes modify the distance properties appreciably for example by connecting two distant nodes which belong to two different communities.

To better explain this example, consider that the structure of communities can be detected from the relationships of friends in the social network. Suppose that 6 and 8 are members of two different communities in the original graph, and the communities are far from each other. By connecting 6 to 8, these communities can become very close or merge to form a single community.

So relying solely on adding links may not be a good solution to keep data useful. To solve this problem, we propose to preserve important properties of graphs, such as distance, the addition of false nodes in the graph. For example, if we simply add a false node to the graph in Fig. 2(a), we can also generate an anonymous 2-neighborhood graph as shown in Fig. 3. In this figure, the distances between the nodes of the original graph haven't changed much.

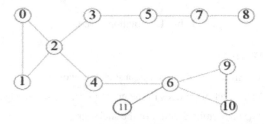

Fig. 3. An anonymous 2-neighborhood graph by adding false nodes

4   Some Concepts of Social Graphs

Before presenting our approach to anonymization, it is necessary to define some basic concepts used in our work.

4.1   Neighborhood and d-Neighborhood of a Vertex

In a social graph G, the neighborhood of a vertex $u \in V(G)$ is the subgraph induced by the neighbors of u, denoted $\text{Neighbor}_G(u) = G(V_u)$ where $V_u = \{v \mid (u, v) \in E(G)\}$ [1]. The neighborhood graph of a vertex u includes all vertices that are in the distance "d" from the vertex u [2].

4.2   Neighborhood Component

In a social network G, a subgraph C of G is a neighborhood component of $u \in V(G)$ if C is a maximal connected subgraph in $\text{Neighbor}_G(u)$. Figure 4 shows $\text{Neighbor}_G(u)$, the neighborhood of a vertex u, which contains three neighborhood components C_1, C_2 and C_3. Clearly, the neighborhood of a vertex can be divided into neighborhood components.

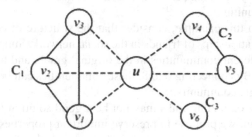

Fig. 4. Neighborhood and neighborhood components (the dotted edges are just for illustration and are not in the neighborhood subgraph) [1]

The following table summarizes the notations used in this work (Table 1):

Table 1. Notations used.

Symbol	Description
G	The initial graph modeling a social network
V(G), E(G)	V: The set of vertices in the graph G, E: the set of edges
G'	The anonymized graph of the social graph G
$\text{Neighbor}_G(u)$	Neighborhood of vertex u
$C_i(u)$	The component number i in the neighborhood of the vertex u
$\lvert V(C_i) \rvert, \lvert E(C_i) \rvert$	The number of vertices and the number of edges in the component C_i

4.3 Graph Isomorphism

Let be two graphs: G_1 (V_1, E_1) and G_2 (V_2, E_2), where $|V_1| = |V_2|$, G_1 is isomorphic to G_2 if and only if there exists at least one bijective function between V_1 and V_2: f: $V_1 \rightarrow V_2$, such that $\forall$(u, v) $\in E_1$, there exists an edge ((f (u), f (v)) $\in E_2$. For example, the two graphs below (a) and (b) in Fig. 5 are isomorphic [6].

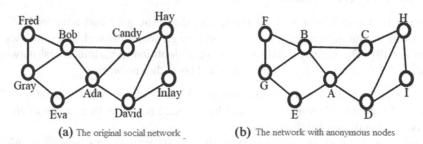

(a) The original social network   (b) The network with anonymous nodes

Fig. 5. Graph isomorphism

4.4 The Subgraph Isomorphism

For two graphs G1 = (V_1, E_1) and G_2 = (V_2, E_2), G_1 and G_2 are isomorphic subgraph if G_1 contains an isomorphic subgraph to G_2. As shown by the graphs from (a) to (c) in Fig. 6, they can find the corresponding isomorphic subgraphs in Fig. 5 (b) [6].

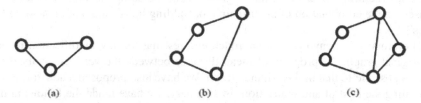

(a)   (b)   (c)

Fig. 6. Example of subgraph isomorphism [6]

4.5 Usefulness of the Anonymized Graph and Structural Properties

When the social network graph is changed, it is a big challenge to balance between preserving privacy and losing the usefulness of the data. In the context of our study, we are interested in utility measures reflecting the structural properties of a social graph G = (V, E), in particular the APL. These characteristics are generally used by analysts, for example to study influence, and forms of communication in social networks, to do viral marketing or to study the patterns of the spread of information and disease, etc. [7]. The result obtained was, on average, six intermediate nodes are sufficient to send a letter to a target individual [8].

5 Proposal For A New Approach to Anonymization

A major challenge in anonymizing a social network is that changing the labels of vertices and adding edges as well as false vertices can affect the neighborhoods of other vertices as well as the properties of the network. It is well recognized that the following two properties are often retained in social networks. These properties help us in the design of our method of anonymization.

Property 1: "the distribution of the degrees of the vertices follows a power law": the distribution of the degrees of the vertices in a large social network often follows the power law [9]. These degree distributions were identified in various social networks, including the Internet, biological networks and co-author networks.

Property 2: "the small-world phenomenon" [8]. It is also popularly known as "six degrees of separation", which states that large social networks in practice often have surprisingly small average diameters.

Our social network anonymization method treats vertices in descending order of degree, and uses the above two properties.

In this paper, the idea is to develop a new technique of social graph anonymization that is not only based on adding links but also on adding false nodes in order to reach a compromise between the preservation of privacy and the resulting utility of the anonymized graph.

Our major contribution is to propose a new efficient social network anonymization algorithm called "AnonSN", which not only preserves the privacy of individuals present in the published social graph, preventing an attacker from being able to identify a user using the neighborhood knowledge, but also which maintains as much as possible the different structural properties of the original graph, including distance. This algorithm is based on the combination of the principle of "adding links" and that of "adding false nodes".

The proposed anonymization approach ensures that for any modification made to the original graph, the property of mean distance between the vertices involved is as close as possible to that in the original graph. We have also proposed a new formula for calculating the cost of anonymization. In summary, we have made the following main contributions:

1. Proposal of a new formula for calculating the cost of anonymization to determine the neighborhoods of the vertices that can be anonymized together.
2. Proposal of a new approach to anonymization based on the addition of false nodes in addition to the addition of links.
3. Comparison of the performance of the proposed approach of adding false nodes to Zhou and Pei's approach according to the preservation of the APL.

The architecture of our anonymization approach is illustrated in Fig. 7 below:

Parameters (α, β, γ and δ) and k

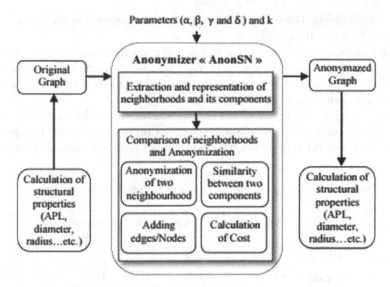

Fig. 7. Architecture of the anonymization approach

5.1 Extraction and Representation of Neighborhoods and Neighborhood Components

The neighborhoods of all the vertices in the graph G are extracted and the different components are separated. To facilitate comparisons between neighborhoods of different vertices, including isomorphism tests that will be frequently performed in anonymization, we have chosen adjacency matrices to represent the different neighborhood components, such as:

$$M[i,j] = \begin{cases} 1, & \text{if } (i,j) \in E \\ 0, & \text{otherwise} \end{cases} \tag{1}$$

Using the "Walid" neighborhood example in Fig. 2(c), the "Walid" neighborhood components and the adjacency matrices that represent them are shown in Fig. 8 below:

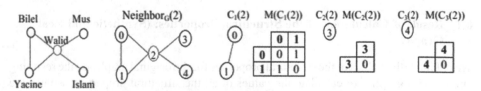

Fig. 8. Neighborhood and neighborhood components of "Walid"

5.2 Measuring the Quality of Anonymization "Cost of Anonymization"

The main goal of social network anonymization algorithms is to develop efficient heuristics to ensure a balance between preserving the structure of the original graph and the privacy of individuals. The strength of an anonymization algorithm can be measured in terms of the loss of information.

In our anonymization model, we have proposed a new formula for calculating the cost of anonymization. There are three ways to anonymize vertex neighborhoods: "generalize vertex labels", "add edges" and "add false nodes". Each of the three methods leads to some loss of information.

Using the social graph presented in Fig. 2 we illustrate on the following table, the values of some structural properties of the graph anonymized using the two anonymization methods: Zhou and Pei edge addition method and our proposed method (Table 2):

Table 2. Structural properties by adding vs links by adding false vertices.

	Original graph	Zhou and Pei	Proposed method
Diameter	7	4	7
Radius	4	3	4
APL	3.109	2.4727	3.1818
Density	0.200	0.236	0.197

We notice that the values of the structural properties of the graph anonymized with the proposed method of adding false nodes are closer to the values of the properties of the original graph when compared with those of the method of adding links, and thus they are better preserved.

6 Experiments

In this part, we describe the different experiments performed on real and synthetic data sets. Thus, we discuss the results to assess and illustrate the performance of our proposed approach by comparing our approach to the existing approach of Zhou and Pei [1].

6.1 Result of Calculation of the Structural Properties: (Synthetic and Real Graphs)

We calculate the values of the structural properties for the original graph and the resulting anonymized graphs. To calculate the values of all the structural properties, we use the Gephi software [10]. Finally, during the last step of our experiment, we compare the values of the structural properties measured for the original social graph with those obtained for the anonymized graphs. The results obtained are shown in Tables 3 and 4. On each table, the row represents the values of a structural property in the original graph and the one anonymized using the two algorithms. The context is defined by the couple: (number of vertices, number of edges).

Table 3. Structural properties of the anonymized graphs generated for the synthetic graph 40 nodes.

	Original graph	Zhou et Pei	"AnonSN"
Context	(40,51)	(40,56)	(41,54)
Nber added edges	/	5	3
Number of false vertices added	/	/	1
APL	5.347435	4.485897	5.332926
Diameter	13	12	13
Radius	7	7	7
Medium degree	2.550	2.800	2.634
Density	0.065	0.072	0.066

Table 4. Structural properties of the anonymized graphs generated for the synthetic graph 345 nodes.

	Original graph	Zhou and Pei	"AnonSN"
Context	(345,355)	(345,374)	(359,374)
Nber added edges	/	19	19
Number of false vertices added	/	/	14
APL	5.061038	4.750640	5.007765
Diameter	14	13	14
Radius	7	7	7
Medium degree	2.058	2.168	2.084
Density	0.006	0.006	0.006

We can notice from the tables that the value of the APL property calculated for the anonymized social graph using our "AnonSN" tool is always closer to its calculated value for the original social graph, so it is preserved. In the histogram below, we illustrate the values of this property (Fig. 9).

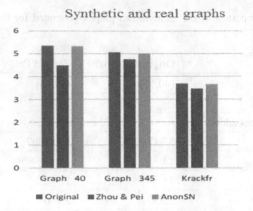

Fig. 9. APL for different data sets studied with k = 2

6.2   Analysis of the Variation of APL According to k

In this section, we study the performance of the proposed approach compared to the Zhou and Pei reference model as a function of different values of the anonymity parameter "k". Figure 10 shows the process of changing the value of APL of the graph "Interest_434" according to different values of k.

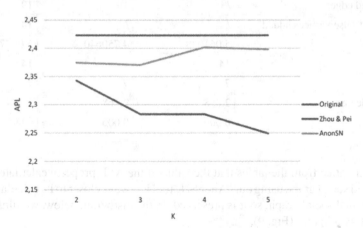

Fig. 10. APL values as a function of k

7   Conclusion and Outlook

In this paper, we have presented and analyzed the results of our proposed "AnonSN" anonymization tool, which considers the distance between nodes compared to the Zhou and Pei algorithm [1]. We have shown that our tool gives satisfactory results according to the tests carried out, it makes it possible to remove the changes in the distances between the nodes and thus better preserve the APL structural property of the anonymized graphs, which will be more useful for data analysis. Our different experimental results demonstrate that the algorithm combining the addition of false nodes with the addition of links can obtain better results compared to that based only on the addition of links and it can generate a graph that effectively preserves the property APL.

1. The results indicate that our algorithm preserves the mean distances compared to the existing algorithm, because we add edges between the closest nodes, and if this addition does not preserve the mean distance, we add false nodes that maintain these distances close to those of the original graph.
2. Measurement of APL: We measured APL according to different values of the anonymity parameter k to confirm whether anonymization could avoid degrading the accuracy of analyzes by changing the distance between nodes. Specifically, we aim to maintain the value of the APL in an anonymized graph by comparing it to its original social network graph before anonymization as this preserves the usefulness of the data for future analysis, and we were able to achieve this goal.

At the end of this work, future extensions and perspectives are envisaged to improve it, namely:

- Deal with the case of d > 1, i.e. when the opponent has basic knowledge about the neighbors of the victim at d jumps.
- It would be interesting to reduce the number of added false nodes, in other words to study the number of added false vertices compared to:

  - to the total original number of vertices
  - the nature of the social graph to anonymize

- We also plan to study other network structural properties to further improve the preservation of utility in social network anonymization.
- Another interesting direction is to consider the implementation of this model in a graph with sensitive labels by introducing the concept of "l-diversity" to prevent homogeneity attacks and better protect sensitive labels while preserving structural properties.

References

1. Zhou, B., Pei, J.: Preserving privacy in social networks against neighborhood attacks. In: 2008 IEEE 24th International Conference on Data Engineering, pp. 506–515. IEEE (2008)
2. Tripathy, B.K., Panda, G.K.: A new approach to manage security against neighborhood attacks in social networks. In: 2010 International Conference on Advances in Social Networks Analysis and Mining, pp. 264–269. IEEE (2010)
3. Zhou, B., Pei, J.: The k-anonymity and l-diversity approaches for privacy preservation in social networks against neighborhood attacks. Knowl. Inf. Syst. **28**(1), 47–77 (2011)

4. Lan, L., Jin, H., Lu, Y.: Personalized anonymity in social networks data publication. In: 2011 IEEE International Conference on Computer Science and Automation Engineering, vol. 1, pp. 479–482. IEEE (2011)
5. Sweeney, L.: K-anonymity: a model for protecting privacy. Int. J. Uncertaintly Fuzziness Knowl.-Based Syst. 10(05), 557–570 (2002)
6. Wu, H., Zhang, J., Wang, B., Yang, J., Sun, B.: (d,k)-anonymity for social networks publication against neighborhood attacks. J. Convergence Inf. Technol. JCIT 8(2), 59–67 (2013)
7. Ghesmoune, M.: Anonymisation de réseaux sociaux. Ph.D. thesis, INRIA-IRISA Rennes Bretagne Atlantique, équipe S4 (2012)
8. Milgram, S.: The small world problem. Psychol. Today 2(1), 60–67 (1967)
9. Faloutsos, M., Faloutsos, P., Faloutsos, C.: On power-law relationships of the internet topology. ACM SIGCOMM Comput. Commun. Rev. 29(4), 251–262 (1999)
10. Wasserman, S., Faust, K.: Social Network Analysis: Methods and Applications. Cambridge University Press (1994)
11. Hay, M., Miklau, G., Jensen, D., Weis, P., Srivastava, S.: Anonymizing social networks. University of Massachusetts Amherst, Technical Report No. 07-19 (2007)
12. Bensimessaoud, S., Badache, N., Benmeziane, S., Djellalbia, A., et al.: An enhanced approach to preserving privacy in social network data publishing. In: 2016 11th International Conference for Internet Technology and Secured Transactions (ICITST), pp. 80–85. IEEE (2016)

Author Index

Abudalfa, Shadi   150
Alexandrou, Dimitrios   48
Alves, Vitor   63

Bogucka, Hanna   176
Bouchard, Kevin   150

Cai, Bai-gen   3
Chatzigeorgiou, Christos   104
Chen, Changsheng   34
Costa, António   63
Cui, Lan-Yu   168

Djomo, Requi   195
Djotio Ndie, Thomas   195

Fdez-Riverola, Florentino   63
Ferraz, Filipa   63

Guo, Zhong-bin   3

He, Jian   168
He, Tingting   17
Hou, Rui   17
Hu, Min   78
Huang, Huan   17
Huang, Ming   139

Kasnesis, Panagiotis   104
Kliks, Adrian   176

Lampathaki, Fenareti   48
Layeghy, Siamak   117
Li, Hao   78
Li, Rui   139
Liang, Xiao-Yue   168
Liu, Jiang   3

Liu, Junxiao   34
Liu, Zhi   34

Meng, Xiangzeng   34
Messina, Domenico   48
Miltiadou, Dimitrios   48
Mo, Zu -Mei   168
Moustafa, Nour   117

Neves, José   63

Patrikakis, Charalampos Z.   104
Perakis, Konstantinos   48
Pitsios, Stamatis   48
Portmann, Marius   117

Rangoussi, Maria   104
Ribeiro, Jorge   63

Sarhan, Mohanad   117
Shan, Minglei   90
Sousa, Lia   63
Spyropoulos, Dimitrios   48
Su, Mi-Qian   168

Vicente, Henrique   63

Wang, Xiaoyan   139
Wang, Yu-Chen   168
Wasilewska, Małgorzata   176

Yang, Jingjing   139
Ye, Xiu-Wen   168
Yu, Tengye   139
Yuan, Shuai   17

Zhao, Xiao-lin   3

Printed in the United States
by Baker & Taylor Publisher Services

Printed in the United States
by Baker & Taylor Publisher Services